'Cultural work has been a lively area of study for some years now, but even the best contributions have tended to lack historical engagement. This excellent collection, expertly edited by three leading figures, fills that gap with aplomb. By doing so, it hugely advances debate and understanding.'

Professor David Hesmondhalgh, *University of Leeds*

Theorizing Cultural Work

In recent years, cultural work has engaged the interest of scholars from a broad range of social science and humanities disciplines. The debate in this 'turn to cultural work' has largely been based around evaluating its advantages and disadvantages: its freedoms and its constraints, its informal but precarious nature, the inequalities within its global workforce, and the blurring of work–life boundaries leading to 'self-exploitation'.

While academic critics have persuasively challenged more optimistic accounts of 'converged' worlds of creative production, the critical debate on cultural work has itself leant heavily towards suggesting a profoundly *new* confluence of forces and effects. *Theorizing Cultural Work* instead views cultural work through a specifically historicized and temporal lens, to ask: what novelty can we actually attach to current conditions, and precisely what relation does cultural work have to social precedent? The contributors to this volume also explore current transformations and future(s) of work within the cultural and creative industries as they move into an uncertain future.

This book challenges more affirmative and proselytizing industry and academic perspectives, and the pervasive cult of novelty that surrounds them, to locate cultural work as an historically and geographically situated process. It will be of interest to students and scholars of sociology, cultural studies, human geography, urban studies and industrial relations, as well as management and business studies, cultural and economic policy and development, government and planning.

Mark Banks is Reader in Sociology in the Faculty of Social Sciences at The Open University, UK.

Rosalind Gill is Professor of Social and Cultural Analysis at King's College London.

Stephanie Taylor is a Senior Lecturer in Psychology in the Faculty of Social Sciences at The Open University, UK.

Culture, Economy and the Social

A new series from CRESC – the ESRC Centre for Research on Socio-cultural Change

Editors

Professor Tony Bennett, Social and Cultural Theory, University of Western Sydney; Professor Penny Harvey, Anthropology, Manchester University; Professor Kevin Hetherington, Geography, Open University

Editorial Advisory Board

Andrew Barry, University of Oxford; Michel Callon, Ecole des Mines de Paris; Dipesh Chakrabarty, The University of Chicago; Mike Crang, University of Durham; Tim Dant, Lancaster University; Jean-Louis Fabiani, Ecoles de Hautes Etudes en Sciences Sociales; Antoine Hennion, Paris Institute of Technology; Eric Hirsch, Brunel University; John Law, The Open University; Randy Martin, New York University; Timothy Mitchell, New York University; Rolland Munro, Keele University; Andrew Pickering, University of Exeter; Mary Poovey, New York University; Hugh Willmott, University of Cardiff; Sharon Zukin, Brooklyn College City University New York/Graduate School, City University of New York

The *Culture, Economy and the Social* series is committed to innovative contemporary, comparative and historical work on the relations between social, cultural and economic change. It publishes empirically based research that is theoretically informed, that critically examines the ways in which social, cultural and economic change is framed and made visible, and that is attentive to perspectives that tend to be ignored or sidelined by grand theorizing or epochal accounts of social change. The series addresses the diverse manifestations of contemporary capitalism, and considers the various ways in which the 'social', 'the cultural' and 'the economic' are apprehended as tangible sites of value and practice. It is explicitly comparative, publishing books that work across disciplinary perspectives, cross-culturally, or across different historical periods.

The series is actively engaged in the analysis of the different theoretical traditions that have contributed to the development of the 'cultural turn' with a view to clarifying where these approaches converge and where they diverge on a particular issue. It is equally concerned to explore the new critical agendas emerging from current critiques of the cultural turn: those associated with the descriptive turn, for example. Our commitment to interdisciplinarity thus aims at enriching theoretical and methodological discussion, building awareness of the common ground that has emerged in the past decade, and thinking through what is at stake in those approaches that resist integration to a common analytical model.

Series titles include:

The Media and Social Theory (2008)
*Edited by David Hesmondhalgh and
Jason Toynbee*

Culture, Class, Distinction (2009)
*Tony Bennett, Mike Savage,
Elizabeth Bortolaia Silva,
Alan Warde, Modesto Gayo-Cal and
David Wright*

Material Powers (2010)
*Edited by Tony Bennett and
Patrick Joyce*

**The Social after Gabriel Tarde:
Debates and assessments (2010)**
Edited by Matei Candea

**Cultural Analysis and Bourdieu's
Legacy (2010)**
*Edited by Elizabeth Silva and
Alan Ward*

**Milk, Modernity and the Making
of the Human (2010)**
Richie Nimmo

**Creative Labour: Media work in
three cultural industries (2010)**
*Edited by David Hesmondhalgh and
Sarah Baker*

Migrating Music (2011)
*Edited by Jason Toynbee and
Byron Dueck*

**Sport and the Transformation
of Modern Europe: States,
media and markets 1950–2010
(2011)**
*Edited by Alan Tomlinson,
Christopher Young and Richard Holt*

**Inventive Methods: The happening
of the social (2012)**
*Edited by Celia Lury and
Nina Wakeford*

**Understanding Sport:
A socio-cultural analysis (2012)**
*John Horne, Alan Tomlinson,
Garry Whannel and Kath Woodward*

**Shanghai Expo: An international
forum on the future of cities (2012)**
Edited by Tim Winter

**Diasporas and Diplomacy:
Cosmopolitan contact zones
at the BBC World Service
(1932–2012)**
*Edited by Marie Gillespie and
Alban Webb*

Making Culture, Changing Society
Tony Bennett

**Interdisciplinarity: Reconfigurations
of the social and natural sciences**
*Edited by Andrew Barry and
Georgina Born*

**Objects and Materials:
A Routledge Companion**
*Edited by Penny Harvey,
Eleanor Conlin Casella,
Gillian Evans, Hannah Knox,
Christine McLean,
Elizabeth B. Silva, Nicholas Thoburn
and Kath Woodward*

**Accumulation: The material politics
of plastic**
*Edited by Gay Hawkins, Jennifer
Gabrys and Mike Michael*

Theorizing Cultural Work: Labour, continuity and change in the cultural and creative industries
Edited by Mark Banks, Rosalind Gill and Stephanie Taylor

Rio de Janeiro: Urban life through the eyes of the city (forthcoming)
Beatriz Jaguaribe

Devising Consumption: Cultural economies of insurance, credit and spending (forthcoming)
Liz Mcfall

Unbecoming Things: Mutable objects and the politics of waste (forthcoming)
Nicky Gregson and Mike Crang

E·S·R·C
ECONOMIC
& SOCIAL
RESEARCH
COUNCIL

Centre for Research on
Socio-Cultural Change

Theorizing Cultural Work

Labour, continuity and change in the cultural and creative industries

Edited by
Mark Banks, Rosalind Gill and
Stephanie Taylor

LONDON AND NEW YORK

First published 2013 by Routledge

2 Park Square, Milton Park, Abingdon, Oxon OX14 4RN
711 Third Avenue, New York, NY 10017, USA

Routledge is an imprint of the Taylor & Francis Group, an informa business

First issued in paperback 2017

British Library Cataloguing in Publication Data
A catalogue record for this book is available from the British Library

Library of Congress Cataloging in Publication Data
Theorizing cultural work : labour, continuity and change in the cultural and
creative industries / edited by Mark Banks, Rosalind Gill, and Stephanie
Taylor.
     p. cm. – (Culture, economy and the social)
   Includes bibliographical references and index.
   1. Cultural industries. 2. Work–Social aspects. I. Banks, Mark.
II. Gill, Rosalind (Rosalind Clair) III. Taylor, Stephanie, 1954-
   HD9999.C9472T524 2013
   331.7'610705–dc23
                2012050795

ISBN: 978-0-415-50233-7 (hbk)
ISBN: 978-1-138-08708-8 (pbk)

Typeset in Times New Roman
by Taylor & Francis Books

Contents

Contributors

Lisa Adkins is Professor of Sociology at the University of Newcastle, Australia, and was previously Professor of Sociology at Goldsmiths, University of London. Widely published in the areas of economic sociology, social and cultural theory and feminist theory, she has contributed most recently to debates concerning the reconstruction of social science through the volumes *What is the Empirical?* (2009, co-ed. with Celia Lury) and *Measure and Value* (2012, co-ed. with Celia Lury).

Mark Banks is Reader in Sociology in the Faculty of Social Sciences at The Open University, UK. He first became interested in the cultural industries during the late 1990s when he worked at the Manchester Institute for Popular Culture. He is the author of *The Politics of Cultural Work* (Palgrave, 2007), and numerous articles on cultural industries, work and identity, cultural value and cultural policy.

Sarah Brouillette is an Associate Professor in the Department of English at Carleton University, Canada, where she teaches contemporary British, Irish and postcolonial literatures, and topics in print culture and media studies. She is the author of *Postcolonial Writers and the Global Literary Marketplace* (Palgrave, 2007), and is currently researching a cultural history of UNESCO (the United Nations Educational, Scientific and Cultural Organization).

Bridget Conor is currently a Lecturer in the Department of Culture, Media and Creative Industries at King's College London. Her research interests include screenwriting work and workers, creative labour, and the dynamics of gender and inequality in cultural production industries. Her previous research analysed the New Zealand film industry and the production of *The Lord of the Rings* trilogy.

Mark Deuze is Associate Professor at the Department of Telecommunications of Indiana University-Bloomington, USA. His research interests are media work and management, journalism studies, digital culture, media philosophy and extreme metal.

Rosalind Gill is Professor of Social and Cultural Analysis at King's College London. She is interested in gender, media, new technologies, labour and intimacy. She is author of numerous books and articles including *Gender and the Media* (Polity, 2007), *Secrecy and Silence in the Research Process* (ed. with Roisin Ryan Flood, Sage, 2009) and *New Femininities* (with Christina Scharff, Palgrave 2011). She is currently writing a book called 'Creatives', and another on mediated intimacy.

Melissa Gregg is Senior Research Scientist and Researcher in Residence at the Intel Science and Technology Center for Social Computing, University of California, Irvine. Her research focuses on the technological configuration of contemporary work, and the synergies between desirable economic and intimate selves. Her publications include *Work's Intimacy* (Polity, 2011), *The Affect Theory Reader* (Duke, 2010) and *Cultural Studies' Affective Voices* (Palgrave, 2006).

Nicky Lewis is a PhD student in the Department of Telecommunications of Indiana University-Bloomington. Her research interests include media psychology and the relationships between media and society.

Susan Luckman is an Associate Professor in the School of Communication, International Studies and Languages and the Hawke Research Institute at the University of South Australia, who teaches and researches in the fields of media and cultural studies. She is the author of the book *Locating Cultural Work: The Politics and Poetics of Rural, Regional and Remote Creativity* (Palgrave Macmillan, 2012); she co-edited the anthology on creative music cultures and the global economy *Sonic Synergies* (Ashgate, 2008); and is the author of numerous book chapters, journal articles and government reports on creative cultures and industries.

Richard Maxwell is a political economist of media and a Professor of Media Studies at Queens College, City University of New York. He has published widely on a range of topics: media and the environment; television in Spain's democratic transition; Hollywood's international dominance; media politics in the post- 9/11 era; and how big political economic forces work in the mundane routines of daily life and culture.

Toby Miller is Professor of Cultural Industries at City University, London, and people can follow his adventures at www.tobymiller.org.

Brett Neilson is Professor at the Institute for Culture and Society at the University of Western Sydney. He is lead researcher on the Australian Research Council-funded project *Transit Labour: Circuits, Regions, Borders* (transitlabour.asia). Together with Sandro Mezzadra of the Università di Bologna, he is author of *Border as Method, or, the Multiplication of Labor* (Duke University Press, 2013).

Kate Oakley is Professor of Cultural Policy at the University of Leeds, UK. Her research interests include the politics of cultural policy, work in the cultural industries and regional development. She is a Visiting Professor at the University of the Arts in London, and worked for many years as an independent policy analyst and writer. She is currently working on a history of cultural policy-making under New Labour with colleagues at the University of Leeds.

Sarah B. Proctor-Thomson is a Lecturer in the School of Management at Victoria University of Wellington, New Zealand. Her research aims to explore the ways in which individuals work in, are recognised by, and identify with their organizations and broader social contexts. Her current focus is on theorising different forms of what she calls 'LoveWork' (or work in which love and passion are said to characterise worker's participation) in domains including the creative industries, science and academia, and community and social services areas. She draws from the fields of feminist studies, sociology and critical employment and organisation studies, and has published reviews, articles and chapters in the areas of creativity, leadership, worker experience, voice and identity.

Andrew Ross is a Professor of Social and Cultural Analysis at New York University. A contributor to the *Nation, The Village Voice, The New York Times* and *Artforum*, he is the author of many books, including *Bird On Fire: Lessons from the World's Least Sustainable City, Nice Work if You Can Get It: Life and Labor in Precarious Times, Fast Boat to China – Lessons from Shanghai, Low Pay, High Profile: The Global Push for Fair Labor, No-Collar: The Humane Workplace and its Hidden Costs* and *The Celebration Chronicles: Life, Liberty and the Pursuit of Property Value in Disney's New Town*.

Matt Stahl is an Assistant Professor of Information and Media Studies at the University of Western Ontario, where he is also a member of the Digital Labour Research Group. His monograph, *Unfree Masters: Recording Artists and the Politics of Work* (Duke University Press, 2013) examines the representation and regulation of recording artists' labour, contracts and property.

Stephanie Taylor is a Senior Lecturer in Psychology in the Faculty of Social Sciences at the Open University, UK. Her long-term research interests concern the social formation of the person and the ways in which ongoing identifications, including gendered identifications, are shaped and constrained by available meanings and cultural associations. She is co-author (with Karen Littleton) of *Contemporary Identities of Creativity and Creative Work* (Ashgate, 2012).

Jason Toynbee is Senior Lecturer in the Sociology Department at The Open University, UK. His research is on cultural production, creativity and race, often with a focus on popular music. He is author of *Making Popular Music* (2000) and *Bob Marley: Herald of a Postcolonial World?* (2007), and has edited several collections.

1   Introduction

Cultural work, time and trajectory

Mark Banks, Rosalind Gill and Stephanie Taylor

The turn to cultural work

After decades of being displaced in media and communication studies by a focus on texts and audiences, and in sociological research on work by the study of industrial and service sector labour, the labouring lives of people working in the cultural and creative industries are now firmly on the research agenda. This recent upsurge of interest – which amounts to something of a turn to cultural work – can be attributed to at least three factors.

First, it can be traced back to the mid-1990s and the wave of enthusiasm that greeted the alleged rise of a 'creative' or 'cultural' economy, seen, for example, in the hyperbole about 'Cool Britannia' in the UK, or in the 'Creative Nation' cultural policy of Australia. The cultural and creative industries,[1] once regarded as peripheral to the 'real' economy, took centre stage in a seemingly unstoppable celebration in which they were hailed as engines of economic growth, motors of urban regeneration, and promoters of social cohesion and inclusivity. Across Europe, regional and national governments sought to rebrand deprived neighbourhoods as 'cultural quarters', or entire metropolises as 'creative cities', and there was fierce competition for the coveted title of 'European Capital of Culture', seen as a means of attracting inward investment, and transforming economic and social fortunes. Similarly, across North America, Australasia and Asia, national and regional governments sought to identify those places and peoples that could contribute most effectively to establishing an economic advantage in the new creative stakes.

The growing interest in the cultural and creative industries prompted explorations of the nature and organization of work in fields such as fashion, design, music, television or new media. These fields were rapidly expanding in the wake of accelerated public demands for more symbolic leisure or entertainment and goods, an enhanced commercial focus on cultivating effective images, brands and marketing, and the rapid technological changes underpinned by the Internet, which began to transform working practices and give rise to entirely new occupations, such as web designer and digital animator. Political and industry changes, most notably a trend towards media deregulation, also contributed to a rapid expansion of the creative and cultural economy, for example spawning a multiplicity of small, independent TV production companies alongside the few 'giant' transnational operations. Broader deregulation and patterns of disintegration, fragmentation and dispersal within large firms and bureaucracies across all creative sectors brought the freelance, 'portfolio' or independent creative worker to the fore. Although today the 'hype' about the creative industries in the UK might be said to be waning from the dizzy heights achieved during the New Labour administrations, the creative industries are nevertheless still regarded as exceptionally important and as a sector that is 'vital to national economic recovery' which can 'get people back to work' (Arts Council England 2009) during a time of financial crisis. Indeed, during the 2012 Olympic Games in London, the Conservative (coalition) Prime Minister David Cameron reiterated his faith in the 'extraordinary' talent of UK creatives whose work had been showcased in the opening ceremony, and called for renewed rounds of investment in creative endeavour.

Second, parallel to these shifts, there were also optimistic voices from the academy backing the turn to cultural work and studies of workers. Richard Florida's (2002) influential 'creative class' thesis, while focusing on a broad set of industrial sectors, nonetheless gave prominence to cultural workers and those engaged in creative occupations as vanguard workers in post-industrial transformation. Flores and Gray (1999) saw the emergence of new, entrepreneurial, DIY (do-it-yourself) biographies – emblematic of media workers – as offering potential for flexibility, autonomy and self-reinvention: liberations as much as cages. Writers such as Charles Landry (2000) and John Howkins (2001, 2010) repeatedly drew attention to the economic and socially progressive potential embedded in the cultural and creative industries, and the kinds of work and social relationships they promised.

A third factor contributing to the turn to cultural work was the arguments of a significant body of critical social theory centred on transformations in the nature and experience of work in late modernity. This scholarship, from writers like Ulrich Beck (2000), Zygmunt Bauman (2005), Manuel Castells (1996) and Richard Sennett (2006), took as its focus the way in which work was changing in conditions variously described as 'risk society', 'liquid modernity', 'network society', and 'cultural', 'new' or 'late' capitalism. Despite important differences, these writers and others together highlighted the speeding up and intensification of processes of individualization that left a large number of increasingly 'liberated' workers alone – without job security or the safety net of state or social welfare protections – to bear the risks of fragmented, precarious and discontinuous working lives. These lives, it was argued, were no longer amenable to narration through the story of a linear career or biography (notwithstanding that this was a narrative that had mostly been restricted to a minority of well-educated, first-world men). In today's 'political economy of insecurity', Sennett lamented, jobs have been replaced by short-term projects, with a withering of organizational ties and loyalties, and with them the valuing of persons, as well as the very possibility of telling a meaningful story of one's life. Manuel Castells drew on metaphors from information technology to capture the way in which work was transforming: in the network society, he argued, people had to become 'reprogrammable', constantly updating their skills in order to meet new challenges, staying agile and mobile, and always 'upgrading the self' (Ashton 2011). Cultural workers have been widely identified at the centre of many of these mooted transformations, or as peculiarly subject to their myriad influences and effects.

From a different critical position, autonomist Marxist writers such as Maurizio Lazzarato (1996), Michael Hardt and Antonio Negri (2005) helped to position cultural labour centre stage in their views of the growth of 'immaterial labour' in a rapidly transforming 'cognitive capitalism' where the production of immaterial and symbolic – rather than material – goods appears to be taking precedence. Hardt and Negri (2001) identified the qualities of labour conditional to an economy now populated by workers subjected to a stringent regime of 'immaterial production' where the ceaseless creation and circulation of ever more complex ranges of symbolic, cultural and informational goods corrals workers into oppressively standardized, 'computerized' and homogenized labour processes – a far cry from the self-liberation that others have associated with cultural work.

Despite the very real divergences between the positions outlined above, much of this social science has consistently positioned cultural workers at the centre of an ongoing transformation of work. For good or ill, workers in media, design and the arts are routinely held to exemplify the working lives and generalized practices of the 'worker of the future'. Perhaps most significantly, artists and 'creatives' more broadly are said to embody the new form of constantly labouring subjectivity required for contemporary capitalism, in which the requirements for people fully to embrace risk, entrepreneurialism and to adopt a 'sacrificial ethos' are often linked to an artistic or creative vocation.

A fourth and final factor that contributed to the coming to prominence of cultural work as a topic of research is the idea and belief that 'we are all cultural workers now' (Coté and Neilson 2014). Although Mark Coté and Brett Neilson present this idea as an interrogative, to raise questions about the extent to which the precariousness that characterizes work in the cultural field has now dispersed across the economy, the notion has a more widespread currency. At its most general, this claim points simply to the 'culturalization' of the economy, in which culture is 'put to work' across a variety of spheres of production (Du Gay and Pryke 2002). In this broader sense, it refers also to the thoroughgoing penetration of all facets of social and economic life by cultural signs, meanings and values, and the apparent indivisibility of the cultural and the economic at moments of production and consumption.

Somewhat differently, the notion of all-pervasive cultural working has been used to account for the allegedly progressive 'convergence' of media technology, producers and consumers (Jenkins 2004). Particularly popularized since the advent of Web 2.0 technologies is the idea that large swaths of the population are now involved in cultural production (and relations of co-production and consumption) in a variety of different and complex ways. People appear routinely to tweet, blog, post videos to YouTube, have websites, update social networking sites, and contribute to debates and threads on various different electronic forums. They may work as 'modders', seeing themselves as co-creators in a liminal space that is both outside and inside the computer games industry. Even those who self-consciously 'opt out' of active 'content creation' on the web may nevertheless 'like' certain webpages, leave feedback on eBay or rate Amazon marketplace transactions. Those who eschew even these newly mundane activities will – unless they disavow technology entirely – nevertheless leave sediments and trails of digital data that can then be mined by media companies, keywords in emails that will be picked up by Google for auto-tailored advertising, and Internet browsing histories that will be bought and sold as commodities. There is, today, in affluent societies, no 'outside' to media and cultural production, giving rise to the idea that – whether or not people are aware of their contribution – particular forms of cultural work have now become generalized across populations.

It is perhaps paradoxical then, that this awareness of the dispersed, networked quality of media and cultural production has helped to animate interest in cultural producers as a relatively *distinctive* group: to raise questions about the privileged autonomy of the artist (Banks 2010a), the 'professional' versus 'amateur' practitioner in journalism (Keen 2008), the particular qualities demanded and afforded by media work (Hesmondhalgh and Baker 2011), and to interrogate whether the 'free labour' (Terranova 2004) routinely given to media and games companies (amongst others) is always and necessarily exploited. If 'we are all cultural workers now', then what makes people who work in the cultural and creative industries – from advertising, to the arts, to film production – different and worthy of study? Is cultural work actually able to be distinguished from other types of work, and, if so, how and in what ways?

Contemporary debates about cultural work

It is clear that cultural work – broadly defined as symbolic, aesthetic or creative labour in the arts, media and other creative or cultural industries – has now engaged the interest of scholars from a broad range of social science and humanities disciplines, sustained by ongoing dialogue with policy makers, educationalists and trainers, and by interactions with cultural workers themselves. The diversity of both the scholarship and dialogue must be acknowledged, but more benign or upbeat readings of the coming to prominence of cultural work in Westernized, post-industrial capitalism have been consistently challenged by critical discussions which converge around four discrete, but interrelated, problems. These are:

- the precariousness of cultural work, including its contested availability and the uneven distribution of its internal and external rewards (among them, pay, working conditions, prospects and status);

- the inequalities within the global cultural workforce and, in the Western cities that are the industries' hubs, the persistent over-representation of the already privileged (white, highly educated, male);
- the celebrated associations of cultural work with the aesthetic and a supposed life–work synthesis of personalization, playfulness, informality and sociality which, it is argued, attracts but also disadvantages many cultural workers;
- the accelerated invasion of cultural work into the previously separate or protected territories of leisure, and personal and intimate life.

These issues have all been well rehearsed, but there is, we contend, something missing from the extended debates. While academic critics have persuasively challenged more optimistic accounts of 'converged' worlds of creative production, seldom have they sought to do so through an explicitly *historical* lens. Despite some cautionary voices (e.g. Ross 2008), the emerging critical language that couches the problems of cultural work in terms of post-industrial 'individualization', 'precarity', 'immateriality' and 'self-exploitation' has leant heavily towards suggesting a profoundly *new* confluence of forces and effects. However, this book asks, to what extent is such an unanchored, ahistorical focus appropriate? What novelty can we actually attach to current conditions, and – the corollary – precisely what relation does cultural work have to social precedent?

The necessity of (re)theorizing cultural work

The first aim of this book is therefore to challenge what we perceive as an historical lack in the critical literature. Our contributors were invited to reflect more fully on cultural work in terms of its (arguably) more complex and variegated social pasts, and the degree to which these impress discernibly upon contemporary conditions. The perceived deficit is not simply historical, however, but more broadly temporal, in all of its dimensions. A further aim, then, is to explore more closely the precise trajectories, or patterns of continuity *and* change that might be discernible in work in the cultural and creative industries as they move into an uncertain future. We have invited situated projections of the cultural work of tomorrow – a world that draws from, but also extends, the work histories of today.

Our further intention is to elaborate the sometimes over-simplified objects and contexts that prevail in many discussions of the cultural and creative industries, countering the tendency for critical understandings of 'new' forms of cultural work – somewhat echoing the fixation of its arbiters and industry advocates – to be restricted in focus to the empirical case in hand and primarily evaluated within a context of prevailing trends, or immediate political concerns. To this end, our contributors have been asked not only to identify and explore some of the more consistent and durable elements that appear to recur in the historically composited cultural and creative work process, but also to consider the specificities of socio-historic locations. In doing so, they bring into question the often-assumed neat boundaries and interchangeable referentialities of 'cultural work' as an object of inquiry, opening the possibility of multiple presents and a plethora of possible futures for both the work and the workers.

By reflecting both on the salience of history in the present, and its consequence for potential work futures, the critical gaze ideally extends beyond the apparent immediacy and novelty of current events. The consequence, we hope, is a more thoroughly temporalized set of theorizations that locate cultural work as an historically and geographically situated process, or processes, that can challenge more affirmative and proselytizing industry and academic perspectives, and the pervasive cult of novelty that surrounds them.

Why is this necessary? First, the time seems (economically) right. As we write, the prevailing and persistent global financial crisis and subsequent economic recessions have not fully muted the optimistic discourse of cultural and creative industries expansion but have perhaps brought to a close an initial 'golden era'. This was characterized by the energetic promotion of various aspects of the allegedly 'new' knowledge and innovation economy, supported by growth of the new (and 'old') media and creative, copyright and intellectual property industries, which, at least in the UK context, roughly coincided with the regime of the New Labour government (1997–2010) and its influential policy proclamations and naming of new sites of cultural work, including the 'creative industries' (DCMS 2001). The current shrinking in employment and revenues in those industries, and the diminution of much of the commercial investment and state subsidy that made them happen in the first place, suggest that cultural work may have reached a moment of pause and reappraisal. Projective talk about the creative economy is now considerably quieter, although still audible (e.g. Arts Council England 2009; GLA 2012).

In particular, if the cultural and creative industries were acclaimed as part of a post-millennial economy that had apparently ended cycles of boom and bust, that had transcended capitalist history in fact, then the rude awakenings of the 2007 crisis offered forceful disabuse. Consequently, if there is a need to accept that the cultural and creative industries have proved suspect in purely economic terms, vulnerable to 'old' economic cycles, then they must, too, be discredited as providers of putatively new models of flexible and responsive work and employment, as they were so frequently portrayed in the years of relative growth. Certainly, they have not (yet?) been able to provide individuals with the resources necessary to ride out the downturn or sidestep exogenous infrastructural shocks. While, of course, we must accept that to some degree all boats are lowered when the economic tide goes out, this failure is further reason to question the novelty of cultural work as part of a re-evaluation of the grounds on which the cultural and creative industries are understood. As the latest political project becomes to (re)consider the role cultural work might play in any anticipated recovery, we must also ask whether such activity is much less than a new form of time-defying, transcendental super-sector, and rather more a set of activities fully embedded within and shaped by history, politics and economy and their characteristic cycles, rhythms and patterns of internal transformation – in short, embedded in a past (or pasts) that, despite all the celebratory rhetoric of novelty, it has failed to escape or transcend.

Second, it seems timely to enquire what has happened to those social futures that the cultural and creative industries promised so volubly to usher in. What became of those egalitarian, meritocratic worlds where lack of application was the only barrier to success, and where tradition – especially in its classed, gendered or ethnicized forms – was meant to evaporate in the ardent heat of innovation and personal creative expression? What we know now is that the cultural and creative industries are actually less inclusive, equal and egalitarian than many of the traditional industries they purported to supplant and surpass (Adkins 2005; Gill 2002, 2013; Holgate and McKay 2009; Randle *et al.* 2007; Skillset 2010). Not only have they failed to detraditionalize progressively by, say, challenging the conventional gender division of labour, or ethnic minority exclusion in the workplace, but they have apparently even helped to ossify and intensify the prevalence of inequality in those social relations.

Moreover, a shift of focus from the industries to their workers has, inevitably, enabled some more nuanced explorations of the experience of cultural working. As accounts of a field are supplemented by accounts from its workers, it is necessary to abandon the hyperbole of either brave new careers or sacrificial labouring driven by the blind and single-minded pursuit of self-actualization. Empirical work shows, for example, that the aesthetic satisfactions of cultural and creative work cannot be dismissed as entirely illusory, and also that many creative workers are as aware of precarity as any discerning academic or policy maker. Research with novices who enter creative fields through the study of art and design, as just one set of specialisms, suggests that they are well aware of the difficult experiences of their predecessors and of the uncertain employment and poor financial rewards associated with their chosen professions. There is therefore a need to avoid the various caricatures of either the cultural dupe or the rational maximizer of information or (economic) benefits, in order to develop a fuller notion of the creative worker as a subtly responsive and interpreting situated subject. History operates in the carried-over affective associations and myths of cultural and creative working, as much as in the practical strategies noted by Ross. For example, to understand why cultural work has been embraced as 'good', it is necessary also to consider why other kinds of work appear worse. The valuing of the personalized nature of cultural work that has been noted by many researchers is linked to the imbuing of 'ordinary' work with Orwellian horrors of mundaneness and constriction and, further, to the perceived need to become 'not ordinary' as a condition of success. This potentially opens up a new project in which career development and self-improvement blur together and, for those aspiring workers who are less than entirely confident, set an idealized and endlessly deferred endpoint of the perfected creative self (Taylor and Littleton 2012).

This book therefore argues that to understand cultural work outside of the complex endowments of history and the social divisions of the present is fundamentally to misunderstand its form and character. We invited contributors to question the status of the cultural and creative industries as exemplars of post-industrial work, to reconsider the roles played by shared and different pasts, presents and possible futures in economic organization and, in particular, to address those forms of work that appear to remain strongly vested with traditional social relations, despite being associated with the possibility of more socially integrated, and personally liberating 'creative' or 'innovation'-led work. The final collection utilizes a range of theoretical resources and supporting case studies to provide a plural and varied analysis of the patterns of trajectory, continuity and change in social worlds of cultural and creative industries work. We do not rule out the possibility that changing patterns of cultural work are leading us into some new and uncharted waters where the temporal and spatial domains of labouring significantly break with previous arrangements. However, on the basis of our contributors' chapters, we suggest that, as well as being reliant on the unstable promise of futurity, the accelerated creation and colonization of a variety of real/virtual social and spatial environments, and the expanded use of 'co-creative' and 'free' labour based on the extension of work and careers into (hitherto) discrete social domains, cultural work might also offer experiences somewhat less revolutionary or transformative.

Conversations ...

The idea for this book arose from open-ended conversations about cultural work, temporality, value and organization, which began at recent interdisciplinary conferences about cultural work organized or co-organized in the UK by The Open University[2] and King's College London.[3] The questions that animated these occasions, and the disparate, interdisciplinary responses we received in response to our various calls for papers, furnished us with a sense of an already existent field that is both exciting and vibrant, and contains multiple, unfolding conversations, some seemingly proceeding in parallel, so fated never to converge. The aims of the book are to pull some diverse voices into dialogue, to take stock, and to prompt new thoughts about what 'the field' is and, of course, to make an intervention into it.

Through example and juxtaposition, the collected chapters raise some well-ecognized quandaries as well as new questions for future research. One recurring issue, already mentioned, is the nature of work more broadly and what constitutes 'good' or 'bad' work (Ross 2009; Hesmondhalgh and Baker 2011; Kennedy 2012). However, like any attribution of value, even one deemed personal and subjective, what is 'good' in relation to cultural work is potentially multifaceted and inevitably dependent on the historicized context. Contributions to this volume show how even such indubitable positives as 'self-actualization' or 'democratic cultural participation' must be understood in terms of what has gone before (Brouillette, this volume; Oakley, this volume). Such background is also relevant to the range of affects attached both to the work and whatever 'culture' it invokes – for example, illuminating the historical processes that contribute to an understanding of the particular potency of 'personalization' and the 'aesthetic' as intrinsic 'goods' that are routinely presented as givens for contemporary cultural workers.

Finally, the collection not only illustrates conversations about the many *other* cultures encompassed by the reference of cultural work – historical, national, professional, artistic and more – but also, in this diversity, raises the classic questions of whose interpretation and whose work is under discussion, what evidence is relevant and who is selecting it. As just one example, if the informal work on the (social and geographic) edge of a recognized industry is to be included (Neilson, this volume; Maxwell and Miller, this volume), then both the definition of cultural work and the delineation of its boundaries are, quite properly, called into question. These and other longstanding issues around both research and definition acquire a new salience in relation to cultural work.

Temporalizing and locating cultural work

The contributors to the book explore the patterned trajectories of cultural work from several different theoretical, temporal and geographical starting points. The chapters are grouped into three broad sections, which look in turn at *Histories, Specificities/transformations* and *Futures.*

Part I of the book considers histories of cultural work, challenging the claims to newness that saturate discourse in this field. Susan Luckman begins by arguing that both the contemporary celebration of the virtues of creative labour and accounts of meaningful cultural work have antecedents in the Victorian period, particularly with the great thinkers of the Arts and Crafts Movement and Victorian socialism John Ruskin and William Morris. Against the modern tendency to dismiss Arts and Crafts thinking as hopelessly romantic and utopian, the chapter demonstrates that the pillar principle of striving for meaningful labour, marked by what Morris once termed the 'impress of pleasure', has obvious analogues with contemporary discourses around the proper constitution of post-industrial work in the cultural and creative industries. Furthermore, in Western contexts, the contemporary renaissance of small-scale craft and local or indigenous production, and the more extended dispersal of creative and cultural industries beyond 'creative cities' and into rural peripheries, suggest that the affordances of this Victorian utopianism are still evident and widespread today. Whether one views this tradition in terms of a conservative or radical purpose, Luckman shows how its influences impact significantly on the contemporary practices of cultural work, as well as on the way that work is evaluated by practitioners and observers alike.

It may be ironic or unsurprising, or perhaps both, to argue that the idea and ideals of cultural work had their genesis in the same society, that of England in the 19th century, in which the soul-deadening labour of early capitalist industry prompted Marx's original theorizations of capitalism and its associated alienation. A less ambiguous historical irony is exposed by Sarah Brouillette, who proposes that many aspects of the image of the artist as the exemplary creative worker – a self-motivating, self-actualizing non-conformist – despite being commonly associated with a vague pre-modern period (for the Arts and Crafts Movement, a fictionalized medievalism), in fact (re-)originated in mid-20th century US society. She examines the work of a number of psychologists who, 'influenced by their research on World War II military personnel, began in earnest to specify the attributes of the kind of creative individual who would help secure the nation's future prosperity'. Brouillette's analysis reminds us that the mid-20th-century period saw many others seeking ways to identify and cultivate conditions for new cultural workers. By the time of *White Collar* (1951), C. Wright Mills had heralded the arrival of the 'new entrepreneurs' of the American middle class, which included an emergent cadre of proto-cultural workers operating in the bureaucratic contexts of new industries selling 'intangible services' (Mills 1951: 95), such as advertising, public relations (PR), mass communications and entertainment. Here dealing predominantly with 'symbols and other people', such workers sought to impose and manifest their own creative per-sonalities, appropriate to the new economic circumstance of post-war USA. Brouillette recalls a time when the creative personality was being further forged in the heat of new demands for self-actualizing, creative thinkers that would become normal – rather than an exceptional – requirement for the capitalism of the future: the capitalism of today, in fact.

This image of the 'creative' has long been cited as part of the attraction of contemporary cultural work, supposedly holding out a promise of self-actualization which becomes a further inducement to self-exploitation (McRobbie 1998). Some contributors to the book also suggest that historical continuities are relevant, though less as cautionary tales than as organizing guides to action. Bridget Conor explores how well-honed accounts of the past have become part of the functional mythology of a particular occupation, screenwriting. Her chapter therefore draws attention to the relevance of the past for cultural workers themselves. Even the celebration of novelty requires a corresponding awareness of whatever past is supposedly being superseded, and, given that so many forms of cultural work centre on communication and image, it is inevitable that the workers will be highly sensitive to their own self-presentation and the depictions foreshadowed by well-rehearsed stories of the past. Conor shows how the self-identification of contemporary screenwriters is intricately tied to their claims to a collective history. She argues that stories around the denigration of earlier writers as 'hired hands', 'liars' and 'schmucks' are functional for contemporary workers, for example, as a rationalization for the difficulties of their profession and a justification for some practical strategies for managing those difficulties.

Kate Oakley also discusses the status of work and labour more generally, but focuses on how this has changed within the history of labour movements and the Left in the UK. She notes that for many of those supporting the development of the cultural industries, as part of regional or urban development schemes or in practice-based settings, the idea of cultural work as 'good work' is held dear. Their concern has often been with securing representation within these labour markets for women, ethnic minorities and working-class people. Oakley argues that this may have been informed in part by an idealized notion of cultural work but it was also animated, in a way peculiar to this work, by the importance of 'voice', the idea that involvement in cultural production cannot be confined to the elite. Yet, in the decades since the first cultural industry initiatives, the marginalization of women, ethnic minorities and the working class from participation in cultural labour markets has grown, not declined. Alongside that marginalization, the virtual exclusion of the politics of labour from the policy-making process allowed the development of a discourse of 'representation' in the workforce that paid no attention to questions of working conditions. This has resulted in the UK's highly unrepresentative cultural sector, with often poor working conditions. Oakley traces this process in the case of the UK, looking at the neglect of both labour and class issues in the debate and considers the political implications of this exclusion.

The work of these writers suggests that contemporary cultural work is 'haunted' by older questions and images, including those of the artist and the factory, and by a labour movement that has always been ambivalently located for artists, writers, crafts people and other cultural labourers.

In the second part of the book, the contributions turn to questions of both specificity and transformation – the extent to which cultural work is distinct from other kinds of work, what marks its distinctiveness, and where its limits or boundaries might lie, particularly in the context of rapid and ongoing transformations that are simultaneously technological, social, global and perhaps even logistical.

Principally at stake in theorizing cultural work is the ontological status of the category itself: how might it be regarded as distinctive or special? Contributors wrestling with this conundrum include Matt Stahl, who identifies cultural work as a 'limit case' of work in general. As the template for an exemplary kind of meaningful and autonomized labour, cultural work is the ideal model that exists at the frontier of possibility for *all* kinds of work – the kind of good work to which mass populations might conceivably aspire. Thus, in contrast to most recent analyses, Stahl argues that the specialness of cultural work lies less in its absolute distinctiveness from other kinds of work, and rather more in its relative propensity to bring into sharpened focus the kinds of conflict that pervade work *in toto*, though usually much less visibly.

These include not only struggles over creative freedom, meaningfulness, or the avoidance of disaffection and alienation, but also fundamental attributes of modern work such as the exchange of property rights and the transfer of control rights. The 'interpretive usefulness' of cultural work therefore lies in its amplified capacity to provoke critical reflection on the qualities and character of work that are often underplayed or disregarded in other kinds of work context. In the second part of his chapter, Stahl shows how struggles over the distinctiveness of cultural work, and the extent to which it is able to expose some of the fundamental problematics of work in general, may vary considerably across different national or systemic contexts. By comparing the Anglo-American and German histories of work and labour, and their distinctively forged 'epistemological maps', Stahl suggests how conceptions of cultural (and non-cultural) work might be more eloquently specified and untangled.

Similarly challenging the idea that work in the cultural and creative industries is somehow qualitatively unique or special, Jason Toynbee's chapter also proposes an end to the separation of cultural work from work in general. Yet here, the foundation of this challenge is first rooted in an unease and political objection to the elevation of cultural work above 'ordinary' work – a charge levelled at a diverse array of thinkers including Hannah Arendt, Alasdair MacIntyre and, in more recent interventions, Michael Hardt and Antonio Negri. Toynbee retains some sense that as a focus for dissent and critique there remains some essential 'promise' in cultural work, but he suggests that such a potential ought to be regarded as constitutive and foundational to *all* forms of work. Drawing on recent work by Mike Wayne, Toynbee identifies a notion of the 'essential creativeness of [all] work' at the heart of Marx's theory of labour, one that has faded from view in mainstream workplace study, but has become prominent in those accounts that attribute special quality to the cultural work process. Like Stahl, Toynbee wants to bring cultural work back into the fold of work in general, and debunk its privileged status, while retaining the possibility that cultural work is able to disclose something fundamental that other forms of work might not so singularly or promiscuously reveal.

A different set of questions is probed by Brett Neilson. His chapter makes an original contribution by locating cultural work within the wider networks and chains of supply, demand, production and consumption, and specifically tracking how cultural work relates to other labour processes and experiences. Set within an account of logistics as central to the social form of contemporary capitalism, the chapter is less interested in cultural work as the labour of symbolic expression, and more concerned with patterns of exploitation and dispossession that link differently positioned cultural workforces. The focus comes from his involvement in a 'transit labour' project which looks at a variety of Chinese and Indian cities/workforces. Politically, the chapter takes us to a new place: rather than posing the problem of the precariat or the capacity of cultural workers to unite as a class, it places the political moment of precarity within a wider network of relations in order to think about the potentialities of linking these through questions about dispossession. It argues that a labour politics for cultural workers must look beyond the cultural and creative industries and generate new liquid solidarities. It requires that we ask new questions, such as how accumulation by exploitation relates and articulates to accumulation by dispossession.

Richard Maxwell and Toby Miller's chapter also pushes at questions about the specificity of cultural work, in a polemical critique of the focus of scholars on a small over-privileged 'creative cognitariat'. Maxwell and Miller charge that this preoccupation comes at the expense of forgetting the murderous toil and exploitation of the people who manufacture and dispose of some of the very gadgets that are central to the lives of 'creatives', like mobile phones and iPads. Documenting the situation of Apple subcontractors in Chinese compounds and coltan miners in the Congo, Maxwell and Miller contest the invisibility of this work to scholarship on the cultural industries. When, they ask, did cultural labour become synonymous with 'immaterial labour' amongst those relatively privileged? Their chapter highlights the all-too-brutal material reality of the lives of those who are essential to cultural work, but unable to enjoy its 'creative' benefits.

Finally in this section, Melissa Gregg interrogates cultural work from another direction, questioning its apparent distinctiveness from (other) forms of less glamorous white-collar work, the way it is seen as 'special' and, moreover, contesting the very boundaries of work itself at a moment when the idea of work and non-work as 'separate spheres' is breaking down. Focusing in particular on work done outside the office, the chapter considers the extensification of work across time and space and the psychological and affective dispositions it engenders. It also looks at how new notions of professionalism are developing in which workers learn to embody responsibility for their work at all hours, and take part in extensive regimes of preparation (before work) and recovery (after time spent in the office). In this way, the chapter questions the usefulness of notions such as 'work–life balance', suggesting rather that work is expanding across time and space to colonize pervasively the sphere of intimate life.

The third part of the book takes off from Gregg's contribution to ask about the futures of cultural work. In a field in which inequalities are getting worse rather than better, Sarah B. Proctor-Thomson's chapter takes a critical look at discourses of gender diversity in the cultural industries. Using a feminist poststructuralist approach that draws on the work of Judith Butler, she explores the ways in which rhetoric about creativity and cultural work is performative of realities of inequality and exclusion. Her chapter identifies a strong tendency in government and development agency rhetoric to link creativity and diversity with positive economic performance, despite the continuing under-representation of women and black and minority ethnic workers in the cultural and creative industries in comparison with the rest of the economy. By analysing a combination of academic and policy discourses and interviews with digital media workers, the chapter shows how a norm of 'difference' is promoted as necessary for creative work. However, this difference is variously interpreted within the boundaries of conformity to norms of the conventional workplace (such as whiteness, maleness and able-bodiedness), or in a simplistic contrast that reinforces the value of women's difference in deeply sexist terms, such as the supposedly 'civilizing' influence they bring to the (male) workplace. The chapter unpacks the idea that women 'bring diversity', arguing that even progressive or positive-sounding statements may actually entrench inequalities. In this sense, it offers a bleak assessment of the possibilities of a more egalitarian future for cultural work.

A contrasting note of caution is sounded by Lisa Adkins who examines the utility of dominant methods for studying cultural work, and finds them unable to grasp the uncertain, precarious and DIY biographies of the new media workers she studies. In particular, her target is the use of biographical methods, organized around the life history interview as a dominant form of data collection. If we take seriously claims about the impossibility – or at the very least difficulty – for contemporary cultural workers to narrate a meaningful story of their lives, because of the radical uncertainties they inhabit and the breakdown of 'clock time', then, Adkins claims, new and different methodological tools will be necessary to apprehend and capture the interrupted and discontinuous biographies of cultural workers.

Contrasted with Stahl and Toynbee's chapters earlier in the book, Mark Deuze and Nicky Lewis's chapter is a testament to the specialness (of cultural work) thesis. They suggest, echoing writers such as Henry Jenkins and John Hartley that patterns of work in the cultural and creative industries *do* mark a distinctive epochal break with previous formations. Their argument is that systems of labour, technology and production have been revolutionized in the context of a new and hybrid 'media ecology' and era of 'convergence culture' marked by the progressive dissolution of historically established social relationships and temporal and spatial boundaries. The political consequences of such a shift are outlined. The cultural worker is identified as an exemplary actor at the vanguard of a new work world – and Deuze and Lewis suggest that with progressive individualization comes the opportunity for workers to 'determine their own destiny' as systems erupt into decentralized, dispersed regimes that offer neither a comfortable security nor a constraining tradition. In offering the strongest statement against the endowments of history and inherited patterns of opportunity and constraint, Deuze and Lewis offer an affirmative counterpoint to the majority of other perspectives in this book.

Finally, in an interview with Andrew Ross, the cultural analyst who has perhaps done most to open up and popularize this academic field, we return to some of the core questions that animate this book. We asked to what extent cultural and creative labour is marked out as distinctive from other forms of work; whether the 'troubles' of creative biographies are new; and what kinds of political engagements are appropriate for intervening in the current moment. Ross reflects at length on the impact of the current recession, arguing that it has been so long and so deep that it may have enacted a seemingly permanent transformation in work mentalities. One area where this is vividly evident is in relation to the normalization of the unpaid internship – a situation which, as Ross points out, not only re-entrenches class privilege and inequality, but also may come to constitute a 'terminal limbo' for people attempting to make a living in the cultural and creative sector. Alongside this, and potentially offering access to individuals from a wider range of backgrounds, is the growing significance of the talent show/reality TV model in which young people are exhorted to believe they can 'make it' in the affective attention economy, as the traditional 'casting call' is 'industrialized' to form a more extensive mode of cultural production.

Ross's reflections on the cultural and creativity 'hype' of the late 1990s and beyond are insightful. Whilst highlighting battles over intellectual property and the cynical use of 'creatives' to push up rents and gentrify neighbourhoods, he also argues that one unintended consequence of the dominance of the cultural and creative industries rhetoric is precisely that cultural workers are 'more conscious of their labour conditions and their serviceability to corporate and political elites than they were 10 or 15 years ago'. In this, as well as in the flourishing of new forms of labour organization and activism around debt, which he regards as a key political issue of our time, Ross sees grounds for hope. His ideas offer a means of (re)connecting the cultural and creative industries to the wider social and political relations in which we are all embedded, theorizing cultural work in terms of both continuity and change.

Notes

1 In academic and non-academic discourse, these terms are often used interchangeably, usually as shorthand to describe various forms of artistic labour, media work or activity that involve the production of symbolic or expressive goods and intellectual property. In different national and regional contexts, each may carry some specific meaning, though this is often contested. Institutional definitions and measures similarly vary. Throughout this book, contributors use both of these terms, often in different ways. It is not our intention therefore to specify or police this distinction too carefully – though we would suggest that the idea of cultural industries carries a deeper connection and value to issues of politics and culture not always present in creative industries thinking, policy and practice – and that our personal preference is to think of creative industries as a particularly modern object and form of praxis emergent from a much longer history of cultural industry thinking and endeavour.

2 *The Future of Cultural Work* (2008), *Cultural Work and Creative Biographies* (2009), *Researching Cultural Work and Creative Biographies* (2009), and, with the University of Leeds, *Moral Economies of Creative Labour* (2011).

3 *Inequality in the Cultural and Creative Industries*, King's College London, June 2010.

Part I
Histories

2 Precarious labour then and now

The British Arts and Crafts Movement and cultural work revisited

Susan Luckman

> I believe the right question to ask, respecting all ornament, is simply this: Was it done with enjoyment – was the carver happy while he was about it? It may be the hardest work possible, and the harder because so much pleasure was taken in it; but it must have been happy too, or it will not be living.
>
> (Ruskin 1903: 218)

All too often, work in the creative and cultural industries is discussed as though it embodies a complete break from the workplace practices and the debates of the past. As the global North adjusts itself into the next major economic and social revolution – the shift to the information society – it is important to remind ourselves that concerns about the vulnerability of the (precarious) creative worker in the face of rapid change are not new. Indeed, as I will argue in this chapter, in many ways, the Arts and Crafts Movement of the late 19th and early 20th centuries represents a key reference point for contemporary English-language discussions of creativity and cultural work. Yet figures such as Ruskin and Morris have not received the attention they deserve in the emerging literature about the creative industries. This is perhaps not surprising given the tendency of recent writing to distance contemporary cultural work from the Romantic figure of the artist, and, moreover, the lingering concerns about Luddism within the Arts and Crafts Movement. However, as I shall argue, the time is ripe for a re-evaluation of the significance of Ruskin and Morris for contemporary analyses of cultural work, at a moment when, as the dust settles on the initial excitement of 24/7 connectivity, the uses to which technology may be put within employment systems is again emerging as an important employment issue (c.f. Gregg 2011).

After briefly introducing the key figures of Ruskin and Morris, this chapter will outline a number of their core concerns including the de-humanizing effect of treating a worker as a 'tool', the importance of a healthy workplace, the organization of cultural labour, the possible uses of machines, the need for social inclusion as a core organizing concern of labour and society, and guild socialism. Then the chapter concludes by suggesting that these Victorian approaches to creative good work offer a useful historical context for present-day discussions of cultural employment.

The contemporary precariousness of cultural work

Space limitations mean I cannot go into any great detail nor do justice to this complex and important body of ideas, which other writers in this volume will examine more deeply, but in order to situate the parallels between current scholarly debates and the Arts and Crafts Movement's legacy it is first necessary to set the contemporary scene. In short, today, creative workers find themselves negotiating a complex new workplace environment and its problematic refashioning not only of the producer–consumer, but also of the work–life, divide. All too frequently, this melding of work and play is lauded as one of the great leaps forward of the creative workplace.

However, a growing body of critique is emerging that throws cold water on some of the grander employment claims implicit in much creative economy discourse, notably including scholarship inspired by Italian thinkers and the conceptualization of 'immaterial labour' (Banks 2007; Berardi 2009; Berlant 2008; Coté and Pybus 2007; de Peuter and Dyer-Witheford 2005; Gill and Pratt 2008; Kücklich 2005; Lazzarato 1996; Negri 2006; Terranova 2000). Some of the potential shortcomings of these kinds of employment models were certainly acknowledged early on in the current moment by many creative industries supporters. For example, Leadbeater and Oakley in their 1999 report *The Independents: Britain's New Cultural Entrepreneurs*, published by the key British think tank Demos, recognized that the cultural industries are 'less socially inclusive in terms of employment than other industries' (Leadbeater and Oakley 1999: 18), and that, owing to the lack of a medium-sized business tier mediating between the transnational global empires that control the majority of the world's copyright industries and small-scale independent entrepreneurs, 'many cultural entrepreneurs run fragile, low-growth companies in industries that have low barriers to entry and a high turnover of talent and ideas' (Leadbeater and Oakley 1999: 19).

Today around the industrialized world when discussing creative industries workers, we are talking about people who grew up taking for granted job flexibility, casualization of the employment marketplace and all the uncertainty that goes with this. Bourdieu argued that job insecurity as a result of casualization has profound individual and societal effects which become particularly visible at the extreme level of unemployment: it leads to 'the destructuring of existence, which is deprived among other things of its temporal structures, and the ensuing deterioration of the whole relationship to the world, time and space' (Bourdieu 1998: 82). The insecurity caused by bouts of over- as well as under-employment, he continued,

> profoundly affects the person who suffers it: by making the whole future uncertain, it prevents all rational anticipation and, in particular, the basic belief and hope in the future that one needs in order to rebel, especially collectively, against present conditions

(Bourdieu 1998: 82)

In many ways, the international video games industry with its phenomenal growth underpinned as it often is by the self-taught and unpaid 'modders', like other digital content growth sectors of the creative economy, has seen this 'work as play' pattern of rewarding but demanding employment speeded up, yielding salient lessons for other sectors of the cultural economy. In particular, it is seen to be defined by long hours with no overtime pay; hours that negate the ability to have a family or maintain a relationship; mobility and the expectation of a willingness to uproot one's life at short notice; the exclusion of women and non-dominant groups from workplace culture; long hours that impact upon a healthy lifestyle (loss of sleep, poor diet, no exercise); the expectation of being creative without a break; and a lack of recognition for copyright (de Peuter and Dyer-Witheford 2005; Kücklich 2005). Frequently, it leads to the loss of experienced workers as their vision of the good life shifts to include non-work commitments.

New technology is enabling a different kind of workplace, one that allows a wider array of mobile work locations. On the upside, this does lead to greater flexibility and potential social inclusion – for instance, working from home is regularly seen as more inclusive of family and other care-giving commitments, whether or not this is true in practice (Gregg 2008, 2011). On the downside, work concerns increasingly leak into personal time (Williams *et al.* 2009; Gregg 2011), which results in longer hours of labour, as workers seek to fit competing responsibilities around occupation deadlines. This is especially the case as women retain the lion's share of child-rearing and domestic responsibilities (Jurik 1998). Further, given that most cultural workers in medium-sized and large creative industries organizations tend to occupy privileged but not powerful locations within their workplaces (Hesmondhalgh and Baker 2011), and not be unionized (Callus and Cole 2002; Gibson 2003; Hesmondhalgh and Baker 2011), their ability to negotiate a fairer deal around these issues is severely compromised.

Victorian socialism and creative labour: John Ruskin and William Morris

> Art is man's expression of his joy in labour.
>
> (Morris 1973: 67, interpreting Ruskin)

Despite the emergence of the creative industries as a discursive economic framework, the current moment is clearly not the first time questions concerning the individuation of the labour force, the negative impacts of new technologies, long working hours, exploitation and unhealthy lifestyles have arisen in cultural and political writing around creative work. As Raymond Williams has written, the Romantic idea of the artist carried over into the late Victorian period of the Arts and Crafts Movement. At this time, key figures such as Ruskin and Morris emerged in the late 19th century as they sought to challenge the dehumanizing assemblages of the Industrial Revolution.

John Ruskin (1819–1900) is a larger-than-life figure increasingly known in the 20th century for his less than exemplary biography, rather than the words that made him famous in the first place. As Kenneth Clark noted in his mid-20th century annotated collection of Ruskin's work, collected together as he felt it was time people read Ruskin's words rather than about him, 'Between 1929 and 1953, at least seven full-length biographies of Ruskin were published; but his own works were almost entirely unread' (Clark 1967: ix). To be sure, he opened the introduction to the book with the statement: 'No other writer, perhaps, has suffered so great a fall in reputation as Ruskin' (Clark 1967: xi). Beyond his personal biography, some of Ruskin's ideas certainly do not hold up as feasible or desirable in a 21st century context; for example, editors of his work have singled out the emphasis on fixed wages Ruskin presented in the canonical volume *Unto this Last* for special attention in this regard (Ruskin 2010: 12). However, whatever his personal biography, Ruskin's words and actions have had a profound influence globally. They inspired some of the key figures of the 20th century (Gandhi, Tolstoy, Bernard Shaw), and are directly linked to the emergence out of the Victorian era of some of the community organizations that continue to work to protect environmental and community interests to this day, such as the National Trust, as well as the welfare state and green movements (Clark 1967; Jackson 2010; Ruskin 2010). While he himself self-identified as a Tory and not a socialist (Clark 1967; Jackson 2010: 80), when at the first meeting of the British parliamentary Labour Party members were asked to name the determining influence on their lives, almost every one answered 'the works of Ruskin' (Clark 1967: xii).

In an 1983 overview that demonstrates how the ideas of the Arts and Crafts Movement would today be as much at home on an 'Occupy Wall Street' website, Raymond Williams wrote of the key tenets of the earlier age that:

> The emphasis on a general common humanity was evidently necessary in a period in which a new kind of society was coming to think of man as merely a specialized instrument of production. The emphasis on love and relationship was necessary not only within the immediate suffering but against the aggressive individualism and the primarily economic relationships which the new society embodied. Emphasis on the creative imagination, similarly, may be seen as an alternative construction of human motive and energy, in contrast with the assumptions of the prevailing political economy.
>
> (Williams 1983: 42)

Certainly, given that the global financial crisis has caused many to reconsider the dominant post-1980s economic rationalist focus on the accumulation of money as a defining *raison d'être* of people and society, it makes particular sense to look again at the Arts and Crafts Movement's challenge to the 'complacent Victorian belief in progress' (Newman 1984: 8). Such a mood clearly resonates with Ruskin's belief that a society, and the individuals within it, will only truly be wealthy when they acquire that wealth under particular moral conditions that have at their core a commitment to honesty – or transparency, as we would be more likely to articulate this call today (Ruskin 2010: 19).

As already indicated, the increasing casualization of cultural work and the fact that much of it remains contract-based is one of those qualities lauded as markers of the 'new' post-industrial era, the post-'jobs for life' economy. Yet the uncertain income arising from seasonality and otherwise inconsistent demand for particular forms of labour was a core concern of Ruskin, which he conceived as unacceptable in a humane industrial system:

> This inequality of wages, then, being the first object towards which we have to discover the directest available road; the second is, as above stated, that of maintaining constant numbers of workmen in employment, whatever may be the accidental demand for the article they produce. I believe the sudden and extensive inequalities of demand, which necessarily arise in the mercantile operations of an active nation, constitute the only essential difficulty which has to be overcome in a just organization of labour.
>
> (Ruskin 2010: 32)

With digital technology and the growth of the creative workforce again destabilizing the dominant modes of production for many workers in the industrialized and industrializing world, the concerns of the two eras have clear parallels. Thus, scholarly discussions of precarious labour and, within this, the valorization of creative employment, contain patent resonances of Ruskin's oft-repeated famous dictum:

> You must either make a tool of [your worker], or a man of him. You cannot make both. Men are not intended to work with the accuracy of tools, to be precise and perfect in all their actions. If you will have that precision out of them … you must unhumanize them. All the energy of their spirits must be given to make cogs and compasses of themselves. In every man there is the capacity for something better than this machine-like labour, some power of feeling and imagination.
>
> (Ruskin 1907: 176–77)

Though Ruskin made his reputation as Britain's foremost art commentator of the Victorian age, as he and his writing matured, he veered away from the more assuredly popular topic of arts commentary and became increasingly concerned with explorations of the organization of creative labour and explication of his own vision of good work. His *oeuvre* is vast, and thus, while many of his later works criticized political economy writ large and sought to provide alternative models of labour exchange well beyond the arts (for example, Ruskin 2010), he arrived at his political critique via an examination of the conditions under which workers can produce good art, architecture and cities. This means that, while his legacy extends far beyond the realms of cultural work, he remains first and foremost a commentator on *creative production*. He was the popularizer of the art of J.M.W. Turner, but when he started to extend his interest in the aesthetics of art into what was ostensibly a socialist concern with the historical conditions of its production – in particular, he held up medieval modes of craft production as his ideal – he was roundly criticized by his middle-class audience, which was much more comfortable with his arts volumes than emerging political radicalism (Jackson 2010: 80). The first clear manifestation of Ruskin's growing interest in the conditions of cultural work begins to emerge in Volume II of his *Stones of Venice* (the three volumes were released between 1851 and 1853). Here, in the section entitled 'The nature of gothic', Ruskin first linked good art to good work. The short section was extracted and circulated as a pamphlet to be distributed free of charge at the newly founded Working Men's College in London (Jackson 2010: 71). Much to the chagrin of his early arts-focused middle-class readership, Ruskin continued to develop his critique of labour relations and the economic organization of society in subsequent writings and most notably in *Unto this Last* (2010 [1862]).

For the Arts and Crafts Movement, labour and the ethics of work were but one part of a person's being that need to be deliberated within a larger vision of a person's life. Consequently, John Ruskin's emphasis on the idea of 'wholeness' (Williams 1983: 139) as applied to the individual artist/craftsperson is analogous to contemporary concerns over work–life balance. One of Ruskin's particularly insightful observations about the organization of cultural labour, which was quite ahead of its time, arose out of his earlier exposure to the relatively autonomous status that artists had under systems of patronage that enabled them to produce quality work without the constant monitoring and threat of punishment emerging as the management system of the Industrial Revolution. Coming out of the arts, he recognized that workers will do their best and work hard if self-motivated – that is, if engaged in self-actualizing work. Not only this, but that under these conditions they are also most likely to be capable of 'perpetual novelty' (Ruskin 1907: 192). He argued that the political economist's emphasis on hard treatment to extract all the labour a worker could give would only work:

> if the servant were an engine of which the motive power was steam, magnetism, gravitation, or any other agent of calculable force. But he being, on the contrary, an engine whose motive power is a Soul, the force of this very particular agent, as an unknown quantity, enters into all the political economist's equations, without his knowledge, and falsifies every one of their results.
>
> (Ruskin 2010: 27)

For as he had written elsewhere:

> It may be proved, with much certainty, that God intends no man to live in this world without working: but it seems to me no less evident that He intends every man to be happy in his work. It is written, 'in the sweat of thy brow,' but it was never written, 'in the breaking of thine heart'.
>
> (Ruskin, 'Pre-Raphaelitism', quoted in Clark 1967: 267)

Therefore, when it comes to practices of good work, Ruskin argued strongly for what he saw as the common sense idea that you get the best out of people (economically and socially) when they are valued as people and engaged in a task they find rewarding: 'Thus worthy work carries with it the hope of pleasure in rest, the hope of the pleasure in our using what it makes, and the hope of pleasure in our daily creative skill' (Morris 1973: 88). Such ideas are clearly antecedents to the relative autonomy and opportunities for self-actualizing work underpinning the idealized 'good work' so desired, if not always realized, in the contemporary creative economy.

Like Ruskin, his contemporary William Morris (1834–96) was a key Victorian progressive; however, unlike Ruskin, Morris was very much an out and proud socialist. This is perhaps ironic given that he is now best known as the entrepreneur and textile designer behind Morris and Co. which brought the handcrafted items of the Arts and Crafts Movement into the drawing rooms of the emerging British middle classes via the Liberty shopfront. However, Morris, who was greatly influenced by Ruskin's ideas – 'Reading [*Stones of Venice*] was a turning point in Morris's life' (Jackson 2010: 72) – offers us a better model for how they might work in practice and in the specific context of a socialist vision of labour (Jackson 2010: 71; Williams 1983: 148).

Perhaps not surprisingly given that Morris was actually a practising creative producer on a significant commercial scale, he was concerned with the pragmatic question of what exactly constituted an optimal workplace for cultural production. He believed that quality work comes from quality processes, and that means a healthy workplace:

> The last claim I make for my work is that the places I worked in, factories or workshops, should be pleasant, just as the fields where our most necessary work is done are pleasant. Believe me there is nothing in the world to prevent this being done, save the necessity of making profits on all wares; in other words, the wares are cheapened at the expense of people being forced to work in crowded, unwholesome, squalid, noisy dens: that is to say, they are cheapened at the expense of the workman's life.
>
> (Morris 1973: 152–53)

Despite a hostility to machines being a high-profile part of his legacy (Harrod 1999: 17), the pragmatist Morris was not against machines if they reduced labour drudgery (Williams 1983: 154). For example, he believed machinery should be introduced to reduce the costs associated with books bound by hand (Harrod 1999: 15–16). His interest, like Ruskin's, was the need to avoid dehumanizing the worker, as per the mechanisms of the Industrial Revolution: as Williams paraphrased, 'The artist's goodness is also his "wholeness", and the goodness of a society lies in its creation of the conditions for the "wholeness of being"' (Williams 1983: 138).

A commitment to social inclusion and respect for the dignity and sustenance of the worker inform both Ruskin's and Morris's political writings. In *Unto this Last*, Ruskin (2010: 42) identified two ways of viewing the economy: 'political' and 'mercantile'. The former foregrounds the economy as but one part of the wider social world of the community, one with the important responsibility to deliver the means of sustenance at its core. The other, the 'mercantile' approach, is the debased economy of accumulation by the individual at the expense of the community. His was a progressive social agenda which did not seek to overthrow capitalism, but sought rather to make it a balanced part of a humane society. While the utopianism of much of both Ruskin's and Morris's writings has been validly identified as a point of weakness, aspirational progressive visions of society that ethically weave together people's working and social lives are once again on the political agenda. In the Victorian era, the Arts and Crafts Movement was highly attuned to the need to skill, educate and provide meaningful employment to the working classes, rural poor and, increasingly, women. Today, issues of social inclusion are again at the fore of creative industries debates. Gender and class remain trouble spots in terms of a larger social inclusion agenda, but are now joined by an increasing awareness of race, ethnicity, sexuality and (dis)ability as sites of contestation in the highly socially networked world of creative employment. Further, with digital communications technologies increasingly enabling more 'intimate' (Gregg 2011) and 'flexible' work arrangements, which are particularly sought out by women who disproportionately bear responsibility for child-rearing, even in the advanced economies of the global North (Jurik 1998), fairness and inclusion remain central concerns for creative work. On this note, we might do well to heed the lessons of early post-mortem examinations of the Arts and Crafts Movement's failure. While acknowledging that the Movement had successfully upheld one of its two key aims – the revitalization and maintenance of traditional skills – later arts intellectual A.R Orage laments the failure of its more radical sociological agenda (Orage 1907). He felt that the virtue had gone out of the Movement, in no small part as a result of its alliance with the emerging labour movement and party, which benefitted far more from co-opting the Arts and Crafts Movement than the latter did out of the relationship (Orage 1907). With creative industries scholarship now being identified by some leading scholars as cultural studies' neo-liberal, market-friendly 'New Right' (Maxwell and Miller 2011: 588), the importance of a 'sociological agenda' as a core agenda of cultural work politics remains. So, too, does the place of collective organization as a possible means by which to counter the worst effects of precarious employment upon the individual worker and their community.

Looking back to medieval modes of work and aesthetics as it did, the Arts and Crafts Movement as inspired by Ruskin and Morris upheld the value of the old guild model of craftsmanship, which brought together otherwise autonomous craft specialists to oversee the training, accreditation and standards of workmanship in any given creative practice. More relevant for today, by the early years of the 20th century, this had been developed further into a more contemporary 'guild socialism', which emphasized the purity of labour and aesthetics less, and thus allowed for the use of machines to reduce repetitive labour, and instead emphasized the importance of the economic model of collective ownership and control as the determinant of good work (Harrod 1999: 154). Perhaps the fullest practical expression of these ideas came in the form of the Guild of Handicraft. Headed by architect, visionary thinker and follower of the ideas of Morris and Ruskin (among others) C.R. Ashbee, the Guild famously moved from its early base in the east end of London to the Cotswolds town of Chipping Campden in search of its vision of a better, more holistic life for its workers and their families. Here 'craftsmen [and women] worked together and shared their leisure hours in sing-songs, excursions and play-acting: Ashbee provided a swimming pool for use by both the Guild and Chipping Campden' (Cumming and Kaplan 1991: 28).

Contemporary cultural work is seen as notable for the ways in which its precariousness is manipulated and sustained by management practices that reinforce the individualization of the creative worker (Banks 2007). This situation is reified by the large surplus pool of labour seeking entry and the relative absence of unionization or any other form of collective organization. While it remained economically viable, the Guild's collective structure furnished its members with a buffer against the precariousness of contract-based work. Individual craftspeople were able to leverage against the economies of scale possible via group membership. Groups could afford to establish comfortable work spaces and a guaranteed quality of life (housing, food, entertainment), and provide shared marketing and distribution networks, for example a London shopfront, not possible at an individual level. Such collective forms of organization continue, especially in the traditional cultural work areas of arts and crafts practice, and notably in rural and regional areas where many independent producers are located, outside of large urban networks (see Luckman 2012). Pooling together can increase the profile and hence income stream attainable by small producers without the benefit of marketing and distribution arms, by affording access to not only physical but also virtual shopfronts. In the online world, this is perhaps most obviously demonstrated by the increasingly popular etsy.com, which has been described as 'eBay for the handmade' (Luckman n.d.). While collective organization can be difficult in sectors of cultural work marked by their competition – for example, the highly contract-based world of digital media and film media production – the pooling of resources by individual workers with complementary rather than overlapping skill sets still enables leveraging of these kinds of economies of scale. In this way, craft models familiar to the Victorians remain useful tools, especially for those workers seeking to maintain a degree of control over their working situation through self-employment, which notably includes a growing body of women seeking to generate an income while working from home.

Conclusion: the Victorian experience and contemporary creative 'good work'

While not wishing to defend or uncritically argue for a return to the Romantic conception of the artist, like Raymond Williams (1983) I believe that the political (rather than aesthetic) writings of such key Victorian figures as William Morris and John Ruskin, among others, are worth exploring in terms of their philosophical and political parallels with contemporary debates around precarious labour. In this way I agree with those few voices in cultural work scholarship who see too much emphasis in current debates on breaks from previous practices, and hence their lessons. As Hesmondhalgh and Baker noted in their recent book *Creative Labour: Media Work in Three Cultural Industries*, 'it would be a mistake to think of cultural industries as always in such a state of permanent flux that there is no stability. Change is often exaggerated at the expense of continuity' (Hesmondhalgh and Baker 2011: 13).

Indeed, to really get a feel for the resonances between the two periods of economic and industrial (and hence cultural and social) change, it is useful to juxtapose Morris and Ruskin's visions of proper labour arrangements with Hesmondhalgh and Baker's recent writings on 'good work', which they distil down to: 'decent pay, hours and safety; autonomy; interest and involvement; sociality; esteem and self-esteem; self-realization; work–life balance; security. Conversely [the] features of bad work [are]: poor pay, hours and safety; powerlessness; boredom; isolation; self-doubt and shame; overwork; insecurity and risk' (Hesmondhalgh and Baker 2011: 17). Hesmondhalgh and Baker's current contribution is but one part of the emerging body of post-precarious labour literature that seeks, like the Arts and Crafts Movement earlier, to clarify and reimagine understandings of the ideal qualities of cultural work, within the pragmatic realities of contemporary economic structures. Both eras feature analogous conceptions of 'wholeness': of the need for cultural work to be an integrated (and not alienated) part of a balanced, healthy lifestyle. Both acknowledge some sense of vocation: of the importance of pleasure and pride in work well done and of a commitment to something larger than simply the work or a job. Thus, an analogous itemization of the overlaps between the mutual concerns of the Arts and Crafts Movement and contemporary cultural workers would include: the desire for non-alienated labour and creative work; a belief in reward for effort, fair pay, a living wage and quality of life issues; concern about the relationship between work and community, in particular the individualizing of society at the expense of social ties; the relationship between family life and creative work, especially in relation to work undertaken from home; the place of women in creative industries; the standing and conduct of craft-based practice; the value of craftsmanship and the place of 'quality' and skills (which resonates in the 21st century in terms of debates over user-generated content and the future of content production professionals); the value of culture and creativity as drivers of regional development, but also of the potential negative impact of tourism; sustaining people through seasonally based or insecure contract-based labour; and alarm at the impact of production on the environment.

At times of profound social and economic change, such as we are experiencing at present, quality of life – what exactly constitutes 'the good life' within the economic, social and technical frameworks in which we find ourselves – is an issue that societies need to revisit in the interests of collective and personal sustainability. To fail to reacquaint ourselves with how these issues have panned out in recent history would be to reinvent the wheel, and we can learn from errors just as we can from successes. It is all too easy to dismiss many of the key writings of the Arts and Crafts Movement as overly utopian and, at worst, patronising, totally naïve and misguided 'middle Englander' Romanticism. That said, Ruskin, Morris and their contemporaries were attuned to a key truth about cultural work: that for most people engaged in it, creativity-based labour is as much about the heart as it is the head, or hands. In its rush to distance creative industries rubrics from the isolated, elite and often economically unproductive Romantic figure of the 'artist in the garret', the affective importance of cultural work within wider structures of feeling has all too often been ignored in contemporary debates. Rather than a weakness, then, at the dawn of the 21st century the desire for social inclusion and its emotive utopianism is perhaps the Arts and Crafts Movement's greatest gift to us.

3 Cultural work and antisocial psychology

Sarah Brouillette

Scholars have sometimes observed that, as work of many types has been increasingly experienced as indivisible from self-expression and self-fulfilment, artists have been imagined as models for all workers (Boltanski and Chiapello 2005: 422; Sholette 2010: 134). However, little research accounts for how particular ideas about artists' work have exerted their influence – ideas about its flourishing in unstable conditions, or about its relationship to economies of competition and prestige, for example. That what circulate are not simple facts about artists but rather aspects of a discrete aesthetic ideology with its own rich and contentious history is often ignored. This chapter considers one feature of this history. It argues that since the early 1950s influential psychologists and management theorists have tended to present the study of artists as straightforward evidence that the social is a form of constraint to be transcended by the effective working self. Their work has had implications for how art is perceived and for how work is organized. They have depended upon and reinforced the notion that making art is the fundamentally insular expression of one's personally directed passionate devotion to 'the task itself', 'the materials at hand', or simply 'the work'; and they have formed and circulated models of good work as a flexible and self-sufficient enterprise averse to social responsibility, human interdependence and collective politics.

Overview

It was in the late 1940s that US-based psychologists, influenced by their research on World War II military personnel, began in earnest to specify the attributes of the kind of creative individual who would help to secure the nation's future prosperity. This work flourished throughout the 1960s and 1970s when, steeped in the countercultural ethos, it morphed into a celebration of the non-conformist as ideal creative personality. It was at this time that influential thinker Abraham Maslow, who had put forward his theory of the hierarchy of human needs in 1943, increasingly emphasized that the 'self-actualization' perched atop it involved an against-the-grain creativity that was the key means to – and indeed ends of – proper human development. In Maslow's research, as in the writing of his fellow humanist psychologist Frank Barron, non-conforming creativity was figured as an innate tendency to eschew the social, to oppose the mundane, the taken-for-granted, the common and banal, formed less by political will than by an inherent tendency toward self-exploration and self-expression. By the 1960s, inspired by the application of his ideas within management theory, Maslow was arguing that the creativity possessed by the self-actualizing person was potentially as important to business innovation as it was to individual self-development. He suggested that the self-actualizing person would, artist-like, lose the ability to distinguish between her work and her person, as the self and the social merged in the subject whose happiness was inseparable from devotion to a kind of work that was simultaneously selfless and self-interested. The actual purpose of that work was irrelevant. One could achieve self-actualization as a corporate executive, professor or artist, as long as one's work fulfilled one's ideal self.

In the 1980s and 1990s, Maslow's concepts – in particular, his theories of the hierarchy of human needs and of self-actualization – were crucial fodder for a growing network of Anglo-American psychologists and management theorists. These thinkers tended to romanticize self-managing employees able to overcome the divide between self and work, or to achieve 'extrinsic' rewards precisely by following 'intrinsic' directives, to use terms derived from the work of Harvard management theorist Teresa Amabile. I argue that Amabile's work is representative in its tendency to present the social as a sphere that, while relevant to some stages of work, exists for the most successful as a sphere to be transcended in heightened moments of creative passion. In less academic versions of this conception – I focus on management guru Tom Peters, but Richard Florida's ideas, or those of former Demos Director Richard Reeves, might be discussed in similar terms – the character of the self-reflexive, expressive and exploratory self is understood to be both economically useful and morally correct. Those who would prefer more stability are thought simply to lack the healthy desire to embrace the art of life, seemingly predisposed by disposition to long for the constraints of the nanny state or the paternalistic daddy corporation.

Creativity as non-conformity

A formative moment of psychologists' interest in creative thinking was J.P. Guilford's presidential address to the 1949 Convention of the American Psychological Association, in which he discussed his own research programme, supported by the US Office of Naval Research, on the aptitudes of high-level personnel. Noting that the generation of new ideas had an economic value already recognized in the business world, and that the US government, itself a major employer of scientific and technical personnel, was clearly interested in identifying potentially inventive people, Guilford concluded that psychologists were falling woefully behind. It would take creative thinking to develop a new economic order in which sufficient employment would remain once machines were doing a lot of the thinking that people once did. He suggested that most forms of knowledge – the kinds of memorized materials and rote skills charted by IQ tests – would be easily covered by machine intelligence. Creative thinking was the exception. To Guilford, creative thinking entailed advanced aptitudes for new ideas, and in order to study it properly psychologists would need to abandon the conventional notion that it is simply subsumed within one's general intelligence, fostered by mass education and measured by standardized IQ tests (Guilford 1950: 446).

Guilford's address coincided with the founding in 1949 of a research centre based on ideas similar to his, where psychologists were trying to define creativity and study it in some depth. The Institute for Personality Assessment and Research (IPAR), on the Berkeley campus of the University of California, was supported at first by the Carnegie Corporation and run by D.W. MacKinnon.[1] During World War II, MacKinnon had headed a station of the OSS (Office of Strategic Services) dedicated to determining appropriate candidates for special military operations. IPAR began as an extension of this research into individuals' effective functioning, but the relationship between personal effectiveness and creativity soon became its primary concern (Barron 1988: 81). Test subjects and psychologists were housed together for days at a time, sharing informal activities like meals and casual conversation in addition to the usual formal observation and testing. Psychologist Frank Barron joined IPAR as a graduate student in its early days, and went on to become one of its most influential scholars. Study of artists and creative writers, as well as observation of subjects' verbal aptitudes and reactions to art images, were all integral to his research conclusions. I argue that the effect of his work was to present the alienated artist as a model of psychological health, and to construct the social as equivalent to forms of mass culture, routine and conventional respect for authority that healthy individuals wish naturally to reject.

Making this case requires looking closely at some of his correlated tests. In the Barron-Welsh Art Scale (BWAS), designed as a measure of subjects' dispositions toward originality, artists and non-artists were asked to like or dislike a series of black and white designs on 3 x 5 inch cards. Barron found that artists liked images 'which were highly complex, asymmetrical, freehand rather than ruled, and rather restless and moving in their general effect' (Barron 1953: 164). Images liked by people in general were, in contrast, 'relatively simple, often bilaterally symmetrical, and regularly predictable, following some cardinal principle which could be educed at a glance' (ibid.: 164), and these same images were described by artists as dull and uninteresting. In a similar measure, the Painting Preference test, Barron and his team showed subjects colour postcard reproductions of European paintings, and then sorted them into groups according to their preferences for particular items. He claimed that the results of the test could be correlated to subjects' self-perceptions. In one group, the relatively non-creative group, the preference was for depictions of religion, authority, aristocracy and tradition, and its members tended to describe themselves as 'moderate, modest, responsible, foresighted [and] conscientious' (ibid.: 194–95). In the second group, made up of relatively creative people, preference was for complex and irregular forms, and for radically experimental, sensual, esoteric, sensational and primitive themes; people in this group tended to describe themselves as pessimistic, bitter, dissatisfied, emotional, unstable, demanding, anxious and temperamental.

At one point in Barron's research, he chose a test group made up of 56 professional creative writers and 10 student writers, their names largely obtained through consultation with faculty in English and in Drama at the University of California. Test group members were asked to respond to the usual roster of tests and interviews, which by now included the BWAS, the Painting Preference test, and also another he had devised called the Symbolic Equivalence Test. The Symbolic Equivalence Test had a literary inspiration. Barron had seen Cecil Day-Lewis give the Clark Lectures on 'The Poetic Image' at Cambridge in 1946, where, in Barron's words, he 'spoke to a point that was to become a central concern for me in the psychology of creativity ... the problem of gestalt transformation in memory' (Barron 1988: 84). In the published version of his lectures Lewis describes one instance of this gestalt transformation – the transmutation of an image from one domain into another – which Barron soon deemed an aptitude for thinking of – or thinking in – metaphors:

> The poet was looking out of his window in blitzed London. A searchlight practice was on. The beams swung about the sky, then leaned together like the framework of a wigwam, and at the apex an aircraft could be seen, silver, moth-like, flying slowly, found, lost, found again by the searchlights. It was a common enough sight just then ... but this time the poet saw it differently, as a dramatic paradox; it seemed to him that candle-beams were desireously searching for the moth.
>
> (Lewis 1946: 89)

With this account in mind, Barron devised a test in which people were asked to think of three metaphors, 'or symbolically equivalent images', for each in a set of ten stimulus images. They were scored for their number of admissible versus original responses; admissible responses were scored for aptness on a scale of one to three; original responses were scored for their degree of originality on a scale of one to five. So, for instance, given the stimulus image of 'Sitting alone in a dark room', respondents would provide equivalents such as these: lying awake at night (scored a one); an unborn child (a two); a stone under water (a three); a king lying in a coffin (worth four); or Milton (worth five). Barron explains that to be highly original, 'to get the highest rating', the response necessarily 'grabs you, it surprises you, it gives you a chill as a great line of poetry can do' (Barron 1988: 88).

Barron extended his findings to argue that high scores on the Symbolic Equivalence Test, as on the BWAS, were significantly correlated with high scores on other tests devised to measure independence of judgement and complexity of outlook. They were also correlated to low scores on tests to measure socialization, indicating a significant resistance to acculturation, or to a socialization process which they perceived as a demand that they sacrifice their individuality, which, Barron judges, 'it often is'. He notes as well a correlation to low scores on tests to measure one's adherence to economic values. Writers' scores put them at the apex of those personality types who were not 'playing' for financial 'stakes' (Barron 1968: 244–45). Indeed, the writers included in Barron's studies had the best scores across the range of tests, becoming models for the kind of iconoclastic and creative self-articulation Barron himself valued and sought to valorize in his research.

That Barron's research was slowly elaborating a model healthy self is quite apparent: his various tests, and the correlated self-descriptions of his subjects, were eventually formalized into measures distinguishing the Complex from the Simple Person. Barron argued that an appreciation for complexity is what allows the healthy individual to experience seemingly contradictory states of being with no real difficulty: she is healthier than others because she has experienced and worked through psychological problems; she can confidently regress because she can return to her mature self with ease; she is free to use her powers of imagination because she never loses her firm grasp on reality; because the distinction between self and object is most secure, it can be allowed to disappear for a time, thus freeing the mind for creative exploration. It is writers who best model the Complex Person for Barron, because they are 'as a class significantly more independent, flexible, and original than most people' (Barron 1968: 242). They are also more comfortable with ambiguity, balancing dualisms within themselves; they are for instance at once sicker and healthier than average, as 'they are much more troubled psychologically, but they also have far greater resources with which to deal with their troubles' (ibid.: 244).

I suggest that the construction of this model self was a notably solipsistic project. Barron and his colleagues were themselves creatively deviating from existing ways of thinking about human intelligence and motivation, and Barron's studies were a version of what they aimed to assess, as was much of the research going on under IPAR's auspices. They are a social science expression of what was to become the countercultural ethos of the 1960s, in this case manifest as a reaction against the limitations of traditional psychology – against, for instance, its conformist acceptance of IQ testing, which connected genius-level intellect to repetition of existing knowledge and worked against the Romantic idea that creative geniuses are emotionally unstable and socially maladjusted (Arons 1996: 63–64). Like Guilford, who claimed success on standardized tests was evidence of convergent thinking, whereas original thinking was necessarily divergent, Barron and his colleagues found that the traits correlated with creativity would not necessarily relate to attaining high scores on traditional tests. These traits were instead thrillingly 'alien or threatening to values dominant in psychology and the society at the time' (ibid.: 65), and they could not be measured by any assessment based upon one's absorption of accepted knowledge. What matters to the genealogy I am constructing here is the way that this model of non-conformity tended to align society at large not with any necessary community or ethics, but with conformity and predictability, with a respect for popularity and authority, and with an unhealthy addiction to tradition. The divergent values associated with creative thinking involved, in contrast, an insistence on the freedom of one's thinking from social constraint of any kind – including, I emphasize, the constraint of social responsibility or political engagement.

Creative non-conformity at work

Barron expressed occasional awareness that business organizations might be interested in understanding how creative people operate, but he was rarely concerned with specifying in any detailed way the applicability of his findings to the workplace. In this, he differed from Abraham Maslow, the premier theorist of the human potential movement to which Barron informally belonged. Maslow actively turned his own conclusions about creative thinking, which are similar in many ways to Barron's, into management principles. Like Barron, Maslow argued that non-conforming creativity rested in an innate tendency to oppose the mundane and the commonsensical. Maslow came also to argue that the creativity possessed by the self-defining person was as important to business innovation as it was to self-development.

Before the 1960s, Maslow wrote of his surprise at being of interest to corporations. He was unsure if his work could be useful to organizations or if he was instead too much concerned with the loner, someone dissatisfied with what exists and apt to work alone in a corner and be perceived as an outsider or bohemian. Nor did he need to appeal to corporations in order to secure his professional standing. His academic star had been rising steadily since he put forward his 1943 theory of the hierarchy of human needs, an account of the dynamic evolution of human motivations. According to this theory, until certain basic physiological needs and safety needs are met, there is no room for worry about whether or not one is respected by others or a member of a functional family. In turn, until one has achieved respect and familial contentment one cannot pursue the highest need, the need for self-actualization, the pursuit of which involves an array of 'higher' values Maslow worked throughout his life to specify. The self-actualized person is the ideal person, the model to which all should aspire, and her needs are as inherent or biological as the need for food and shelter. Maslow refers to these higher needs as B-Values (or Being-Values), and they are both intangible and tangible qualities, including truth, beauty, newness, uniqueness, goodness, elegance, cleanliness, order, justice and completion.

In the early 1960s, Maslow's description of the self-actualizing person motivated by B-Values dovetailed significantly with his conception of the creative person. In 1962, he wrote that 'it is as if' creativity 'were almost synonymous with, or a *sine qua non* aspect of, or a defining characteristic of, essential humanness' (Maslow 1962: 137); in 1963, he notes that 'the concept of creativeness and the concept of the healthy, self-actualizing, full human person seem to be coming closer and closer together, and may perhaps turn out to be the same thing' (Maslow 1971: 57). Around the same time, he began to conduct his studies from within business organizations. In 1962, he spent a summer at Non-Linear Systems, Inc., a digital voltmeter factory in Del Mar, CA; in 1969, he started a four-year fellowship at the Saga Corporation, funded by a wealthy businessman. It is no surprise then that he was beginning to see his findings about self-actualization and creativity as important ones for business management. It was Non-Linear's President Andrew Kay who invited Maslow to visit the company. Kay had been using books by two progressive management theorists, Douglas MacGregor and Peter Drucker, as guides to how to structure the company, and he was impressed by the overlap between these studies and Maslow's research. Maslow was excited by the fellowship in part because he noticed that, though working as a management consultant, Drucker had reached conclusions about human nature that were similar to his own, Drucker insisted that employees thrived when they perceived themselves to be respected by their bosses – that is, in Maslow's term, when their B-Value desire to be respected was met, a point that Elton Mayo had started to develop decades before. For Douglas MacGregor's part, his 1960 study, *The Human Side of Enterprise*, derived much from Maslow's theories, as he wrote against what he labelled Theory X Management, the authoritarian approach found in most workplaces, which assumes that people dislike work, and because of this must be coerced and threatened to do it. MacGregor proposed Theory Y Management instead, arguing that a person will self-direct to fulfil objectives to which she is herself committed, and that the organization should be attuned to workers' own needs, such as the need for self-respect.

Maslow's work at Non-Linear built upon MacGregor's and Drucker's respective approaches. I argue that he goes much further, though, in arguing for the veritable absorption of the worker's subjectivity into organizational directives, and in creating a fantastical image of the magical transcendence of divisions between self and society, in which the self in pursuit of its own authentic self-realization will lead inevitably to utopian community. He called the book that resulted from his time at Non-Linear *Eupsychian Management*. 'Eupsychia' was his neologism for the 'culture that would be generated by 1,000 self-actualizing people on some sheltered island where they would not be interfered with' (Maslow 1965: xi). Within this utopia, the only ethical mandate to which people would be beholden is their own self-realization, and this can be achieved through *any* correctly managed professional employment. Yet producing one's individual ends would not be opposed to helping others. Instead, one's pursuit of one's own goals would happen independently of, but also somehow never detract from, anyone else's. Indeed, Maslow notes elsewhere a general tendency toward resolution of dichotomies in self-actualizing people: their selfishness is ultimately unselfish; their duty is their pleasure; their work is play; they are childlike and mature; they regress without being neurotic; they are strong egos but also self-transcending. They are, in a word, whole.

Maslow uses artists as models of the kind of wholeness of being that he recommends. Artists become for him particularly important figures because of what he construes as their thriving in insecure conditions and their motivation by internal directives. Having what Maslow called 'peak-experiences' means seeing a thing, an event, a situation in and for itself, separate from any sense of its expediency. To clarify, this is true during the primary phase of creativeness, which is distinct from the secondary working out phase. During the primary phase, rooted in the process itself, one is unconcerned about the products of one's work or its results in success and acclaim. Maslow's subjects tended to describe it as a loss of ego, as transcendence, as integration of self with non-self. It is a kind of 'nakedness' in the situation, or innocence before a task. In its pursuit, we become free of concern for other people and external judgement; we become our authentic or 'Real Selves'. Alienation from this authenticity is the product of what Maslow deems a neurotic involvement with others. Its realization requires that we forget any audience and, ceasing to be actors, become, for the moment, un-neurotic, un-anxious, not sick. He finds a model for this attitude in what he deems the 'artist's respect for his materials' and attention to the 'matter-in-hand'. We thus see here how one particular conception of aesthetic experience is given as self-evident truth: the artist treats her work as 'an end, something *per se*, with its own right to be, rather than as a means to some end other than itself' (Maslow 1971: 68). Thus, her behaviour is a model to the extent that it is non-instrumental, or produced by a 'lack of willful "trying," a lack of effortful striving or straining, a lack of interference with the flow of the impulses and the free "radiating" expression of the deep person' (ibid.: 70).

Maslow acknowledged that secondary processes are necessary. He claimed healthy individuals should be capable of being both poet and engineer. Deliberation must follow spontaneity. Hard work and control must follow regression into our inner beings and receptiveness to inspiration. At some point, instead of being subject to an experience, we make a product *our* subject. Nevertheless, according to Maslow, primary processes are where the deepest human values are realized. It is through them that the healthy self expresses itself. Hence, though secondary processes are needed for one to receive financial compensation for one's work, increasing one's wealth cannot be the goal of a self-actualizing person. Instead, B-work, 'work at the level of being', is its own intrinsic reward; the paycheque is merely a 'byproduct, an epiphenomenon' (Maslow 1971: 305). Ideal, self-actualizing work is one's intrinsic values incarnate; it is pursuit of these values, and not work *per se*, that the healthy person loves (ibid.: 307).

It is notable that Maslow's take on the primary phase of creativity, the phase at the heart of self-actualization, consistently lionizes insecurity.

He argues that 'creativeness is correlated with the ability to withstand the lack of structure, the lack of future, lack of predictability, of control, the tolerance for ambiguity, for planlessness' (Maslow 1965: 188); it is akin for him to the ability to 'loaf', to float for a time in a purposeless void without a distinct future. Neurotic people are uncreative because they have no self-confidence. Creative people, self-actualizing people, thrive precisely when conditions seem most threatening; they are 'attracted to mystery, to novelty, change, flux', because they feel able to manage the world (ibid.: 192–93). Moreover, Maslow argues that any thriving society would need to commit itself to producing precisely this kind of person: a person who is able to improvise in the face of change, who enjoys flux, who is able to face with confidence and strength situations 'of which he has absolutely no forewarning' (Maslow 1971: 58). He claims that it is only unhealthy selves who need to 'staticize' the world in a frozen present; they need, pathetically, to 'do what their daddies did' (ibid.: 59). For Maslow, healthy people, self-actualizing, creative people are instead able to face with confidence their lack of knowledge of what will come. Moreover in order to thrive, societies would have to find the means to produce and support such 'aggridants [his term for the superior members of any species] innovators, geniuses, and trailblazers' (ibid.: 59).

Managing non-conformity

Organizational psychology and management theory appear to have absorbed wholesale Maslow's arguments about the ideal person's motivations at work. This absorption is clear evidence for Luc Boltanski and Eve Chiapello's claim that the 'artistic critique' of capital so palpable by the 1960s – a critique positioning authenticity and autonomy against routine, management and monotony – was easily stripped of any political impetus and turned into fodder for new models of capitalist accumulation. Teresa Amabile's influential recommendations to business organizations about how to nurture creativity are a good example of the mainstreaming of Maslovian thinking. Her early work was not primarily directed at corporations, but the 1996 edition of *The Social Psychology of Creativity*, renamed *Creativity in Context*, is revised with applicability to business organizations in mind. She notes that a number of concrete traits of creative people have already been 'revealed' in repeated research. These include self-discipline, an ability to delay gratification, perseverance in the face of frustration, independence of judgement, tolerance for ambiguity, a high degree of autonomy, an internal locus of control, a rejection of conventional norms, and a propensity for risk-taking and self-initiated striving for excellence (Amabile 1996: 90). Adding to this work, Amabile's 'social psychology of creativity' is meant to 'identify particular social and environmental conditions that can positively or negatively influence the creativity of most individuals' (Amabile 1983: 5).

Yet, despite her claims to a unique focus on the social circumstances that allow for the elaboration of creativity, I argue that at bottom Amabile's work wholly affirms the conceptions of the innate tendencies of the creative person that had been circulating amongst psychologists since the early 1960s. She states, for example, that she is interested in the influence of social factors on creativity, social factors that include:

> a concern with evaluation expectation and actual evaluation; a desire for external recognition; a focus on competition and external reward; a reaction against time pressures; a deliberate rejection of society's demands; and a preference for internal control and intrinsic motivation.
>
> (Amabile 1983: 14)

Hence, 'social factors' are for her primarily negative barriers to the natural inclination of the creative person to desire freedom from the social. What matters to Amabile's conclusions is the various ways in which the contextual factors she identifies are rejected by creative people, such that creativity is once again overwhelmingly presented as a reaction against any social determinants that might influence one's natural internal directedness. Creativity 'in context' turns out to be creativity that is free to reject context. In other words, when a creative person tends to refer her work to some social world of reward and calculation, her work suffers; when she refers her work to internal rewards removed from any social determination, her work benefits. The social is thus always positioned as the extrinsic; or the terms 'extrinsic' and 'social' are virtually synonymous, and are construed as negative.

Taking up Barron's and Maslow's mantles, Amabile, too, supplements her lab research with case studies of writers' biographies, in this case deriving psychological truths from her reading about the lives of Anne Sexton, Sylvia Plath and Thomas Wolfe, amongst others (see also Amabile 2001). In *The Social Psychology of Creativity*, she argues, for example, that Sexton struggled with extrinsic motivations, and was self-conscious about her own concern with making money and achieving external recognition for her work. However, because she worked against these tendencies in herself and learned to function instead as her own worst critic, she was able to achieve despite herself the higher state of intrinsic motivation, finding in her work a positive outlet for her introspective worrying. Plath fares less well, as Amabile reads her overwhelming concern with recognition and her tendency to compare her own success with that of other writers as a crippling encumbrance. Wolfe is said to have suffered a related paralysis, due in particular to the phenomenal success of his first novel; the external expectations that were put upon him were thereafter too much for him to handle.

These studies of respected writers, coupled with her more conventional lab findings, lead her to conclude that extrinsic motivation is detrimental to creativity – a claim she later revised to acknowledge the possibility of some productive synergy between internal and external drives, but which has nonetheless continued to be cited in encyclopaedias, handbooks and surveys of the field as a major finding for the study of organizational behaviour. Her intrinsic motivation hypothesis resonates profoundly with Maslow's and Barron's work and with the aesthetic ideologies upon which their works depend. This hypothesis holds that creativity involves the refusal of conformity and rejection of social approval (Amabile 1996: 90), the ability to engage in an activity for its own sake (ibid.: 109), and motivations that stem from the individual's engagement in some feature of 'the task itself' (ibid.: 115).

'Liberation' management

If Amabile's work is its academic expression, the popular apotheosis of Maslovian thought is the work of management guru Tom Peters, who has been since the early 1980s a highly sought-after international speaker and consultant. Peters echoed Maslovian psychology when he claimed in 1987 that emerging economic conditions mean that winning workers will now need to perceive chaos and flux not as problems but as opportunities. His 1992 study *Liberation Management* is a working through of this emphasis on the wonders of chaos. It is nothing if not a celebration of Maslow's 'aggridants', as he encourages companies to retain only those employees who view work as the fulfilment of their own 'creative ambition' (Peters 1992: 173). Peters links the transformations he observes in progressive companies to wide-scale changes in society to which all workers must adapt. Most tellingly, he connects his recommendations about 'deconstructing' the corporation (ibid.: 479) to postmodernism and its movement away from hierarchies and toward 'flexibility, choice, and personal responsibility' (ibid.: 468). The successful employee now has to embrace postmodern complexity and accept all its paradoxes. Liberation means a lot of sleepless nights and the abandonment of certain comforts. The new kind of organization is disorganization. Meanwhile, market necessities, indistinguishable from psychological necessities, mean that passionate pursuit of one's goals must lead to the equally passionate destruction of whatever one has already created.

In the late 1990s, Peters shifted his main work to motivational speaking and writing for employees wishing to perceive themselves as self-managers and, ultimately, as brands. It is in this more recent work that artist figures have taken on particular importance, though Peters had claimed before that he would, for instance, look to see who is reading Chekhov when he boards an airplane, and then 'bet on his or her stock' (Peters 1992: 609) since reading Chekhov is a sure sign of one's comfort with complexity. By 1999, though, he would claim that after seeing Placido Domingo perform in *Simon Boccanegra* at the Metropolitan Opera he wondered why 'a day-at-work-in-the-Purchasing Dept' couldn't be 'more like Placido's evening-at-the-Met?' (Peters 1999a: 19). He concludes that it can be if one is willing to embrace the right attitude and pursue the right work. All work should be like the artist's work: it is a performance rather than a job; it is an act of unbridled passion rather than 'puttin' in time'; far from being 'Faceless', it is the 'epitome of character'; far from being predictable, it is a 'plunge into the unknown'; rather than treating the customer as an afterthought, it changes 'the users' universe'; it is a growth experience rather than just another span of lost time that will never be recovered (ibid.: 20).

In *The Brand You 50, Or Fifty Ways to Transform Yourself from an 'Employee' into a Brand that Shouts Distinction, Commitment, and Passion*, Peters continually places faceless, predictable, unartful jobs in an older age that emphasized security, in which what he calls the 'so-called safety net' in fact drained workers of their 'initiative, drive and moxie' (Peters 1999b: 24). In this light, pursuing Brand You is more than pragmatic: it is equal parts self-reliant liberation and self-definition. He states that his growing interest in artists' lives has led him to conclude that all successful employees are now performance artists: 'Accounting' is a 'Performing Art' when 'It is Your B-e-i-n-g, the Presentation of You, that is under discussion' (ibid.: 125–27). One notes that 'B-e-i-n-g' here – one's very selfhood – is thus inseparable from the performance of one's brand distinction, and that Peters collapses the process of discovering and achieving one's highest values into market rationality. Indeed, examples of this collapse abound in his work: 'I am urging you to think – long and hard – about your I-D-E-N-T-I-T-Y. In BMW-ian terms' (ibid.: 129) he tells us; we are also all 'Rapidly Depreciating Assets', and must counter the rapid decline of our human capital with 'Aggressive Investment' (ibid.: 154). Uncovering our most deeply held values is, in short, a matter of marketing.

Peters acknowledges that cultivating your own brand takes a lot of time. It can even include, as it has in his own life, neglect of friends and family, but, he admits, 'I don't know how else to do it?!' (ibid.: 72). One notes a tinge of despair in this last statement, with its twinned interrogative and exclamation. Peters even admits to being 'gloomy' and using Prozac, and discusses his dedication to his work as nearly pathological. Yet an ostensible accord between suffering and success again echoes Maslow's – and Barron's – emphasis on the successful subject's ability to live with contradiction, transcending conventional distinctions between, for instance, sickness and health, happiness and suffering, selfishness and selflessness. We might note here that Peters fought in the Vietnam War, inventing a gun emplacement that was written about in engineering magazines; worked for several years at the consulting company McKinsey Co., which helped many firms downsize and become attuned to flexible specialization; worked for a Pentagon project to establish a naval base on Diego Garcia in the Indian Ocean; and, while working for the State Department in 1973–74, spearheaded a project to eradicate the opium trade in Mexico. These are the activities that he presents as the highlights of his own working life before he became a management writer, tasks to which he dedicated himself with such passion. These were his self-actualizing endeavours. Yet, at the very same time, his new persona – and Brand You is self-invented, ever-changing and fundamentally free from the past – can recommend the constant incorporation of 'cool people' like Che Guevara into his 'network', and can celebrate the kind of commitment to changing others' views about what is possible evident in Lenin's devotion to Russian serfs or Martin Luther King's to African Americans (ibid.: 181).

Tensions like these are not a problem for Peters. They are in fact a constitutive feature of the new age of liberated work. While Brand You deploys caring and empathy in constructing her marketable persona, she does so only temporarily and can readily transfer such skills to any new workplace. Her devotion to mastery of a task is simply equal to her willingness to move on to the next thing. Identity is a matter of marketing but also a matter of life's meaning. It is something one must contemplate 'long and hard', but also quickly and incessantly. Peters acknowledges the tensions, calling them 'an irony' or 'paradox' (ibid.: 149), but he states that they are a source of personal energy rather than of psychological harm and alienation, political indifference and quiescence.

Conclusion

I conclude with Peters because his thought is a summation in stark terms of several features of the tradition of thought this chapter highlights: its use of artist-figures as models; its treatment of self-realization as a process that can occur in the absence of any judgement about the impact of one's work on society; its presentation of the economy as a reflection of human nature, while at the same time, contradictorily, market realities are necessities to which we must accommodate ourselves; its stigmatization of collective politics and workers' interdependence; its lionization of an elite cadre of creative innovators and sidelining or outright omission of industrial, service and manual labour; and its insistence that the individual worker shoulder the burden of establishing a secure future.

This burden can mean vacillation between unemployment and overwork, and can entail ceaseless self-promotion, including presentation of oneself as a marketable brand or commodity. Yet creative-economy boosters, in the tradition of thought charted above, rarely mention increased rates of anxiety and depression, or decreased rates of political participation amongst the elite they imagine and typically address. Nor are they troubled by evidence that people forced to move from job to job, or from fashion to fashion in their self-presentations, struggle with and against a pressing lack of permanence and coherence, and find self-referencing introspection to be insufficient grounds for the establishment of a lasting sense of life's value (Sennett 2006; Heelas 2002). Instead, they put forward quite unquestioningly a psychology that celebrates the anti-social and the insecure as the triumph of human innovation and development.

I argue that reconstituting the history that these conceptions of the self eschew is a way of questioning the presumed permanence and naturalness of contemporary capitalism. Brian Holmes (2002) suggests that rigorously exposing, situating and undermining mainstream celebrations of the flexible personality is part of the work of narrating new subjectivities. It is part of the collective work of imagining new ideals of autonomy and authenticity to counter the old critique of massification, with its demand for liberation of a limitless human potential from all social constraint – a demand that proved highly serviceable to management discourse. These new ideals will not arise from yet another innovative discovery originating in the inherently creative intellect. They will emerge instead from old roots that need only be uncovered and valorized. In Boltanski and Chiapello's (2005: 491) compelling formulation, they will stem from sensitivity to others' conditions of existence, and from the 'incrimination' of any model of the self that assumes and privileges its egoism. In concert with these other theorists, I suggest in sum a two-pronged approach to forwarding a fundamentally social conception of the self. We need to challenge the model of the asocial or antisocial flexible individualist by stressing that she is produced by the same social circumstances she disavows; and we need to circulate more socially responsive visions of human agency and identity – visions of a subject not sufficient to itself, a subject whose anti-egoism and need for sympathetic community are no less essential or natural than the predilections of the flexibly creative individual.

Note

1 For an interesting parallel to IPAR in post-war Britain, see Rose and Miller 1988, especially pp.182–87.

4 Hired hands, liars, schmucks

Histories of screenwriting work and workers in contemporary screen production

Bridget Conor

Introduction

New-ness, difference and temporal restructuring are now undeniably central to our understanding of how culture is produced in particular industries, and at macro-, meso- and micro-levels of analysis (Havens *et al.* 2009; Hesmondhalgh and Baker 2011). As well as this, particular production roles and creative and craft professions are historically and temporally embedded, circumscribed and understood via histories of practice and subjective experience.[1] This chapter illustrates the importance of considering discursive and material histories of cultural work and the ways in which historical, mythologized figures and traits percolate through the lives of contemporary workers.

Screenwriting offers a unique case study in this respect. Empirical investigations provide evidence of the ways in which screenwriters as creative subjects understand and make sense of their working experiences and daily lives. On the face of it, historical accounts of invisible or marginal 'scribes' as 'hired hands', 'liars' and 'schmucks' indicate that bad working practices are the norm for screenwriters and always have been; that indices of bad work, such as the practice of multiple authorship, or the ubiquity of horror stories within 'development hell', were established in Hollywood's early days and continue to be enacted in contemporary settings such as the London-centric UK film industry. However, this chapter complexifies this zero-sum account. As well as screenwriting histories illuminating the longitudinal effects of bad cultural work, this case study also highlights some of the ways in which today's screenwriters can be understood to be speaking back to a collective history of their profession – calling up particular figures, events and conditions as they pursue and undertake contemporary screenwriting labour.

Screenwriting histories

I wish to consider a number of durable historical discourses that foreground the standardization of industrial screenwriting within Hollywood, the concomitant separation of craft from creativity, and the marginalization of screenwriters as autonomous workers. The crudest and most potent version of this role, the marginalized screenwriter acclimatized to bad working practices and beholden to other 'creatives' from directors to producers to financiers, is evoked again and again in the writings of Hollywood-based individuals.[2] The histories of professional screenwriting on which I draw in this research (Rosten 1940; Powdermaker 1950; Schultheiss 1971; Staiger 1982; Stempel 1988; Hamilton 1990; Norman 2007) are a representative sample, as the publication dates indicate.[3] They offer a number of insights into an ongoing process of professional theorization and mythologization on the part of the screenwriting community and commentators within this community, and this is a process that in temporal terms is not always linear and chronological; particular origin stories, figures, events and grand narratives are repeated across and within the histories.

Historical accounts of the origins of writing for the screen in Hollywood and the development of the profession of the early 'scenario writer' stress multiplicity and promise in relation to the first modes of industrial screenwriting. The general perception gained from reading accounts of the development of screenwriting as a form of work in the pre-studio era – the era of the scenario writer or scenarist – is a time of a proliferation of opportunities for budding writers, a time in which creative roles in the new industry of screen production are multiple and multivalent. This is also a time in which there are a large number of women working as scenario writers (see Francke 1994), and this point is regularly emphasized as another facet of early professional freedom and flexibility.[4] The very early development of the screenwriting profession is viewed as one of freedom and creative ferment – scenario writers, the histories report, commanded prestige in this new field, often juggled a number of creative roles, were prolific, well remunerated and well respected. Scenario writers for silent films also read and evaluated story material from outside sources (much like the contemporary labour of 'coverage') and early writers undertook multiple roles within the company to which they were contracted. These early scenarists are multivalent workers with portfolio careers, much like contemporary 'professional creatives' (Ryan 1991). For example, Gene Gauntier, a prominent early writer, wrote, edited, acted, directed, made costumes, sets, props and performed stunts. Stempel writes: 'For her first scenarios Gauntier was paid US$20 per reel while the director was paid only US$10, an indication of the relative value the company placed on writers and directors' (Stempel 1988: 8).

The early historical record deploys facts and figures here in generally positive terms, supporting the freewheeling writer and illustrating the rapid turnaround of the work; anecdotes emphasize the dashing-out of a deluge of short scenarios and the increased demand for scripts and stories. Norman quotes Gauntier herself: 'The woods were full of ideas … A poem, a picture, a short story, a scene from a current play, a headline in a newspaper. All was grist that came to my mill' (cited in Norman 2007: 26). Most screen stories at this time were bought, filmed and released within three months and the high turnover created a palpable demand for story material so that, by the mid-1910s, the rates of pay for scenarios were steadily increasing (Hamilton 1990: 7).

However, the temporal relations embedded within this example are also reminiscent of the bulimic 'crunch time' working patterns of workers in creative labour literature (cited by Gill and Pratt 2008). Thus, early screenwriters are flexible, multivalent and time pressured, becoming rapidly accustomed to boom and bust creative work patterns. By the early teens, the mythic narrative is already preoccupied with the theme of the standardization of the form. Early examples of multiplicity and flexibility (these terms, of course, become hegemonic in contemporary discussions of work in the new cultural economy) are quickly eclipsed by narratives of marginalization, creative degradation, and thus multiple manifestations of bad work or what Caldwell (2008: 221) terms 'trade pain'. Processes of rationalization and standardization in the development of screenwriting as a creative profession are characterized in various historical accounts as exemplifying the inexorable movement away from creative freedom and multivalency and towards increased efficiency and continuity.

Particular historical figures serve as conduits for broader themes. For example, Thomas Ince, a prominent early writer-director (what Ryan, 1991, terms a 'contracted artist'), is widely cited as developing the classical narrative style of Hollywood filmmaking by emphasizing continuity in scenario writing and filming (Stempel 1988: 41). In this respect, Ince is a classic example of the empowered and fully autonomous writer with full control over his scripts, which were precise in their detail, including instructions on costumes, shots and blocking of actors. Ince reportedly rubber-stamped all his scripts 'Produce exactly as written' (Norman 2007: 44). For Staiger (1982), Ince's continuity scripts represent something more insidious: the separation of the conception and production phases of scripting and filmmaking that exemplifies a Taylorist division of labour. Maras (2009) argues that, from the earliest moments in the history of screenwriting, the separation of conception and execution was a process used to differentiate screenwriting from other forms of dramatic writing. Ince is also cited as ushering in a process that emphasized organization but sidelined creativity and artistic freedom. Norman writes: 'Ince took assembly-line techniques, perfected by manufacturing giants like Henry Ford, and applied them to the movie industry' (Norman 2007: 44). An historical figure such as Ince is thus deployed to illustrate the degradation of the screenwriter's creative process under the strictures of an industrial production system. As Staiger writes, the application of scientific management to screen production leads to a separation that 'destroys an ideal of the whole person, both the creator and the producer of one's ideas' (Staiger 1982: 96).

Mack Sennett, who produced comedies for the Keystone Company, is another villainous character looming large in early historical accounts, embodying the producer-driven desire to separate out the heads and hands of his screenwriter lackeys. Norman recounts Sennett's tactics of marginalization;

for example, Sennett hired teams of 'gag writers', but the gags conceived to be filmed were never written down. Instead, they were spoken to one another and then 'pitched' to Sennett.[5] Norman also writes that 'Sennett nursed a perpetual mistrust of his writers ... he built a tower on the lot with a glassed-in penthouse so he could glower down at his writers', and that he had an 'aversion to the written word' (Norman 2007: 58). These anecdotes are presented as evidence of Sennett's calculated strategy of degrading his writers' craft and skills as well as a wider trend whereby producers maintained a 'collective anonymous output' in order to control both story conception and production. For Norman, this illustrates an underlying and perpetual antagonism between producers and writers, a theme that can be variably traced through histories of screenwriting in Hollywood. As Mayer notes in relation to the earlier anthropological work of Rosten (1940) and Powdermaker (1950), 'In their narratives, the elite emerges as a social grouping of rootless eccentrics, superficial neurotics, and self-indulgent narcissists' (Mayer 2011: 5).

By the late teens, independent Hollywood production companies were beginning to form major studios and, for the new studio moguls, vertical integration of the production system, including control of distribution and exhibition, optimized profit margins. For the heads of production, control of a project could be harnessed through the script, and a strict division of labour enabled greater control over the entire production process, according to Stempel (1988: 51). Tension was mounting by the early 1920s, then, between writers and directors (who were again being separated out within studio structures). Stempel quotes William de Mille on the consequences for screenwriters' work: 'The two crafts (writing and directing) became theoretically separated but never actually untangled' (ibid.: 56). MacDonald (2007) also notes this in his discussion of British silent filmmaking from 1910 to 1930, arguing that early British screenwriters 'picturized' the films they wrote as well as dramatically structuring them (i.e. they specified shot sizes and offered instructions for actors, for example), but that, by the 1930s, industrial practices inherited from Hollywood were 'rationalizing' the dominance of the director as the principal author of a film.[6] The theme of separation of conception from execution comes to serve as an intelligible device, ensuring a wrenching historical account of the newly minted screenwriter as almost immediately alienated from her/his own labour.

The Hollywood studio system is said to mark the beginnings of the centralized corporate control of industrial screen production, which, whilst it saw a number of subsequent iterations, has continued to dictate the organization of mainstream filmmaking inside and outside Hollywood. At this point, the histories converge on a number of powerful figures (the studios and their bosses) and a number of now-familiar and enduring images – writers as 'schmucks', as inherently and necessarily replaceable, as 'faceless labourers' as Mayer (2011: 6) summarises it. The head of Warner Brothers, Jack Warner, referred to writers as 'schmucks with [U]nderwoods' (ibid.: 85) and is rumoured to have sneaked to the writers' rooms on his studio lot to see if the writers were typing.[7] Another anecdote of the time has the head of Columbia, Harry Cohn, listening to the clacking of typewriter keys from his writers and screaming 'Liars!' (Norman 2007: 136).

Schultheiss quotes Raymond Chandler, who vividly describes how the studio system debilitated 'the author's efforts of creation':

> It makes very little difference how a writer feels towards his producer as a man; the fact that the producers can change and destroy and disregard his work can only operate to diminish that work in its conception and to make it mechanical and indifferent in execution ... There is little magic or emotion or situation which can remain alive after the incessant bone-scraping revisions imposed on the Hollywood writer by the process of rule by decree.
>
> (Schultheiss 1971: 25)

As these histories play out, then, the enlightened but vulnerable figure of the screenwriter is pitted against the brutish, efficiency-obsessed producer or studio boss, determined to control the outputs of writers and to deny those outputs the 'creative' label by effectively severing the ties between hand and head. Yet, no matter how crude or dramatic these characterizations, the rhetorical effect is to make the screenwriter intelligible as a player in the screen production industries – often a 'maverick' or a 'pioneer'[8] with the potential to command a central and multivalent position within this new realm of cultural production but also subordinated by those who recognize this potential but wish to deny screenwriters such centrality and creative flexibility. This historical project is populated with rhetorical devices – themes, personalities, events – that promote the intelligibility *and* marginality of screenwriting work as it develops as a form of industrial creative labour.

Screenwriting as creative labour

This collection of scenes and players sets up a number of devices and ideal traits that animate the persona of the screenwriter and the language used to construct her/his work. These are also devices that I argue resonate in the domain(s) of contemporary screenwriting work: screenwriting as potentially flexible but also as standardized, degraded and de-skilled; screenwriting as lucrative but also compromised and thus impure; as commercially but not artistically legitimate. These evoke ideal subjective traits for writers past and present – screenwriters must accept their secondary status and be supplicative; they must disinvest from their work at an early stage, remaining sceptical and cynical in the face of more powerful elites; and perhaps in a compensatory fashion, confidence, even egotism, becomes necessary in order to survive the slings and arrows of the industry.

In the following sections, I draw on qualitative data gathered from a larger research project that involved labour market analysis, interviews and observations of screenwriting as labour, practice and pedagogy in the UK in 2007–10. Some 17 interviews were conducted with 'professional creatives' (Ryan 1991) – screenwriters, script editors, consultants and screenwriting teachers – and textual analysis involved the close reading of 'how-to' screenwriting manuals (32 in total) and course materials from Masters-level screenwriting courses.

The London-based screenwriters with whom I engaged during this research aligned with and emulated the myths or ideals of the screenwriter (as marginal, as egotistical, as invisible) in discussions of their work and the daily micro-tactics (see Havens *et al.* 2009) that typified their careers. Because they, too, were operating in an industry dominated by Hollywood funding, Hollywood-oriented standards of structure, character and conflict within screen storytelling, and standardized genre categories, writers in London were conditioned to a similar set of devices of intelligibility and at particular times, spoke with and through these.[9] I now highlight three examples in which professional creative screenwriters in London directly evoked or echoed historical subjects and long-term industrial conditions: 1) hired hands; 2) multiple authorship; and 3) professional horror stories.

Hired hands

First, London-based screenwriters to whom I spoke and whom I observed made, at times, direct reference to the history of their profession, to the fact that screenwriters have been, and continue to be, viewed and treated as 'hired hands'. These screenwriters were discussing the strategies they deployed to navigate British, European and Hollywood producers, commissioners and production companies. The daily working practices recounted in interviews ranged from pitching for projects, taking meetings, identifying material for adaptation, various forms of collaboration and script rewrites. As Sandra K[10] explained the uncertainty of her professional life, she made a poignant connection between the norms of bad work within her industry and the history of the work itself:

> I think there's a significant problem in that if you come with an original piece, you can often be put in the position of having to sell everything, sell all your rights to it in order to get it off the ground, and then you can be taken off your own project, and I think that's morally reprehensible, you know it's legally reasonable but it's really inappropriate, you don't buy a piece of art and then go I think I'll have this repainted by Damien Hirst, if you want to commit to somebody's own personal project then you have to commit to it in a serious way, so there's a big problem *and I think it's a historic problem, that writers started off as being studio hired hands* [my emphasis].

Sandra makes a powerful case here for the effects of historical and continued marginalization on her profession. The status of screenwriting as a special and specially tormented creative profession is evoked in everyday narratives of work in the London industry as it was by de Mille or Chandler in studio-era Hollywood. As a less experienced writer, Todd D put it: 'It's so easy to feel fraudulent when you're writing a story, when you're writing for hire, when someone has paid you, for allegedly your expertise, your ability, it's very easy to feel like a total fraud.'

However, it is important to note here that, although the image of the screenwriter as writer for hire or hired hand suggests it is an a priori subject position – that contemporary writers such as Sandra and Todd have passively accepted their 'work for hire' status just as their predecessors did – I would caution against such a neat conclusion. Both Sandra and Todd went on to speak about strategies they used to ameliorate practices and feelings of marginalization – working with guilds and unions, sharing tools and tactics with peers and collaborators, working on a variety of projects at once to spread out creative investments and disinvestments, and working in a variety of modes, often beyond 'screenwriting' itself (such as screenwriting teaching, new media writing, how-to manual writing and script consulting, for example). These are examples of what Banks (2007: 67) calls 'the practical capacities of individualized cultural workers to counter corporate instrumentality'. My initial point here is that the screenwriter as hired hand resonates across subjects and industries, but so do other subject positions that are not always so neatly spelt out: the screenwriter as tactical, as collegial and as historically reflexive.

Multiple authorship

Multiple authorship is often tied to the notorious studio boss Irving Thalberg, the head of Metro Goldwyn Meyer (MGM) in the 1920s and 1930s. Thalberg both respected and charmed his writers, according to Stempel (1988: 71), pioneering an extreme division of labour, more so even than Thomas Ince before him. Multiple authorship practices (which infiltrated other studios) involved the hiring of more than one writer or teams of writers to write the same script, often without the others knowing it.[11] A variation of this strategy to maximize output was to assign 'several screenwriters on several ideas per star at the same time, knowing some of the scripts would work, some wouldn't' (Norman 2007: 15). Powdermaker (1950: 156–57) recounts a number of examples of multiple authorship for 'A pictures' in the 1940s, one on which 16 writers worked simultaneously or serially, another with a tally of 18 writers. This practice clearly affected the view the writers had of their vocation, as William de Mille (writing in 1939) explains:

> The writer naturally lost his sense of artistic responsibility. Constantly rewriting the work of others and knowing that his own work, in turn, would be changed and changed again, he simply did the best he could and took comfort in his salary.
>
> (cited in Schultheiss 1971: 26)

Historical examples of multiple authorship again evoke a set of views still routinely cited by contemporary writers like Sandra K and Todd D: that their work is never their own, that their writing is always at the behest of others, thus reinforcing their 'hired hand' status. This is a truism, screenwriters argue, that would be unthinkable ('really inappropriate', as Sandra put it above) for any other mode of authorship. In fact, multiple authorship represents a kind of entrenched, serial instability and is pathologized in both historical and contemporary terms. Powdermaker (1950: 125) refers to a powerful producer she encounters in her study as 'Mr Schizo', and a producer and script consultant I spoke to in London in 2008 echoed this:

> It's easier to blame the writers, so I think that writers have a hard job … because I think they have to answer to several masters and the masters don't always agree … so it's a schizophrenia that the writer really has to try to stay on top of.

The schizophrenic creative subject[12] engendered via multiple authorship was highlighted during another contemporary conversation with Dale T, a writer whose first feature film had been produced in the UK and had had a long and difficult gestation. Dale had juggled the notes of multiple producers for various versions of the script, had been through a number of development programmes and production companies, and had had a falling out with the director who claimed a co-writing credit that the producers enforced. The writer took a 'realistic' approach to his 'difficult' experience of multiple authorship, acknowledging that the film had been made (an achievement in itself in the British industry) and that he had had to simply 'get over it', a variation on de Mille's resigned advice to just 'do the best you can' (in Schultheiss 1971: 26). In one view, therefore, screenwriters dealing with multiple authorship – a long-term, structural feature of the industry – represent the ultimate self-responsible, self-exploitative creative workers.

In addition, multiple authorship has for some time worked to foreclose the possibilities for larger-scale collegiality or collective resistance for screenwriters. It is the root cause of many a professional horror story, which again signals the normativity of bad work practices for writers past and present. Caldwell (2009: 163) argues, in fact, that four 'sanctioned and well-oiled industry practices and conventions' determine Hollywood's lacerating labour relations across occupational categories: 'idea theft', 'distributed creativity' (both results of multiple authorship), 'work-for-hire' (the hired hands I discussed above), and the vast oversupply of workers and aspiring workers (which ensure unrelenting competition for all these other practices). The responsibility for dealing with all this is placed in the hands and heads of the individual screenwriter. They must 'stay on top of it', 'get over it', or they suffer the effects (economic, psychological, physical, etc.) of 'trade pain' (Caldwell 2008: 221) or what Gill and Pratt (2008: 16) refer to as the 'individualized shame' that is endemic across and within cultural production industries. However, I wish to resist an entirely pessimistic account of screen-writing as bad work by examining some of the multiple functions (and associated meanings) that screenwriters ascribe to their professional horror stories.

Professional horror stories

Professional horror stories can serve a *productive* purpose for writers both past and present; they are a potent form of currency within the screenwriting community.[13] This was highlighted within my encounters with London-based screenwriters in which 'difficult' production stories were recounted – with wide eyes, pauses for effect, the finest points of detail (such as numbers of rewrites or collaborators) in the development process listed. This reflected a need to make sense of these encounters (especially if they were difficult, as Dale's was) and, more elaborately, to prove one's own endurance and long-evity as a writer. Professional horror stories indicated that one had 'done time', had faced the slings and arrows of the business and was still standing, with credits to one's name. At certain points, too, these stories were also connected to historical subjects: the studio-era writer for hire, the tortured but brilliant writer, the necessarily egotistical writer. The history of screenwriting as a specially tormented creative profession was repeatedly evoked and, whilst this perpetuates those well-worn traits – acquiescence and supplication – as the norms of multiple authorship suggest, tactics of resistance are also visible within professional horror stories.

These tactics were/are designed to protect the core elements of narratives and scripts, to promote forms of good work even in the context of bad prac-tices. Donald Ogden Stewart describes his resistance and strategizing in the 1930s: 'I used always to write three or four scenes which I knew would be thrown out, in order that we could bargain with Joe Breen for the retention of other really important episodes or speeches' (cited in Norman 2007: 145).[14] When I spoke to Todd D in 2009, a similar set of tactics were again recounted:

> One project I was working on, I was working with another writer, and whenever we took a meeting about things we'd written, there were always four or five people in the room, either the producer, the director, then the company's head honchos, finance person ... in every scene, we would build in a couple of lines, a couple of beats that were mis-steps, that were badly conceived, slightly clunky, slightly mis-written, purposefully ... and we would build them so that in cutting them, in changing them, it would be a better scene.

Todd D went on to admit that this tactic could be viewed as 'profoundly cynical' but, in both historical and contemporary accounts, professional horror stories also engender tactics that encourage good work: 'important episodes' in 1930 or 'better scenes' in 2009.

The development and deployment of such tactics also signals the growth of professional confidence for screenwriters across industries and time periods. Much like writers cited in Hollywood histories, writers I spoke to in London readily admitted that, although they dealt with difficult producers or forms of development hell, they also had 'a massive ego' (Karen H), or were 'horribly arrogant', even masochistic (Ben J), that screenwriting was 'hard graft' (Karen H again) and required nerdy obsession and fetishization of the profession and its crafty origins (Todd D). All these traits were also framed in terms of dedication to this particular creative form (collaborative screen-based storytelling) and the sharing of that dedication with others. Importantly, Todd D noted that professionalism stemmed directly from obsession with the work:

> There is perhaps an element of sparring for the love of it but there's also, it becomes apparent that people kind of think deeply about this stuff … On the one hand, as I say it's about trying to arm yourself with the sensation at least that you understand and can act the mechanics of this world … The second thing is that as soon as an idea moves from being entirely your own, conceived on your desk, into conversations with people, you need a shared language and actually talking with development execs … it professionalizes that relationship.

Again the figure of the screenwriter as fostering a 'shared language' resonates far beyond this contemporary setting, illustrating a dynamic oscillation between processes of speaking back – to a perceived collective and mythic history of screenwriting as profession and practice – and speaking forward – to collaborators, to audiences, to financiers and to other screenwriters.

Conclusion

Theorizing cultural work as necessarily historical as well as contemporaneous allows us to see beyond the strident claims of new-ness embedded within the discourses of the new cultural economy. This chapter has shown that it also enables a focused reading of the ways in which professional myths and narratives link up workers across time and space – screenwriters as hired hands from Hollywood to London, from 1940 to the present day.

These complex and non-linear linkages between past and present are not only about recounting abuses or experiences of bad work ad infinitum. As I have shown, particular rhetorical devices – themes, personalities, events – are used to understand, first, the particular marginality of screenwriting work. Hired hands, schmucks and liars are figures that embody the creative frustrations and disappointments screenwriters often face. These devices are also used to promote professionalism in the face of marginalization. To conjure up the historical image of the screenwriter as hired hand, for example, or to recount a professional horror story, enables contemporary writers, in small-scale but important ways, to reflect on the multiple functions and meanings of their work.

This means that, although forms of bad screenwriting work abound in both historical and contemporary industries, collegiality can also be fostered via these devices. The shared language(s) and forms of currency that have developed through histories of the profession enable screenwriters to talk to one another, to talk to other collaborators and to understand the particular appeals of the work. A sense of collectivity and shared purpose is fostered across screenwriting histories in terms of the writing itself and its standards which are taught both formally, in screenwriting training courses or how-to manuals, and informally, through anecdotes, horror stories, tales of mavericks and villains.

These devices also work to make screenwriting intelligible and knowable to producers, audiences and writers themselves. They illustrate the ways in which tactics have been, and still are, deployed to pursue good work for screen-writers albeit on a modest scale. The histories of their profession enable screenwriters to share those tactics, to build confidence, to foster forms of solidarity and collegiality even as the vicissitudes of the new cultural economy and the restructuring of its temporal relations may discourage collective measures and actions (see Adkins 2009).

As well as this, screenwriters are trying to speak ahead – that is, to engage with and adapt to the possible directions of their work at a time in which the future(s) of the screen production industries are often characterized as opaque. This relates to the more general restructuring of time in the new cultural economy that Adkins (2009) has highlighted, and to the concern in many studies of creative labour that the temporal relations of that labour are no longer stable or legible. A particular example of this instability for main-stream screenwriters is the new models of remuneration for screenwriting work that proliferate across a range of media and increasingly via online platforms and mean that current or future earnings cannot easily be predicted or weighed up against day-to-day writing schedules and deadlines.

Theorizing cultural work requires us to examine the processes of continuity and change that circumscribe it. This case study illustrates that professional histories percolate through the daily lives of cultural workers, highlighting the ways in which forms of both good and bad work are sought, dealt with, accepted and resisted. Today's screenwriters working in and outside Holly-wood, pursuing studio finance and professional recognition, working with and resisting Hollywood standards of screen narrative, conflict or character-ization, can be understood to be speaking back to a collective history and the mythic persona of the screenwriter that versions of this history conjure up and maintain – calling up those figures, events and conditions in their own daily working lives.

Notes

1 This point has been made via a number of analytical pathways. See for example McRobbie's (1998: 150) analysis of fashion design work which she characterizes as a 'hybrid of old and new', and Banks's (2006: 464) work on Manchester's various social, political and cultural 'scenes'.

2 This self-perception has also appeared in particular onscreen portrayals of writers from *Sunset Boulevard* (1950) to *Barton Fink* (1991) and *Adaptation* (2002).

3 Often, these histories have flowed from writers themselves (such as Marc Norman), and writers based in Hollywood at different points in time have contributed to the self-mythologizing process in numerous ways, through novelizations about Hollywood, for example, often with screenwriters as central characters – Nathanael West's *The Day of the Locust* (1939) and F. Scott Fitzgerald's *The Last Tycoon* (1941).

4 The overall mythologization of the professional screenwriter is highly gendered (cf. the masculine pronouns routinely used in historical discussions of screenwriters), a key finding from this larger research project.

5 A nice echo of the rise of 'pitching' culture in contemporary film and television production in Hollywood and London. Caldwell (2009: 164) argues that the industry is now a 'pitch-driven free-for-all', which is aided by the fact that Hollywood writers legally 'work for hire'.

6 Clearly, this could be viewed as a precursor to the rise of auteur theory (see Conor 2010).

7 An Underwood was the ubiquitous brand of typewriter used at the time.

8 These are also masculine characterizations, as I noted in note 4.

9 For a contemporary televisual rendition of the British writer's working life vis-à-vis Hollywood, see the BBC series *Episodes* (2011–present).

10 Pseudonyms are used throughout this section.

11 Norman (2007: 135) notes that this practice was called 'following' within the business, and Caldwell (2008) has more recently discussed this as 'industrial auteur theory' and writing by committee.

12 Interestingly, Caldwell (2009: 162) has also characterized Hollywood entertainment conglomerates as undertaking 'schizophrenic' posturing in order to reduce risk and hedge bets and he notes that this is how Hollywood studios responded to the rise of television in the 1950s.

13 Other studies of cultural labour have also made this point. For example, Banks (2007: 60) discusses the role of entrepreneurial 'war stories' in his analysis.

14 Note that Stewart is referring to his screenwriting work in the context of the Hays Code in studio-era Hollywood, a censorship code for filmmakers enforced by the aforementioned Joseph Breen between the 1930s and 1950s.

5 Absentee workers

Representation and participation in the cultural industries

Kate Oakley

Introduction

As the problems of cultural labour markets become more apparent, an appropriate political response seems elusive. Should public policy, as it does in the UK, continue to concentrate on issues of access to the labour market (via apprenticeships, regulated internships and so on), without concerning itself about working conditions within the cultural industries? Can workers' organizations, either those based on precarity[1] or established trade unions, reverse the tide of disorganized capitalism in these sectors? Who represents cultural industry workers in these debates?

As Banks and Hesmondhalgh (2009) comment, public policy has tended to ignore or gloss over the problems of cultural labour markets, in part at least because of the assumption that such work is inherently good (desirable, enjoyable and so on). For many of those supporting the development of the cultural industries, whether as part of regional or urban economic development schemes, or in practice-based settings – teaching in community arts, drama, music and so on – the idea of cultural work as 'good work' is held dear (Rimmer 2009).

The concern of those involved in such initiatives has often been with securing representation within these labour markets for women, ethnic minorities and working-class people. This may have been informed in part by an idealized notion of this work, but it was primarily driven by other factors. For those concerned with economic development in regions facing mass unemployment, cultural work was 'rooted' work, tied to and, in some ways expressive of, place, and capable of producing long-term employment in an age when, as Andrew Ross puts it, industrial restructuring has not been 'kind to the cause of secure or sustainable livelihoods' (Ross 2009: 20).

However, it was also animated, in a way peculiar to cultural work, by the importance of voice, the idea that involvement in cultural production cannot be confined to the elite, if there is to be any hope of a more democratic culture or indeed society. Who gets to make culture, in its widest sense from advertisements to TV news bulletins and situation comedies, matters, because it is how we understand ourselves as a society. The origins of cultural industries policy in the UK lies in the 'municipal socialism' of cities like Sheffield, Manchester and London, where the aim was, as Peck puts it, 'to pluralize the sphere of cultural distribution and consumption, to broaden access to cultural markets and to cultural work, and to recognize the creativity of marginalised social groups' (Peck 2011: 47).

Yet in the decades since the first cultural industry initiatives, the marginalization of women, ethnic minorities and the working class from participation in cultural labour markets has grown, not declined (Skillset 2009). The politics of cultural industries policy making has shifted from municipal socialism to neoliberal urbanism (Peck 2011), albeit in a variety of forms (Larner and Craig 2005). Changes in the wider organization of capitalism, post-Fordism in particular, which for some appeared to hold out the promise of better working conditions, are part of this story. Alongside that, the virtual exclusion of the politics of labour from the policy-making process allowed the development of a discourse of 'representation' in the workforce that paid no attention to questions of working conditions. The result of that is the development of a highly unrepresentative cultural sector, with often poor working conditions.

The chapter draws on the experience of the UK, particularly in the last 30 years or so, but it is part of a much wider international debate. The popularity of cultural industries as an economic development strategy is now global (Cunningham 2007), as are the growing movements of young people, both precariously employed and unemployed, and of students, who wish to work in these industries.

The trouble with work

The development of cultural industries policy in the UK, and thus the realizations of these ideas about the nature of work, took place under a government – the modifier 'New' notwithstanding – that derived its existence from the labour movement (Oakley 2011). Parties of the 'centre left', from Brazil's *Partido dos Trabalhadores* to the German SPD (Social Democratic Party), have been, if anything, keener on promoting the development of cultural industries than their counterparts on the right.

I have argued elsewhere (Oakley 2011) that, in the case of the British Labour Party, this reflects the centrality of work to much of the New Labour project.[2] In part, this was a response to what was regarded as a shameful tolerance of long-term unemployment and its social consequences by the previous Conservative government, but, beyond this, a reformed labour market was believed by New Labour to offer political success in a variety of areas. At the 'top' of the labour market, skills were seen as the key to improving Britain's economic competiveness, while the answer to the problems of poverty and social exclusion at the 'bottom' was believed to be via integration into the labour market. Throughout society, higher skills were seen to be linked to adaptability and resilience, helping to produce the neoliberal subject, who could not only cope with, but also thrive on, the sort of changes that the economy was understood to be delivering (Seltzer and Bentley 1999; Gibson and Klocker 2005).

Despite this emphasis, however, questions about *quality* of work, work organization and control of working lives rarely troubled New Labour. A minimum wage was introduced for the first time in the UK; there were some changes to the previous government's anti-union legislation[3] and statutory paid paternity leave was launched, alongside slightly improved maternity leave. However, issues of workers' control and ownership and the democratization of economic decision making, which had been a prominent feature of Labour Party discussions in the 1970s and 1980s (Thompson 2002), were regarded as anachronistic, if they were acknowledged at all. Indeed, the current revival in the UK of interest in cooperatives and other forms of mutual ownership owes as much to sections of the paternalistic or 'red' Tories (the UK Conservatives) as it does to Labour or the trade unions (Norman 2008; Blond 2009, 2010).

A long-term debate on the Left would see this resulting from a widespread, if not universal, decoupling of political parties of the Left from the labour movement. From a Marxist point of view, this represents a fundamental loss of faith in the working class as the primary agent of the progress towards socialism, and the replacement of its crucial role with the politics of identity and social movements (Wood 1986). For others, it was a necessary adaptation to the alleged 'withering away' of the working class, at least in the global North (Hobsbawm 1981).

For the New Left, the need to develop a political movement beyond white, male trade unionists was not only necessitated, but also facilitated, by changes in the structure of capitalism. As a consequence of this, work lost its centrality in the politics of the Left, a change that would have implications for all workers, and indeed for those who defined their politics in other ways, such as in terms of anti-globalization or as social justice. Not the least of these was the collapse in the spending power of working people and con- comitant rise in personal debt, which underlie so much of the continuing financial crisis.

Alongside this, I would argue, is a change in the idea of what good work and particularly good creative work means. As a 'patron saint' of the British Labour Party (MacCarthy 1994), William Morris is often credited with informing its ideas about 'good work' (Morris 1884). While distrust of 'profit mongering', as Morris called it, never ran that deeply in the Labour Party, his notion of the working life as a source of education, and of the inseparability of mental and manual work, both described and predicted the experience of the labour movement as a counterculture, which concerned itself not only with daily working conditions, but also with the education, recreation and self-expression of an entire class (Wills and Simms 2004; Mason 2007). One can sees echoes of such views through a variety of forms of workers' education, the community arts movement of the post-war period, and in what is sometimes called the non-formal learning sector (NFLS) today (Samuel 2006; Sefton-Green 2008; Rimmer 2009).

While daily working conditions under Fordism were anathema to all that Morris would have promoted, it was its collapse that brought an end to a labour movement that could ensure, albeit partially and highly unequally, levels of security and links to training and education that could in part compensate for an often brutal daily reality. The criticism of this 'gas and water' socialism was that the notions of mutuality and self-sufficiency that had animated Victorian reformers had been sacrificed for efficient economic growth and a social wage (Bevir 2011). However, while the collapse of Fordism produced a new and optimistic narrative about work in some parts of the Left, one where the flexible, skilled worker could be made to look like Morris's well-rounded and independent artisan (Kelly 1982), the loss of collective power that ensued drove rapidly widening inequality and helped to produce today's fragmented insecurity. It also produced an account of labour markets from which class issues could be safely excised.

A new dawn? The post-Fordist labour market

Noel Thompson has characterized the enthusiasm in some sections of the Left for what was believed, from the 1970s onwards, to be the changing nature of work as 'post-Fordist socialism' (Thompson 2002). 'Flexible specialization', that is, firm strategies based on multi-use equipment, highly skilled workers and strategies of competition through innovation, appeared to some thinkers on the Left as a re-valorization of work and workers, not a diminishing of them. Such attitudes were highly influential on the British Labour Party as it reconstructed itself during the 1980s and 1990s, and indeed fed into many 'cultural industry' debates of that period and later.

Robin Murray (1988) argued that post-Fordism saw labour as the key asset of modern production, while others argued that it produced 'flatter', less hierarchical workplaces, allowing both productivity gains and the development of a more contented workforce (Sabel 1982; Handy 1995). We can see this sort of language directly echoed in later writers on the 'creative economy', such as Florida (2002).

Such expertise, 'knowledge of industrial processes, markets, even the character of key personnel', is what Paul Hirst called 'intimate knowledge' (Hirst 1989: 276). It was deemed vital to the triumph of the post-Fordist enterprise, relying, as it often did, on tacit, embedded forms of know-how, particularly suited to small firms in specific locales. Economic success was seen to depend not on 'cut throat competition among atomistic entrepreneurs', but on a complex set of sub-contracting relationships that both required and engendered high levels of trust and cooperation (Zeitlin 1989: 369).

Some went so far as to claim that the post-Fordist production paradigm means that democratization of industry became essential, and that workers who 'experience a sense of empowerment and responsibility at work that was denied them under conditions of mass production' could be expected to take a greater interest in community and wider political affairs (Mathews 1989: xiv).

In this way, the goals of economic (and wider) democracy could be allied to economic revitalization, both of the firm and, ideally, the region or nation in which it was situated.

For a time at least, this notion of post-Fordism was allied to a debate about ownership and participation at work. Opening up company boards to worker involvement, amending company law to broaden the accountability of boards of directors and mandate wider social goals, enshrining rights to training and education, the promotion of worker co-operatives: these and other matters were advocated by some post-Fordists (Hirst 1989; Mathews 1989; Kelly 1982). All this tapped into a long history on the Left, but it was a history that was often recast as being free from the failures associated with statism and Keynesian economic policies. The decentralization of economic activity away from the head offices of large corporations was seen as being paralleled by a decentralization of economic policy-making, away from national governments to regions, and the diffusion of industrial relations negotiations from the national offices of the 'big' trade unions, directly to the skilled workforces in the local firm.

However, this discourse often appeared to have little to say about the larger international context in which such developments were taking place. The growth in international capital movements during the 1980s and 1990s, and the resulting increased volatility of the global economic system, together with the growing power of transnational organizations, was largely ignored by some post-Fordists on the Left, preoccupied as they were with the local and the regional, the idea that the future belonged to the small, the flexible and the deeply embedded. Peck (2011: 49) argues that, in the case of the Greater London Council (GLC) at least,[4] the cultural industries project was simply terminated too early, 'leaving unresolved a series of searching questions concerning its political-economic sustainability'.

The degree to which its interventions into elements of cultural production and distribution could ever have been 'scaled up' to a national level remains unanswerable, but, as cultural industry schemes drifted into 'creative industry' policies for urban regeneration, concerns about issues such as media ownership, access to distribution chains or intellectual property were dealt with in a way entirely consistent with neo-liberal, deregulatory approaches, with little attempt to intervene on behalf of national or local firms (Garnham 2005; Hesmondhalgh 2005).

The role of the national state or local government in this vision was essentially a permissive one, helping to equip local firms and local workers to compete in what was seen as the real agent of change – the market. As Thompson has commented, responding to customer demand in this way was seen as the surest way to ensure high-quality products that demanded skill and imagination in their production (Thompson 2002). The Morrisonian craftsman may have come back into fashion, but his idea that good creative work can only be realized in producing useful things, not in adding to over-consumption, fitted less well with the spirit of the times.

Not at the table – organized labour and the cultural industries

In this *zeitgeist*, trade unions, for so long the active agent of change in the labour movement, were relegated to a subsidiary role. Levels of unionism were relatively low in many of the craft-based firms so beloved of post-Fordists, and small, geographically scattered workplaces made unionization difficult. The distinctions between more highly skilled craft labour and other, more casualized, sub-contracted labour were often strong, even in the paragon regions of post-Fordism such as Emilia Romagna (Thompson 2002).

Some post-Fordist writers sought to draw distinctions between 'continental' European unions, who they argued were in favour of 'job enrichment' processes, and those in the UK who preferred the 'comforting incantation' that capital puts profits before people, and were not persuaded by talk of the more humane workplace (Kelly 1982: 15). In such cases, it was suggested, unions had 'a fatalistic attitude to the prospect of progressively reforming work' (Kelly 1982: 16), preferring to concentrate on maintaining wage levels or the re-grading of particular types of work.

In the cultural industries, the debate was somewhat differently framed. When alighting on these sectors as part of the 'new economy', the discussion of boring, repetitive or demeaning work was largely absent. This was depicted as useful work, not useless toil. However, here too the decline of unionization is a major part of the story of work. The cultural industries, particularly when grouped under the looser heading of 'creative industries', have always had differing levels of unionization, with the media sectors such as journalism and broadcasting traditionally heavily unionized, alongside some performing arts such as acting. Other activities, from crafts and visual arts on one hand, to advertising and architecture on the other, have been much less so. The largely self-employed character of individual makers in the arts is one reason; those in creative services such as advertising, design and so on more resemble 'knowledge-based' workers such as IT professionals in having relatively low levels of unionization.

The story of declining union representation in the cultural industries as they reconstructed themselves along post-Fordist lines is well told (Christopherson and Storper 1989; Ursell 1998, 2000). Such changes made it easier not only to celebrate the cultural industries as archetypal new economy sectors (Cunningham 2002), but also to conduct policy conversations in which the issues of labour – working conditions and hours, access to training, ownership and control – were easily ignored.

In its New Labour incarnation, engagement with trade unions was a minimal part of cultural industry policy making. As Hesmondhalgh and Pratt (2005) pointed out, one of the problems of cultural industry policy making from the beginning was 'the intertwined story that we are told of the development of the cultural industries as big businesses and the development of local and national cultural industries policy'.

In other words, policy was supposed to deal with both multinational organizations and single artists. In practice, given that most of the work was carried out at the regional and local level, the cultural businesses in question were generally small businesses or loose networks of individuals. When real money was at stake, such as in discussions of intellectual property or broadcasting, larger rights-holders were of course party to discussions, but the 'average' cultural industries intervention was characterized by an emphasis on small firms and individuals, even if the individuals were recast as entrepreneurs, and the small firms as 'high growth'. When issues of exclusion were discussed, as they were, given the presence in cultural industry policies of ideas of social exclusion and regeneration (Oakley 2006), the representatives of such concerns were more likely to be community arts organizations or publicly funded networks,[5] rather than representatives of labour.

The 'social conscience' of the cultural industries

As Banks and others have argued (O'Connor 1998; Banks 2007; Prince 2009), local cultural industry initiatives generated a set of cultural intermediaries whose concerns often embraced wider ethical and political issues. Indeed, as the policy concept of creative industries began to circulate, more individuals became creative industries 'experts', and more clients, needing creative industry advice, were, for a while at least, created.

However, not all of these individuals or organizations were new to the game. Many had previously styled themselves as 'arts consultants' working on instrumental cultural policies linking the arts to health, education or other social amelioration projects. Some had worked within local government: the Greater London Council's cultural industries experiment was a notable source of such people. Others, those in small organizations rather than individuals, had often started life as community arts organizations. For them, the goal of helping people to work in the cultural industries was less important as a way of securing a decent livelihood, or even of regenerating declining local economies (important as that was), than it was to secure representation from marginalized groups in industries that were seen as so important to our shared understanding of ourselves.

As Rimmer (2009) argues, this particular group, many of which started life in the 1970s or before, had by this period taken a variety of organizational forms, and indeed their rationales had evolved in response to policy and funding changes. In the process, they had moved away from a focus on art making as an element of democratic cultural participation, and towards one on vocational learning. Ensuring labour market entry for those from underrepresented groups became a key goal, and what had previously been seen as supporting democratic cultural participation was recast as helping young people to find work in the cultural industries.

It was in this guise that such organizations were often agents and indeed recipients of public funding in creative industries initiatives such as the

Mayor's Commission on the Creative Industries in London, which was set up in London in 2002 (Oakley 2012). While featuring a couple of representatives of big business, the Commission also featured representatives of community development organizations. Alongside the usual concerns of investment, ensuring access to affordable space and helping small firms get intellectual property (IP) advice, there was strong emphasis within the Commission's discussions on issues of diversity (generally understood in terms of ethnicity, but also gender), and on ensuring that training and skills development was as widespread as possible to help develop a more representative labour market (LDA 2003).

It follows from this that work itself – the experience and nature of it – could not be the problem; the 'problem' was getting people into work and this involved what was often described as 'working with the grain of the sector'. Mentoring schemes, work placements and internships that would enable young people to secure the mix of freelance and unpaid work deemed vital to entering these sectors thus became part of the vocabulary and practice of community arts and similar organizations. When the egalitarian culture that was the heritage of such organizations came into conflict with the realities of a socially stratified labour market, the result was often a strong resistance to acknowledge such problems, perhaps fearing that such conversations would lead people to conclude that cultural work was best left to those who could handle it, which in practice meant those with relatively high levels of cultural and economic capital.

What was at stake here was in some cases a confusion between the promotion of cultural industries growth, on one hand, and improving the employment prospects of marginalized young people, on the other. Though rhetoric about cultural industries has often run these two things together, there is in fact no essential relationship between them. One could easily have 'successful' cultural industries growth predicated on a narrow social basis, and indeed that is what we appear to have.

The promotion of cultural industries growth and the potential of the cultural industries to offer sustainable employment to relatively large numbers of people, at all levels of the labour market, was what motivated local authorities and regional development bodies to get involved in support schemes. However, for many of the cultural intermediaries with which, and through which, they worked, this was less important than securing representation within these sectors for voices that they felt would otherwise be silent. The policy mechanisms in which they involved themselves were essentially meritocratic and involved working within the cultural industry's often exploitative employment practices. Through a combination of industry nous and connections, mentoring schemes and work-based learning, such organizations sought to diversify the composition of the labour market in ways that ensured that it had very little to say about its 'dark side' (Neilson and Rossiter 2005).

The issue of social class exclusion was one privately acknowledged by many community arts workers and cultural industries advocates, but public discourse tended to focus on visible difference such as ethnicity, gender or disability – in part aided by the measurement of such categories in national statistics and thus the implicit permission to consider this as an issue. The result was that, while many cultural industry interventions explicitly concerned themselves with questions of social inclusion, the labour market itself was not seen as a battleground. The politics of organized labour were as distant from cultural industry policy making as they were from our TV screens and our classrooms.

Absentee workers

Where participation ties into issues of representation and voice, the question of participation, who gets to be a worker in these industries, is of course vital to understanding the sort of symbolic texts our cultural industries produce and thus a major part of our self-understanding as a society. However, while there is research that looks at the representation and portrayal of class in the media and other cultural arenas (Grindstaff 2002; Skeggs 2004; Wood and Skeggs 2008), there are relatively few such studies that link this to issues of labour and participation in labour markets.

One great exception, Michael Denning's account of the US 'cultural front' in the 1930s and 1940s (Denning 1997), attempts to link working-class participation, unionization and cultural expression. He argues that the influence of labour unions and leftist politics not only ensured better representation of working-class people and better working conditions, but also shaped the popular cultural output of the time: 'for the first time in the history of the United States, a working class culture had made a significant imprint on the dominant cultural institutions' (Denning 1997: xx).

Sadly, no such account of the links between the politics of workplace organization and what Denning calls 'aesthetic ideology' (Denning 1997) exists in a British context. It is tempting to argue, though difficult to evidence, that what has been called the 'demonisation' of the working class in the British media and in popular culture in recent years (Jones 2011) can be traced to a declining level of working-class representation in these industries.

Certainly, it is the case that participation in many media fields is more and more socially skewed (Sutton Trust 2006). As Robertson (2010) argues, the socially unrepresentative profile of top journalists is accompanied by the fact that workers and their representatives in the unions are rarely featured as commentators on economic affairs in any major news bulletin. The degree to which a tax change, a piece of legislation or the takeover of one firm by another is 'good for business' is often the only issue considered, while union commentators are required only when justifying an industrial dispute.

Clearly, there is no simple link between representation and portrayal, any more than there is to consumption. Newspapers like *The Sun*, which feature frequent attacks on 'chavs' or 'the underclass', have a large working-class readership, while some defence against the tide of anger at the so-called 'feral underclass' that followed the English riots of 2011 came from the bastions of high Toryism in *The Daily Telegraph* (Oborne 2011). However, it does reflect a wider culture, not only of anti-unionism but also one where members of the working class are generally absent, when they are not being denigrated.

The removal of the working class from their central position in the politics of the Left, whether one sees it as a political betrayal, a pragmatic adjustment to a changing society, or a welcome embrace of other forms of leftist politics (or as something else entirely), has made work a less vital political issue. Voters are addressed as consumers, taxpayers, family members and even, occasionally, citizens, but very rarely workers. As I have suggested above, this has major implications outside the workplace, not least in the rapid growth in inequality since the early 1980s (Dorling 2010); it also has implications for the development of a notion of what constitutes good work, and for the portrayal of workers and the working class in our media and wider cultural life.

In the case of the cultural industries, many of those engaged in local developments had struggled with the issue of representation for years. Ensuring a more diverse workforce was their mission. However, by failing to engage with the reality of cultural work, indeed by subscribing to the view of such work as unproblematic and desirable, they failed utterly to engage with the real nature of exclusion, which was often economic. Those who could not afford to work for low pay, or no pay, for long periods of time were often from working-class backgrounds, and on this crucial issue their intermediary representatives had very little to say.

Conclusions

The argument of this chapter is that the exclusion of work from cultural industries policy is part of a wider story of the exclusion of work, and therefore the politics of work, from mainstream politics, the media and wider public discourse. In the UK, this can be seen explicitly in the policies pursued under New Labour, both at the level of central government and, perhaps more puzzling, by local authorities and voluntary groups, many of which were less than fully signed up to many aspects of the New Labour project. It is not a uniquely British story, however, but one that can be seen in many territories where the idea of the cultural industries as a source of economic growth has been embraced (Ross 2009).

The sources of this exclusion are complex and contested and no one narrative can claim to capture it all. As Banks and Hesmondhalgh have argued (2009: 416), policy documents of the time portray this work as not only desirable but also 'progressive'. It was a view, I would argue, that was shared by many of those intermediaries involved in what they would see as community-level economic development, including community arts organizations, artists' networks and informal learning organizations.

It cannot be overstated how little success there has been in terms of tackling under-representation in terms of gender, ethnicity or social class in the cultural industries, and most of the data show the problem to be getting worse rather than improving (Skillset 2009, 2010). Yet such concerns still matter. The point is that they cannot be treated in isolation from debates about quality of work, about ownership and control in the workplace and, in the case of the cultural industries, about questions of representation and portrayal.

Angela McRobbie has recently called for a renewal of 'radical social enterprise and co-operatives' in the cultural sector (McRobbie 2011: 33), and beyond the cultural industries we do seem to be witnessing a rebirth of interest in all things mutual and cooperative, even if such organizational forms remain very much in the minority. Other have argued that the current UK and other governments' interest in happiness or well-being could make workplace politics more central to policy concerns, given the evidence that work is the source of so much unhappiness or ill-being (Davies 2011). The current politics of protest, whether in the forms of the various 'Occupy' city movements or in the case of tax justice or student protest movements, clearly offer potential for alliances with the labour movement, which has already been taken up in many cases. The possibilities for making common cause between social movements and labour organizations has not seemed stronger for some time, given the economic crisis and the fear for a 'lost generation' of young, unemployed people.

However, such times can also, of course, be difficult for those campaigning for better working conditions. The cultural industries have often been held up as an indicator of the way work is going, whether that is in optimistic accounts of 'work as fun', or concerns that precarity is becoming the norm across the economy. Talking to those trying to enter the cultural sectors, particularly students in higher education, often seems to reveal a mood of resignation, combined with a lack of historical awareness of the progressive changes that were brought about by workers' acting together. Social and ethical concerns are often seen by such people as a major driver of their desire to engage in cultural work; the need for these to be linked explicitly to a politics of the workplace has never been greater.

Notes

1 For example the Precarious Workers Brigade, Carrotworkers Collective, EuroMayDay.
2 The term 'New Labour' generally refers to the British Labour government of 1997–2010. The notion of the New Labour 'project' is generally dated from Tony Blair's accession to the leadership in 1994 and refers to a process of moving the Labour Party in a rightwards, less social democratic direction.
3 The Employment Relations Act 1999 introduced statutory procedures for trade union recognition in firms with more than 20 employees, gave employees the right to be accompanied by a trade union representative during disciplinary procedures and mildly amended the law on strike ballots.

4 The GLC was London's local government, which, from 1981 to 1986, pioneered cultural industry policies the emphasis of which was firmly on culture as a source of production, and indeed of jobs for Londoners, particularly those from working-class backgrounds and ethnic minorities.

5 The New Labour period saw the establishment of a number of public-funded networks in the UK, the aim of which was to support small creative industries by a programme of events, information provision and advice.

Part II
Specificities/transformations

6 Specificity, ambivalence and the commodity form of creative work

Matt Stahl

[W]e cannot separate literature and art from other kinds of social practice, in such a way as to make them subject to quite special and distinctive laws. They may have quite specific features as practices, but they cannot be separated from the general social process.[1]

Introduction

Work and the status and experience of working persons are problems of market society, continually posing conundrums and dilemmas befitting their importance in social life and social change. Waged work in market society is ambivalent through and through: from the standpoint of working people, it is a means of social inclusion and participation and of isolation and disempowerment; it is evidence of freedom and social mobility and of (gendered and racialized) oppression and social constraint; it is engaged in voluntarily and under dull compulsion; it is a site of initiative and self-realization and of soul-crushing boredom and disappointment.[2] Many of the conundrums and dilemmas associated with work and working people that emerge in the course of social change are legible in terms of these and related tensions, and scholars in numerous fields have been applying themselves to these issues for many years.

Work's ambivalence can be multiplied by ambivalence in the perspectives brought to bear in the analysis of work. Two principal divergent cultural conceptions of work and the working person – carried not only in scholarly and popular discourse but also in institutions, laws, industrial techniques, accounting systems, workplace layouts – shape how these conundrums and dilemmas are understood, and determine to a great degree what kinds of reform appear feasible, or appear at all. From one of these two principal Western perspectives, work appears as an instance of the timed subordination of one party by another; from the other, some variation on the exchange of properties by equals. Rooted in the distinctive industrial histories of Germany and Great Britain, these diverging ideas about the nature and meaning of work undergird contrasting perspectives. Scholars steeped in either of these ideas are bound to perceive or at least prioritize very different aspects of the same case; the relationship and influence of these ideas are important to the development of analyses of work and of approaches to its reform or transformation.

Explosive growth in the communication and entertainment sectors has opened up new and altered existing spheres of work and employment. One result has been the rapid institutionalization in the late 20th and early 21st centuries of a new interdisciplinary specialism: the study of creative work in the cultural industries. Scholarship in this area draws on many of the methods and approaches of earlier studies of work and finds many of the same conundrums and dilemmas in play. However, one novel preoccupation is the argument concerning the distinctiveness of creative work in relation to the rest of the social division of labour. The specificity of creative work is often held to reside in the unusual degrees of autonomy and expressiveness it offers, and is often linked to the signifying aspect of cultural goods. Yet, despite general agreement about the ways in which creative work differs from more routine forms of work, ambivalence remains. Contrasting cultural conceptions of labour and the working person shape how scholars perceive and understand specific conundrums, dilemmas and ambivalences associated with creative work. Specified and disentangled, these conceptions of labour can advance analysis and normative prescription; unspecified and tangled, they can introduce snags.

In this chapter, I seek to clarify these cultural conceptions, to show how they influence scholarly perceptions of and normative prescriptions for creative work, and to advocate a further broadening of disciplinary perspectives. I argue that critical awareness of the role these conceptions play in setting limits and exerting pressures on what we see when we investigate creative work (and how we imagine changing it) will advance analysis and sharpen normative arguments.

First, I propose that scholarship in the 'cultural industries' tradition supports the perception of creative work as a *limit case* of work in general. It is a case with an exaggerated character that brings into high relief features that are common to the category but harder to see in the run of cases. I then turn to a major recent contribution to the field, Hesmondhalgh and Baker's *Creative Labour: Media Work in Three Cultural Industries* (2011), which exemplifies not only a high-water mark of rigorous and authoritative social-scientific research in the cultural industries tradition, but also the difficulties that can arise around implicit invocations of contrasting cultural conceptions of labour. In a perspectival shift apparent in that work, I perceive an ambivalence regarding the nature and meaning of creative work: is labour conveyed to employers in the transfer of rights over labour power or in the transfer of rights over intellectual property? Both transfers are typically in operation and are largely indistinguishable in most work; creative work's limit case brings the two into the foreground. Both concepts and principles appear in *Creative Labour*; their relationship in that text outlines the gap this essay seeks to address.

In the second half of the essay, I turn to major contributions in the sociology of culture and the comparative study of law that focus directly on these
concepts. Biernacki's (1995, 1997, 2001) comparative studies of conceptions
of labour borne by German and British weavers working in the 17th to the
early 20th centuries show how very different ideas about the nature and
meaning of labour developed in these two national industrial cultures. Ahlering and Deakin (2007) extend this line of comparative analysis to show how
these different conceptions of labour have become embedded as assumptions
in the very different regimes of labour and corporate law that developed
in Germany (and France) and in Britain. Following Ahlering and Deakin
(ibid.: 899), I see these assumptions as basic features of historically derived
'epistemological maps' of work and the economy. These maps continue to
serve as common sense within distinctive national-cultural contexts (even as
the ongoing implementation of neoliberal policies undermines aspects of their
material contexts) furnishing members of their respective societies with very
different understandings of the roles and status of workers and managers.
I conclude by suggesting that we may advance our analyses, critiques and
proposals through a more inclusive perception of how work's conundrums
and dilemmas have been differently imagined and addressed in divergent
cultural and political-economic systems.

Ambivalence and the specification of creative work

Influential claims about the specificity of creative work as a general category
of activity focus on the meaningful, communicative nature of its products
(e.g. Hesmondhalgh 2007: 15; Hesmondhalgh and Baker 2011: 59, 165) and
the autonomous nature of its relations of production (e.g. Ryan 1992; Banks
2010a). These explanations are tempered, themselves ambivalent: some of
these meaningful things are of poor quality; some creative workers are less
free than others. Nevertheless, these explanations are freighted with (sometimes
distracting) controversy. Their substantiation requires arguments about what
constitutes a meaningful product or autonomous labour process (and, necessarily, products and processes not meaningful or autonomous). 'Specificity' in
either case is founded on arguable distinctions.

Yet by invoking yardsticks of meaningfulness and autonomy, these explanations propose forms of ambivalence and marginality that suggest an alternative
or additional axis of specification, of an alternative logical type. Creative
work presents a limit case of work in general: it is an example the extremity
of which discloses logics essential to the category in heightened form. Creative
work's appearance as a limit case is what renders its forms of alienation and
exploitation so apparent. More to the point, however, its appearance as a
limit case gives creative work a specific interpretive usefulness in that it renders
work's essential logics themselves controversial and more susceptible to analysis. If this argument seems circular, that is because creative work and other
forms of work are equally participant in the general social process, even as

their specific features differ. Because of the ideological freight of its specific features, creative work heightens and denaturalizes normal principles of work. In creative work's marginal context, normal principles of work seem to contradict broader social values.

I argue elsewhere that literature in the 'cultural industries' tradition, treating creative work as a social form of its own kind, supports this limit case hypothesis (Stahl 2013). Theorists impute specificity also through spatial and temporal ambivalences, often implicitly, alongside explicit assertions about categorical specificity. Banks, for example, uses spatial metaphors to position creative workers at the outer limits of the institution of work. Janus-wise, the creative worker simultaneously faces outward, toward the unknown, and inward, toward the mundane (Banks 2010a: 262). Banks argues that this dual orientation is the social product of the 'art–commerce relation', a term that captures an ideological component of creative work's specific features (Banks 2007; see also Ryan 1992). In this view, the creative worker mediates visions of 'meaning beyond the commercial' (Banks 2010a: 263, citation omitted) for those of us bobbing along in the mainstream. More common is the use of temporal terms to specify the creative worker. Again, a Janus-faced figure emerges: facing and reiterating work's past, intuiting and prefiguring its future. Some scholars highlight creative work's atavistic presentation of 'remnants' or 'holdovers' of pre-, proto- or non-capitalist 'artisanal' or 'craft' forms of labour (Ryan 1992: 40–41; Hesmondhalgh 2007: 67; Banks 2007: 33; Miege 1989: 67, 72, 91). This conception is generally coded positively, as the exceptional preservation of autonomous moments in the contemporary economy (Hesmondhalgh 2007: 67; Banks 2007: 33; Ryan 1992: 41). On the other hand, the creative worker is perceived to anticipate the 'model figure of the new worker' (Menger 2002: 10). This view highlights the ways in which increasingly artist-like workers – self-responsible, highly committed, bearing low expectations of security or stability – suit the labour force desiderata of many employers. This view is coded more negatively: the exportation of norms of artistic or creative work into other fields appears mainly to promise peril and disaffiliation (Menger 2002: 10; Ross 2000: 11–12; see also Stahl 2008: 241–44).

Scholarly positioning of creative workers at the outer edge of the institutions of work, or at the juncture of past, present and future political forms of those institutions, renders dynamics basic to the institution of employment questionable, even controversial. In these accounts, creative workers are sometimes troubled by problems brought into relief by their liminal positions. Indeed, as Hesmondhalgh and Baker (2011: 28, note 7) report, for creative workers, 'control over the means of production and over managerial direction are not distant utopian concerns', but immediate and practical ones. The analytical move I am advocating here entails an inversion of the approaches outlined above: the flipside of creative workers' autonomy is constrained managerial power. The relationship envisioned here may be viewed as the economic version of the relationship between the rights of citizens and the power of governments (Stahl 2010).

Contrasting conceptions of creative labour

Scholarly ambivalence is evident in assessments of creative work's expressiveness, quality, and autonomy, and in the theoretical location of creative workers in relation to the mainstream and history of the institutions of work. A further form of ambivalence has to do with the conceptions and definitions of work borne by creative workers, managers, employers, and the scholars who study them. This ambivalence emerges in exemplary form in David Hesmondhalgh and Sarah Baker's *Creative Labour: Media Work in Three Cultural Industries* (2011). My purpose in focusing on this work is to show how contrasting conceptions of work can influence the analysis of creative labour. Briefly recounting certain of their principal themes will set the stage.

Hesmondhalgh and Baker's wide-ranging interview- and participant observation-based account of creative workers' experiences in music, television and publishing focuses on what the authors call 'good' and 'bad' creative work, in terms both of work processes and resulting products. The main characteristics of 'good work' are workers' 'autonomy' and 'self-realisation'. Their converse, workers' 'control by or dependence on others' and 'frustrated self-realisation', are paramount features of 'bad work' (Hesmondhalgh and Baker 2011: 36). The nub is that creative workers 'are experts and skilled workers with little or no supervisory or managerial power' (ibid.: 18); their abilities and reputations buy them room to work relatively autonomously but do not secure for them much in the way of workplace *political* power (ibid.: 67–70); managers retain power of command and can constrain workers' autonomy at will (see also Stahl 2010: 285–86). In numerous cases, 'bad work' appears as the supervisory frustration of creative workers' autonomy and self-realization (often in response to structural change and budgetary constraint;[3] other culprits include audiences and even the workers themselves).

The book culminates with two specific prescriptions for making 'good work ... more widely available and more equally spread' (Hesmondhalgh and Baker 2011: 222). First, the good features should be distributed more equitably among all workers through '*adjustments*' to the social division of labour (ibid.: 231, emphasis in original). This proposition is worthy of further discussion, but my interest here is in their second prescription, that 'political choices [are] to be made about which institutional arrangements are most likely to encourage fairness and at what cost'. These choices, they argue, should not be left to market mechanisms but pursued with attention to 'ethical questions regarding notions of the human good' (ibid.: 233). Hesmondhalgh and Baker propose the '"co-ordinated market economies" such as [that of] Germany' as the model to be consulted in making these choices. Such economies, they point out, 'have been able to offer, to a greater degree than the Anglo-American liberal market model, workplaces with "autonomy from close monitoring", "opportunities to influence the decisions of the firm", a high level and range of skills and so on – all features of good and meaningful work, according to a wide range of definitions' (ibid.: 233, citations omitted).

I agree that Germany has much to teach the Anglo-American world. However, this suggestion appears as an unexplained departure from the analytical terms established in the book's antecedent chapters. These chapters downplay questions regarding the national ideological and labour policy contexts of the workplaces they study, how particular UK laws and customs might have direct effects on workers' experience of autonomy, self-realization or influence. Hesmondhalgh and Baker's prescription, however, invokes exactly the national regulatory contexts responsible for the 'good and meaningful work' they perceive as the norm in Germany. The difficulty is not that they ignore managerial prerogative; in fact (as I mentioned above), it often appears central to many of the experiences of 'bad work' they report; rather, it is that the manager's right to command and the system that legitimates it appear as givens. When they note, for example, that the 'creative manager will [at times] have to obey the dictates of commerce in hiring and "releasing" staff' (ibid.: 87), this observation is offered as an explanation, not something to be explained, as the German perspective would require. Indeed, in establishing their analytical frame, they draw extensively on a study of Canadian nightclub workers whose workplace autonomy was radically circumscribed following a change in management (ibid.: 41–43). In this case, management's right to command employees to adhere to the new regime or risk termination does not appear as a factor to be considered in an analysis of workplace autonomy. Yet in the German system this right is controversial; its constraint is pivotal to that system's distinctiveness. A new frame appears in Hesmondhalgh and Baker's final prescription, in tension with the established terms of their analysis: state-enforced restrictions on managerial fiat become a reasonable and desirable consideration.

Such analytical disjuncture is possible and understandable because of creative work's appearance as a limit case of work. Creative work's specific features point beyond the general social process even as (and exactly because) they reveal that process in a highly concentrated manner. In this context, managerial fiat seems less just and worker autonomy seems more just. However, in the Anglo-American conceptual context, the appearance of managerial fiat as a problem itself poses a problem: it threatens a confusion or clash of models. It is an ugly duckling, the appearance of themes that seem to contradict the dominant model, and which make sense only in terms of an alternate model. The German conception perceives managerial prerogative as a social problem; the British conception (the root of the US model) perceives it almost as a fact of nature. To point to the German model as desirable is implicitly to argue that the British model is insufficient, or is unsusceptible to reform, if it is not downright unjust. Here, further investigation of creative work's specific conceptual and practical ambivalences will bear fruit.

The ambivalent manner in which creative workers convey their labour to their corporate paymasters brings contrasting conceptions of labour into high relief. On the one hand, creative workers convey their labour through the transfer of (rights to) the intellectual property they create or to which they contribute while on the job: the conveyance of creative *products* (or fractions thereof). On the other hand, they do so through the contractual employment relations by which they grant employers (often exclusive) access to (and the right to control) their labour for the duration of the contract: the cession of workplace *authority*. These two transactions typically operate as indistinguishable facets of a single, compound relationship.[4] Their apparent distinctiveness in creative work is evidence in support of the limit case characterization: employment in general involves both the transfer of property rights *and* control rights; the public-ness of (star) creative workers' struggles over attribution or authorial rights (on the one hand) and contractual control of labour (on the other) remind us of employment's otherwise obscure dual nature (Stahl 2013). The distinguishability of these two moments of transfer in creative work's limit case reveals their real distinctiveness in the run of cases. Yet, because we in the Anglo-American world generally lack a clear sense of how our employment system fuses these two forms and transfers of rights, their distinctiveness in creative work can be the source of confusion, even mystification. Our Anglo-American disinclination to see employment as an authority relation fosters a conception of creative work that emphasizes the transfer of property rights, imagined as an exchange of properties (rights in creative works for wages or rights to royalties or residuals), and downplays the significance of the transfer of control rights. This tendency limits perception of the scope of the 'art-commerce' relationship as it plays out on the shop (or studio) floor and constrains the range of imaginable possibilities for reform.

The ambivalence of creative employment corresponds to divergent cultural concepts of the commodity form of labour characteristic of the two market systems (in)directly invoked by Hesmondhalgh and Baker. These concepts developed in 'the period of industrialization in the eighteenth and nineteenth centuries[, which] was a formative one in the emergence of modern legal and economic institutions' (Ahlering and Deakin 2007: 893). In the following section, I examine studies of these contrasting concepts and their integration into contrasting market systems.[5]

Two cultural concepts of labour's commodity form

Two contrasting ways of understanding labour have become institutionalized over the last several centuries. Both approaches 'interpret a paradox in the employment relation. The worker's labour may generate the value of the finished product, but this labour, since it consists of an ongoing activity, is not a thing and has itself no exchange value' (Biernacki 1995: 60). Each approach highlights logics that are supported by the social facts of employment in capitalism: neither is incorrect, but neither is definitive. The differing 19th-century German and British cultural conceptions of labour are readily summarized: 'German owners and workers viewed employment as the timed appropriation of workers' labour power and disposition over workers' labour activity. In contrast, British owners and workers saw employment as the appropriation of workers' materialized labour via its products' (ibid.: 12). These contrasting concepts of labour ramified into particular labour relations: German weavers claimed remuneration for idle time; while on factory grounds they understood themselves to be under the command of employers, even if they weren't active. British weavers did not imagine such a claim.[6] On the other hand, British weavers did not perceive a personal relation of command; they sometimes could and did send others to work in their stead, often without the permission of an overseer. Wages were figured in terms of the product and not the worker; the employee-employer (an impossibility in Germany) was responsible for paying his substitute(s). Paving the way for the imagined relations of record companies and recording artists (Stahl 2013), an 1891 article in a British employers' journal 'cast the employers as investors who get a return by furnishing the means of production, not as innovative organizers and controllers of the use of living labour', while German workers employed 'labour power' as an everyday conceptual tool long before Marx published it for the first time (Biernacki 1995: 89, 42).

These divergent cultural conceptions 'structured the most fundamental aspects of industrial relations, including methods of remuneration, calculation of output and costs, disciplinary techniques, rights to employment, articulation of grievances, mill architecture, and even the apperception of time and space' (Biernacki 1997: 176). In other words, these were not simply examples of differing workplace vocabularies; 'the techniques of manufacture [themselves] were organized and executed as signifying practices' (ibid.: 175). Similarly, for today's recording artists, writers, producers, illustrators, composers and other creative workers, the delivery of a finished 'master' (e.g. camera-ready art, manuscript, digital file) and the technical forms of budgets, royalties, licence fees or residuals may also be understood as signifying practices (re)producing practice-based conceptions of the commodity form of creative labour. Many of these social forms enact the conveyance of labour as materialized in products, obscuring to workers, to employers, and to observers the ever-present governance relation.

Biernacki's analysis also shows how workers in these different regimes imagined the locus and nature of exploitation. German workers of the 19th and early 20th centuries – not just weavers, and not just socialist workers, but also anti-socialist Christian workers – perceived exploitation and class division as an immediate consequence of their subordination at the point of production (ibid.: 187). German weavers 'contracted for the disposal over their personal labour time itself and had to show up in person'; they 'distinguished themselves by demanding compensation for commitment of minutes, however inappreciable, to tasks after the official close of work, such as waiting in line at the exit to punch time cards'. German employers 'treated unpunctual attendance as a denial of labour power, whose loss could be calibrated and precisely counterbalanced' with fines (ibid.: 176, 184). British workers did not perceive the exercise of authority in production and thus did not attribute exploitation to relations of production. Rather, they perceived their exploitation to be attributable to employers' and workers' unequal access to the market and opportunities to realize profit. According to British pamphleteers, 'people who did not have the working capital needed to maintain their independence could not exchange their labour for its true commercial value' (Biernacki 1995: 225, note 46). This is exactly how contemporary recording artists and their advocates frame their own political-economic debility (Stahl 2013). For the British, 'the exchange of labour as a commodity could be not only separated from but *contrasted* with the exercise of authority. "You are no master of mine", a rule-maker told his employer in the 1840s, "but only a man who buys my labour for a good deal less than it's worth"' (Biernacki 1995: 193, my emphasis). This formulation 'acknowledged a relation that included both formal equality in the marketplace and real exploitation' (ibid.: 193).

Each of these conceptions offers a very different set of everyday analytical tools for dissecting the relationship between worker and employer and for determining what is and is not fair, reasonable and just in this relationship. The 'varying cultural incarnations' of these analytical tools 'impart critically different logics to economic functions that appear deceptively similar' (Biernacki 1997: 188). Biernacki finds that 'the striking correspondence between the definitions of exploitation in workers' collective movements and the symbolic form of German and British factory techniques shows that the workers' experience of the execution of these techniques configured their reception of formal ideologies' (ibid.: 188), predisposing them toward contrasting political-economic self-understandings, social movement goals and political appeals.

Creative workers' experience of forms and techniques of creative work – as well as scholars' perception of those experiences – condition their (and our) 'reception of formal ideologies' and hence their (and our) abilities to imagine desirable and feasible action toward reform. The two very different appearances taken by the conveyance of creative labour in the cultural industries – transfer of intellectual property versus submission to employer authority – nestle comfortably alongside the respective British and German conceptions outlined above *and* extend and reify the apparent disjuncture between them. Both conceptions are supported by the social facts of (creative) work. The emphasis on property may be supported by observation of the activities involved in the production of masters for record companies or manuscripts for publishers, but, in downplaying authority, such an emphasis widens the conceptual distance that must be bridged if we are to turn, with Hesmondhalgh and Baker, to the German model for help expanding and making more equitable the distribution of 'good work'.

Historical development of 'liberal' and 'coordinated' market regimes

The British 'liberal market' system and the German 'coordinated market' system owe their existence and distinctive forms not to political choices made by policy makers based on conceptions of 'the human good' at particular historical turning points, but to complex interactions of cultural concepts of labour and the asynchronous developments of industrialization, market economies, political liberalization, and regulatory/legal regimes in England and on the continent of Europe. The key difference is that in England industrialization predated the development of a market for labour and the modernization of law governing enterprise, while, in much of Europe, industrialization, the market for labour, and corporate law developed more or less simultaneously. These developments explain why the contemporary Anglo-American employee (creative or not) bears the imprimatur of (pre-industrial) servility, while the German (as well as French and Scandinavian) employee enjoys greater autonomy and influence and is more likely to experience 'good and meaningful work'.

In England, the worker entered the dawning factory system under the banner of effectively medieval legal and socio-political conditions, retaining his or her status as servant, while the employer retained his status as master. In the absence of a liberal conception of the labourer and employer as juridical equals, medieval relations of master and servant were carried into industrializing domains of production (see also Bendix 2001). Features of this regime included the criminalization of workers failure to perform, the setting of wages by government authorities and the prohibition of geographic mobility. 'In consequence', writes Biernacki, 'labour could only be envisioned as an article of *free* commerce when it was embodied in a product and vended by independent producers' (Biernacki 2001: 176, my emphasis). This perspective was expressed and reinforced by early political economists such as Steuart, who identified two types of workers: subjugated sellers of labour power ensconced in 'feudal or colonial orders' and autonomous sellers of products participating in a 'liberal commercial order' (ibid.: 176).

As British industrialization and enclosures proceeded, and as paternalistic legislation seemed of diminishing utility to capitalist economic development (Polanyi 1944), labour came to be treated increasingly as an article of commerce, and its public understanding developed in a fashion that belied its socio-political form. Despite its actual servile character – and political economists' understanding that the sale of labour power reiterated feudal political domination – 'the labour conveyed through the engagement of wage workers was still conceived as a general social substance only as it was embodied in a product' (Biernacki 2001: 177). In England, labour for hire became a market commodity with a double character: a servile, compulsive *status* contained within an autonomous, voluntary *appearance* (Pateman 1988: 131–32). By way of the political economists' influential interpretations, and a rejection by labourers of a servile self-conception (evident in the discounting of employer authority: 'you are no master of mine'), the cultural conception of the autonomous artisan incorporated and obscured the persisting political-economic debility that gives labour in 'liberal market' economies its particular character.[7] The contemporary doctrine of managerial prerogative ('duty to obey' in the US) is evidence of the persistence of servility as a core characteristic of Anglo-American employment.

In Germany and France, the more or less simultaneous development of industrialization and a market for labour in the early 19th century (the latter achieved through the progressive abolition of vassalage and of guild domination of production) meant that labour power appeared as a commodity that could be traded by formally free individuals. The reason that this kind of trade can be distinguished from the exchange of properties imagined by British workers and employers is that Germans perceived that the commodity labour power is the timed subordination of workers. Perceiving authority relations as essential to the conveyance of the labour commodity, workers, employers and policy makers inscribed a more democratic ethos in the employment relationship as these systems developed. In the French system, influenced by political liberalization that predated widespread industrial development, the parties to employment were understood as contractually equal. However, rather than simply ascribing equality to relations of social domination through a voluntarist interpretation of the relationship, the state 'assumed, by way of symmetry, a responsibility for establishing a form of protection for the individual worker', who was understood to be placed, through contract, 'in a position of "juridical subordination"' (Ahlering and Deakin 2007: 897). In Germany, the abstract formal equality of the employment relation was similarly substantiated through the general conception of the enterprise as a community. 'German law', write Ahlering and Deakin, 'came to recognize the "personal subordination" of the worker in the form of "factual adhesion to the enterprise" ... a process that conferred "a status equivalent to membership of a community"' (ibid.: 898). In the developing European political economies, 'the view emerged that property and responsibility were two sides of the same coin' (ibid.: 902). Cutting against the Lockean logic of British liberalism, property rights in a European firm did not give owners unfettered control.

The later onset of industrialization in Europe, in relative synchrony with the abolition of illiberal feudal and guild institutions, posed subordination and adhesion as social problems, not legitimate features of a private relation. Cultural, legal, economic and political systems evolved to substantiate formal equality with a 'universal floor of [worker] rights', incorporating 'the principle of worker protection while at the same time recognizing the primacy of capitalist modes of economic development' (ibid.: 876, 899). This principle of worker protection – a product of two centuries' habituation, codification and formalization of conceptions and practice into expectations, legislation and rights – is what makes possible the more routine appearance in Germany of workers who enjoy 'autonomy from close monitoring' and 'opportunities to influence the decisions of the firm'.

Conclusion: epistemological maps and the intelligibility of creative work

As a limit case of work in modern market society, creative work renders two principal political components of work – the exchange of property rights and the transfer of control rights – visibly distinctive, controversial and question-able. However, in the English-speaking world, it does so in a cultural context in which the former is the hegemonic interpretation of work and the latter is a dissenting view. Even as much scholarly work challenges the legitimacy of some particular exchanges, an emphasis on the former is confluent with the hegemonic view. In the hegemonic view, only exceptionally are subordination and exploitation perceived as problems at the point of production.[8] By inveigling us into identifying the conveyance of the creative labour commodity with the transfer of intellectual property from someone resembling an artisan/seller to someone resembling a client/buyer, bearers of the hegemonic understanding of creative work (not just people or media but techniques and systems) downplay the relations of authority that are the obverse of this apparent exchange.

Yet occasions when managerial fiat is exercised to the degree that it con-tributes to experiences of 'bad work' nevertheless remind us that managerial prerogative might indicate a systemic rather than an exceptional problem. Especially in the wake of decades of union busting and attacks on social provisions, these occasions remind us that the limits of autonomy in the Anglo-American workplace are largely determined by management. Here again is the creative worker as Janus figure, mediator not only across social boundaries and between then, now and soon, but also between familiar and unfamiliar conceptions of work. Encountering managerially imposed limits to autonomy in often dramatic and public ways, the creative worker's 'bad work' reveals subordination at the heart of what appears to be a relationship of free and voluntary exchange. This perception is unremarkable to the German outlook, but counterintuitive and sometimes irritating to the Anglo-American. The perception that employer domination and employee subordination are the preconditions of exploitation (Pateman 1988: 149) smacks of crude, theory-driven Marxism. However, Biernacki shows – and comparative analysis of the historical development of British and German epistemological maps and corporate and employment law affirms – that during the early 19th-century formation of present-day institutions and epistemological maps of work, 'German workers did not wait for Marx to use "labor power" to describe the extraction of surplus' (Biernacki 2001: 179).

Without necessarily privileging one over the other, it is not difficult to see that the diverging systems' different epistemological maps attribute different meanings to 'deceptively similar' social processes and legal-political struc-tures. The naturalization of these meanings supports their operationalization as assumptions in different interpretations of workers' relationships with employers. These interpretations set limits to and exert pressures on our ability to imagine targets, projects and scales for reform. The suggestion that we look to routine work in Germany as a model for the improvement of already gen-erally 'good' creative work in the Anglo-American world is provocative indeed. It suggests that creative work's illumination of otherwise obscure logics destabilizes common-sense epistemological maps. Hesmondhalgh and

Baker's analyses of the injuries and indignities of 'bad creative work' may put readers more in mind to question the legitimacy of managerial fiat, to perceive authority relations in work, and to perceive them as unjust than analyses of other types of work relationships. Their final prescription prompts us to consider explicitly what is appealing about the German system, to understand its cultural and political-economic aspects, and to consider realistically what it would take to integrate the parts that we like about the German system into our own. Such a consideration would mean explicitly recognizing the embeddedness of the servile status of employees in our received concepts of work.

This historical-cultural context accounts not only for the structural underpinnings, but also for our very definitions of 'good' and 'bad' work, at least as much as do the discourses of art and artist and the cultural capitalist's dual requirement of novelty and predictability. In the perspective I've outlined here, 'good work' in the cultural industries appears as a cluster of exceptions in the 'liberal market' economy, as moments in which servile norms are constrained and convention provides meaningful (but necessarily tenuous) opportunities for autonomy, self-realization and participation. In this light, as Hesmondhalgh and Baker intuit, the systemic logic and path-dependence associated with England's troubled period of industrialization appear unlikely to support the normalization of 'good work' in the 'liberal market' economies.

I am suggesting that expanding our analytical horizons can aid us immensely. Hesmondhalgh and Baker's parting gesture toward the desirability of regulation – the police power of the state to restrict freedom of contract in favour of social values – suggests an unease with the British conceptual model that undergirds the bulk of their empirical presentation. Their intuition is confirmed by the comparative legal analysis: it appears that the epistemological map associated with the 'liberal market' system is generically less disposed toward seeing or treating workers as *substantively* rather than simply *formally* equal participants in production processes. If that is the case, then 'good work' will continue to be an exception, enjoyed primarily by people whose value (in this case, their creative abilities along lines proven valuable in markets for cultural goods) gives them advantages – 'freedom inside the organization' (Ewing 1977), 'institutional autonomy' (Toynbee 2000: 7–13) – that enable them to enjoy conditions that contravene the normal servile status of workers in the 'liberal market' system.

In this chapter, I have borrowed analyses from other disciplines that shed light on scholarly perspectives on creative work in 'liberal market' societies. These analyses are contributions to ongoing disciplinary arguments and do not pose a last word in their home disciplines nor for ours. Nevertheless, they present compelling evidence that the 'liberal market' and 'coordinated market' economies in which we work and think owe their configuration to, and embed within themselves (and us), very different cultural conceptions of labour and signifying practices, related to differing national-historical paths to industrialization, liberalization and marketization. The 'liberal market' and 'coordinated market' economies pose contrasting examples of how labour may serve as a social medium and figure in '[e]nduring institutions [that] have a "self-enforcing" and "self-sustaining" character' related to their functionality, and not necessarily to their political character or ethical desirability (Ahlering and Deakin 2007: 869, citations omitted; see also Postone 1993).

I have emphasized creative work's Janus-like linking of distinctive regimes and conceptions of work and its appearance as a limit case of work – an instance of the general social process distinguished by specific social-symbolic features. The exercise of managerial fiat is not of a qualitatively different kind in creative work than it is in other forms of work: whether by direct contractual command or impersonal market forces, creative as well as other workers may be made to obey or face penalties. By further exploring and exploiting the reasons why creative work seems to pose exceptions to the hegemonic Anglo-American perspective on work, we may sensitize ourselves, our students and others to the internal logics of an alternate (e.g. German 'coordinated market') normality. Such a sensitivity, I believe, will go some distance toward rendering more useful what have long appeared as radical, theory-driven approaches to the conundrums and dilemmas of (creative) work and toward cultivating and normalizing the appealing features of the 'good work' we perceive in the 'coordinated market' system.

Notes

1 Williams 2005: 50. By permission of Verso.
2 I do not take up the philosophical distinction between 'work' and 'labour' in this analysis, though I do not discount its importance or usefulness (see Standing 1999: 3–9).
3 All manner of supervisory discretion is relevant here, from the enforcement of 'pub' sociality to the translation of commissioners' imperatives into workplace commands (e.g. Hesmondhalgh and Baker 2011: 153–55, 168–70).
4 'Independent contracting' is a form of work in which these two operations are (often only putatively) disentangled (see Davidov 2002; Stahl 2010: 272–74; Stahl 2013).
5 These analyses also concern patterns in and predictions for corporate governance and investment, which I do not address here.
6 This distinction appears in arguments about whether data entry workers should be compensated for the time it takes for their computers to boot (start) up every morning, during which they cannot enter any data (Baldas 2008).
7 Domenico Losurdo (2011) suggests that this recoding of labour in England may have been aided by the expansion and intensification of servility in British colonies.
8 Garnham's frequently cited observation that cultural distribution and not production *'is the key locus of power and profit'* (e.g. Hesmondhalgh and Baker 2011: 103, original emphasis) appears in this light as a striking encapsulation of this view.

7 How special?

Cultural work, copyright, politics

Jason Toynbee

It is an obvious point but still worth making, I think: to treat cultural production as an elevated kind of work, or even beyond work altogether, has been the common sense of the middle classes in the West since Kant and the Romantic movement. Among reading publics, educated audiences and artists themselves, the cult of the artist as free-ranging genius continues to rule. If this is a lay orthodoxy, then the contrast over the last 30 years or so is with the small world of cultural and media studies. Here the strong tendency has been to treat as myth any claim that making symbolic artefacts constitutes a high point of human endeavour, or else simply to ignore it and look at other dimensions of cultural work.

There are some good reasons for scepticism of this sort. One is that the specialness claim depends on notions of aesthetic value, which tend to be both ineffable and elitist. So, in film and cultural studies, the concept of authorship has been criticized as an ideological construct with strong authoritarian implications – a critique heavily influenced by Roland Barthes and his 'death of the author' thesis (Barthes 1993). Meanwhile another, empirical strand in media studies has approached work in the cultural sector simply as an 'occupation' (Tunstall 2000), in this way side-stepping issues of distinction altogether. No doubt, behind some of the scepticism about specialness is its strong association with individualism. Sociologists, notably Howard Becker (1992) and the 'production of culture' school in the USA (e.g. Hirsch 1972), have shown that the process of making symbolic goods is actually social through and through. Any distinctiveness of the field has to do with material or organizational dimensions rather than the elevated character of individual producers and their creative processes. However, perhaps the most sustained attack on the specialness thesis has come from Pierre Bourdieu (1990) in his research into the 'field of cultural production'. Bourdieu suggests that the claim for artistic autonomy by artists is little more than a pretext. One makes such claims in order to acquire cultural power, and no more so than in the case of 'restricted production', that is avant-garde or alternative formations outside the mainstream.

These sceptical or agnostic takes on the specialness of cultural work formed the main body of literature that I had to negotiate when I started my PhD on popular music making in the early 1990s. Certainly, I found such critiques persuasive, but I also had a lingering feeling that there *was* still something rather special about music making. Off and on over the years, I had sung and written songs for rock bands, and perhaps this gave me some insight into what was at stake. Or maybe the experience just made me more susceptible to the idea that authorship mattered, in a self-serving kind of way *à la* Bourdieu. Most likely there was a bit of both involved. In any event, I ended up by trying to show how creativity was indeed a characteristic of popular music making, while at the same time rebutting those notions of romantic self-expression that remain dominant in everyday discourse (Toynbee 2000). In their production of sublime new sounds, popular musicians were, I suggested, 'social authors' who depended on other cultural workers, re-used existing musical materials, and only made small steps in innovation at any one time. On this view, cultural work was special, but modestly so. So, while popular music makers might be characterized as 'exemplary agents', they were nevertheless always positioned within a 'radius of creativity' which both constrained and enabled the rather limited autonomy they had over the organization of musical resources.

As I soon realized, other researchers were taking a similar approach, trying to find a middle way that acknowledged both creativity and its structural limits, enumerated the social dimensions of cultural production, and explored its location in the capitalist market economy, while always recognizing the values inherent in symbol making itself. The work of Barry Shank (1994), David Hesmondhalgh (2002) and Mark Banks (2007) strikes me as being particularly important in these respects, but in an important sense all the contributors in this book belong to the new revisionist camp.

Recently, though, I have started to think again about my own version of revisionism. Can a moderate, socialized view of the special nature of cultural work really explain what's at stake in it – at least in the way I was setting out in earlier writing? The problem, it now seems to me, is not with the account itself, which I think does a reasonable job as far as it goes. Rather, the challenge is to look beyond the substantive field of cultural work to identify the thorough-going contradictions that extend from the larger domain of work in general into the labour of making cultural goods. Over the course of this chapter, I am going to attempt an analysis of this kind. It will involve several steps: examining the origins of the claim for specialness, looking critically at latter-day justifications of it, and showing how a version of it has been taken up by the cultural industries as a rationale for copyright, in other words, the means by which the commodity status of cultural goods is enforced. In the last sections, I suggest that, notwithstanding the problems with theories of specialness, or the ideological mobilization of it by corporate copyright, there is actually an important kernel here. To recover it, I examine recent research which finds the origins of Marx's anthropological theory of labour in Kant's characterization of art making. If, as this writing suggests, autonomy and creativity are at the heart of work in general, what are the implications for a progressive politics of labour?

Origins of the claim

Historically, the special value of cultural work has been associated with two related antinomies in Western thought. The first is aesthetic autonomy set against utility. Here culture making is conceived as autonomous in its resistance to the ratio-centric, means-ends system which has come to order the modern world. The classical statement about the autonomous status of art and artistic practice is found in Kant (1790). The second antinomy pitches human creativity against alienation. On this view, culture making involves realizing the potential of what it is to be human in the face of an industrial system that degrades and denies humanity. An early exposition can be heard in the poetry of the Romantic movement, and perhaps most programmatically in Wordsworth's *Prelude* (1805). Both the above antinomies, of course, emerge in the period when capitalism and reason are developing together in powerful, yet ambivalent, combination from the late 18th century onwards.

Autonomy and creativity are also key values of the broader political movement for emancipation, and as a consequence connect making culture with radical politics more generally – from the Jacobins to Marxism to critical theory to radical democracy. It is a link that involves some kind of mutual legitimation of the struggles for good art and for good life, but if this is a necessary link it also involves, as Jacques Rancière (2002) puts it, the 'emplotment of autonomy and heteronomy' – in other words, a messy entanglement of art, politics and the actually existing world of dominated social relations.

Crucially, however, this emplotment does not occur simply at the level of ideas but has its basis in the material conditions through which culture emerged as a distinct sphere in the first place. Martha Woodmansee (1996), for example, has shown how high art as an institution, and the claims for autonomy that underpin it, were very much a response to the new market for culture which was replacing patronage at the end of the 18th century. Artists and authors distinguished themselves from their counterparts in the commercial world of popular culture by making a case for their special status. A similar argument has been made by Raymond Williams. As he puts it, 'the artist's claim to "freedom" and to "create as he wishes" was much more commonly made after the institution of dominant market relations, and must be both positively and negatively related to them' (Williams 1981: 46). Williams does not elaborate on this, but I think we can reasonably infer that by 'positively' he means to suggest that the claim to autonomy is a form of resistance to the market and exchange value, while he uses 'negatively' to refer to the way in which it is also a strategy of accommodation. That is, autonomy provides a shell for the artist inside which she can retreat as the trade in art carries on all around.

The material origins and entanglement of specialness discourse with market relations form a crucial dimension of the present argument then. The implication is that the specialness claim is an integral part of the *contradictory* nature of cultural work, and no more so than at the moment of its inception.

Not merely an enlightened idea the time of which had come, artistic autonomy emerged as a response to emerging capitalist social relations. Now it seems to me that this historical and materialist perspective is valuable, and a necessary corrective to a narrow history of ideas approach, focused on aesthetics. Nevertheless, on its own the materialist account cannot properly explain the nature of the contradiction. To try to develop such an explanation, I want to examine some more recent defences in social and cultural thought of the special status of certain kinds of labour including, but extending, outside cultural work. Identifying problems here can help not only with pointing up the political dangers of the celebration of cultural work, but also with the task of recovering a progressive and sustainable understanding of specialness, beyond the enigma.

Problems of specialness

The first and biggest problem with theoretical claims for the specialness of certain classes of work is the way such claims involve the relegation of 'ordinary work' to a lower status. Now this is very far from being the case in most of the literature I have described as revisionist. For instance, Mark Banks (2007) shows how cultural work may constitute a practice where 'internal goods' deriving from the particular kind of art making at stake in it can predominate over 'external goods' like money or status (as in Bourdieu's conspectus). The key point for Banks is that 'while much cultural work remains in service only to the accumulation imperative, cultural industries should not be understood as sites of a standardised and general exploitation, but as loci for a contestable and transformable political economy of work' (Banks 2010: 266). It is the critical possibilities of cultural work and its virtues in relation to work in general that count for Banks.

   Yet, in a book that provides some of the social theoretical underpinning for this argument, Alasdair MacIntyre's (2007) *After Virtue*, a sharp distinction is drawn between work that reaches the threshold of a 'practice' and that which does not. Unlike with Banks, there is no normative case being made here for the need to transform impoverished forms of work. Rather, there just *is* a duality in kinds. For MacIntyre, a practice means 'any coherent and complex form of socially established cooperative human activity through which goods internal to that activity are realized in the course of trying to achieve those standards of excellence'. However, by means of examples, he makes clear in the starkest possible way that only activities that reach a certain level of complexity can qualify. So, '[b]ricklaying is not a practice; architecture is' (MacIntyre 2007: 187). The complexity of a practice is, in effect, a requirement for the exercise of creativity by its practitioners. What is more, while 'the ideals and the creativity' of a practice are always 'vulnerable to the acquisitiveness' of institutions that sustain them, nevertheless the independence of practices tends to be ensured by the virtues of 'justice, courage and truthfulness' (ibid.: 194). In other words, virtues beyond those pertaining to the practice itself help to maintain its elevated standing.

The response of Daniel Putman (1997) is that 'the intellectual bias of virtue ethics' on show in MacIntyre's analysis produces an artificial dichotomy whereby a distinction between mere skill and real virtue is conflated with a distinction in lifestyle. As Putman shows, this is illegitimate. For even the most apparently humble of human activities, like bricklaying or repetitive factory work, is actually capable of being practised virtuously. If MacIntyre's criteria for a practice are to be met – namely that it should be coherent, complex, cooperative and depend on standards of excellence (MacIntyre 2007: 187) – then there is no good reason to set the threshold between brick-laying and architecture. For the values MacIntyre describes are historical, such that mere skills may become practices over time, and it would surely be more just and true to recognize, as Putman (1997: 309) argues, that '[a]ll intentional voluntary human activities can be done more or less well'. None of this, it should be added, invalidates the concept of practice, but it does mean that we should use it inclusively, and not to produce a distinction between classes of work as MacIntyre seems to do.

Hanna Arendt sketches a parallel dichotomy between kinds of work, which also has implications for arguments about the specialness of symbol making. Her distinction is between repetitive *labour* undertaken to satisfy the immediate need to consume, and *work* which results in enduring products for use, namely 'works', and therefore too a 'world' (Arendt 1998: 79–100). As with MacIntyre's practice, Arendt's category of work depends on autonomy and independence from compulsion. As she puts it, *homo faber* (the one who works) is 'master of himself and his doings … Alone with his image of the future product, *homo faber* is free to produce, and again facing alone the work of his hands, he is free to destroy' (ibid.: 144).

Sean Sayers, however, criticizes the dichotomy between work and labour from a materialist perspective. As he points out, the two 'are necessarily and inextricably combined in human productive activity' (Sayers 2003: 116). Even in the case of apparently 'pure' labour for consumption, social relations of production are produced. Conversely, in what might appear to be strictly productive work resulting in artefacts, there is also consumption of these artefacts – they sustain us. Now even if we could allow this distinction as being between 'ideal types' (something which Seyla Benhabib (1996) argues), Arendt is complicit, Sayers suggests, in the reduction of labour to an essentially sub-human, animal realm, and as a corollary the raising of work to a transcendent level above the material. This is simply to revert to the aristocratic world view of the ancients, which was itself built on slave labour.

Ultimately, then, the categories that MacIntyre and Arendt create are incoherent because they fetishize autonomy and abstract it from human action which in all its guises is both fully social and material, or else they falsely associate autonomy with high status. Neither writer wants to acknowledge that, in the actually existing world ordered by inequality, autonomy is always compromised, that it always emerges awkwardly at stress points in conflicted social relations.

A quite different, but equally mistaken, attempt to make a distinction between kinds of work is Marxist in provenance, and apparently depends much less on normative considerations. Based on the earlier work of their autonomist comrade Maurizio Lazzarato, Hardt and Negri (2001, 2005) argue for the advent of 'immaterial labour' in post-Fordist capitalism. Immaterial labour is characterized by the fact that it produces immaterial products. By 2005, in *Multitude*, there are two kinds: 'symbolic' and 'affective' labour (Hardt and Negri 2005: 108).

Symbolic labour yields intellectual, linguistic or more broadly symbolic products. Clearly, cultural work is included here, although Hardt and Negri's symbolic labour is actually a larger category, much closer to a 'creative industries' conception. The major problem with symbolic labour as a type is quite simply that it is *not* immaterial. For, as Sean Sayers (2007: 446) points out, '[a]ll labour operates by intentionally forming matter in some way'. Hitting the keys on a computer has material consequences in the sending of electrical impulses to the processor and then screen or printer. Or think about an example where creativity and expression seem to be more immediate, namely acting. Actors don't just imagine their roles, but also transform their bodies and the physical space in which they are located. That is, they contribute materially to the *mise-en-scène* on stage or before the camera. There is a corollary to this, namely that ostensibly material labour has a dimension of knowledge. The bricklayer has to calculate and plan her work, but also constantly monitor the interaction of her body with the external world.

It appears then that Hardt and Negri, just as much as MacIntyre or Arendt, are unable to produce a coherent typology that might support the proposition that cultural work is special. Of course, none of these writers confines themselves strictly to cultural work. They are concerned with work or meaningful human activity in general, and then identify a type of activity ('practice', 'work' or 'symbolic labour') as being particularly significant. In all three cases, though, culture making is clearly and explicitly located within that type, and it is this location that makes their arguments so important. For if the social theoretical case for the specialness of kinds of activity which include cultural work can be rebutted, then this rebuttal is of a strong and supervening kind when it comes to cultural work itself. To put it slightly differently, the specialness of cultural work is cast into doubt in a particularly powerful way when the criticism does not rely at all on aesthetic, and therefore parochial, arguments.

Copyright and the ideology of cultural work

We will come back to this line of criticism shortly, but at this stage I want to broaden the critique of specialness by going beyond arguments made in the academy to examine ideas about cultural work advanced by the cultural industries. These ideas are important because of their impact in the public sphere, and in turn on states that define the terms and conditions under which culture is produced and exchanged. Crucially, the so-called 'content' industries, in other words, those that own and control intellectual property, pose the specialness of cultural work as a key part of their defence of copyright and the exceptional, monopoly form of the commodity that it prescribes.

Copyright represents a response by the capitalist state to the difficulties of restricting access to cultural goods. In order for the 'Money-Commodity-Money' circuit of accumulation to be completed (Marx 1976: 200ff), control must be exerted over the commodity at the point at which it is exchanged. However, whereas non-symbolic commodities can be held physically behind the counter, in the warehouse or shop, symbolic commodities are less easily corralled. Once the expensive process has been completed of producing and publishing the first copy (manuscript, final cut, master and so on), it is relatively easy and cheap for others to replicate. Economists have developed crypto-normative explanations for this circumstance which are then used to justify the granting of copyright, in other words, a legally enforceable monopoly in cultural products. The best known of these is the 'free rider' argument, in which the public-ness of cultural goods, in other words, their replicability at marginal cost, is rendered as a problem for which the solution is copyright.

Now, historically, copyright has been the subject of contention between copyright owners (the so-called 'content' industries) and corporate users of copyright content (chiefly the media, but also shops, restaurant, venues and the like). Quite simply, the former want to defend an expansive copyright regime and the accumulation strategies built on it, while the latter wish to push back the scale and range of copyright control so as to reduce costs of exploiting copyrighted products, notably music. The struggle over copyright between the radio industry (exploitation) and music publishers (content) in the USA in the early 1940s is a case in point (Ryan 1985). Historically, such contest has rarely become a public issue. On the contrary, conflict around copyright has for the most part been a matter of inter-sectoral lobbying, and 'technical' debate.

However, since the rise of digital communication and the Internet, which have made copying and dissemination of copies much easier, there has been a growing crisis in the legitimacy of copyright among citizens. Increasingly, end-users of cultural products see the economic rationale for copyright as serving the interests of content owners, and may even view copyright itself as illegitimate, or simply a 'rip-off' in everyday language. The Pirate Bay website and movement in Sweden, the party of the same name in Germany, the Electronic Frontier Foundation and other organizations in the USA, but most of all the millions of people across the world who download music and other genres from unofficial sites: these individuals and groups attest not only to the widespread sidestepping of copyright, but also active resistance to it.

Hence, the attraction to the cultural industries of rationales for copyright that apparently intercede on behalf of the cultural worker, posing the special nature of the work she does and therefore the need for copyright. Now it is true that in many cases copyright does in the first instance belong to the creator, rather than cultural and media corporations, but even in these cases labour market conditions, whereby supply greatly exceeds demand, mean that the cultural industries are able to insist on the signing over of rights from the creator to the cultural industries via a publishing contract of some kind. Thus, the argument that copyright, and the industrial system based upon it, protects creators *per se* – rather than the corporations – is especially disingenuous. Still, it is this case that is increasingly made by cultural capitalism in the struggle over copyright in the public sphere.

Take the report *Investing in Music* published by the international recording industry lobby body the International Federation of the Phonographic Industry (IFPI) in March 2010. Its subtitle, 'How music companies, discover, develop and promote talent', sets the agenda. Inside, the thrust of the document is that 'music companies' (note that this replaces the older and more instrumental designation of 'record companies') enable music makers to flourish. As John Wenham and Alison Wenham put it in their introduction:

> whilst the direct route afforded by the internet is open to all, mixing the talents of business and creativity is often a minefield, with creativity often compromised by the challenges of running a business, which requires totally different skills. Artists generally prefer to leave the complex administration of a rights based business to someone else.
>
> (IFPI 2010: 4)

The idea of the vulnerability of the cultural worker, her elevated calling and need for protection and development, is not a new one in the cultural industries (see, for instance, Martha Woodmansee's (1996) discussion of the issue in the context of 18th-century publishing). However, what is important now is the way this discourse is being deployed as a central part of the international record industry's public relations strategy in a moment of acute crisis not only of capitalism in general, but of cultural capitalism in particular. Music makers are the 'subjects' of the music industry, we're led to believe, and their special creativity can only be fostered by responsible music companies and the system of rights that sustains them. This ideological offensive is, of course, taking place at a time when the contradiction between the public-ness of cultural artefacts and their privatized commodity form has reached a new height. The struggle for public opinion and the support of legislators in enforcing corporate ownership in the digital domain is therefore reaching a new peak of intensity too. Having previously claimed that unsanctioned downloading of music is a crime, it now seems that the music industry has changed tack and is presenting itself as the benign protector of music makers. We can expect this to be an increasingly important position as the copyright wars intensify.

The point to draw out, quite simply, is that industry mobilization of the specialness claim raises the stakes in the debate. It is not just a question of trying to produce better knowledge, but also of resisting the way inadequate arguments about the nature of cultural work are being used to build public support for, and bring the state to bear down on, the side of rights-owning corporations in the contemporary crisis. There could hardly be a plainer case of ideology, of false ideas serving the interests of power; nor then a plainer case for ideology critique.

Creative work: special or what work itself really is?

Or is it as simple as that? I have already suggested that the claim for the special status of cultural work is contradictory. On the one hand, the potential distinctiveness of such work is capped by its fully material nature and belonging to the larger category of work in general. On the other hand, the specialness claim consists in a long historical tradition, one emerging in the revolt against instrumental rationality, market relations and industrial capitalism. This normative aspect is key. It suggests that, to the extent that cultural work encompasses an idea about what work in general *could* be like, then we ought to take it seriously. An appreciation of the gap at stake here is, of course, exactly what is lacking in MacIntyre's account of practices, in Arendt on productive work, and in the discussion of symbolic labour by Hardt and Negri. The problem common to all is a failure to acknowledge that the best kind of work exists only for the few, but ought to exist for the many. In other words, a critical dimension is missing in regard to actually existing conditions of labour. Instead of developing such a critique, the theories we looked at earlier move precipitously to identify benign forms of work in an historical era when the nature of most work is shaped by the domination of capital over labour. Even for the fortunate artist, this social relation tends to deny the very autonomy that is promised by cultural work.

Perhaps, then, rather than trying to approach specialness as an actually existing social formation, we should explore the normative, in other words, the *promise* of creativity and autonomy in cultural work. In one sense, of course, this is to go back to the origins of the specialness claim in romanticism and the early theorists of aesthetics, but I would suggest that instead of returning there (where this chapter started) the key analytical task now is to rethink work in general – having gained some insights into the potential of work posed by the specialness claim. In attempting this, I want to call on Mike Wayne's (2010, n.d., forthcoming) bold and original argument about the aesthetic theory of Kant, and the way Marx's theory of labour is strongly influenced by it.

Wayne begins by showing how Kant is more of a materialist than is commonly appreciated. In the *Critique of Judgement*, Kant proposes that making art is free labour in that it depends on reason rather than understanding (the latter being merely a reflection of the natural world of necessity). However, reason, and specifically the judgement used in art making, is not unbounded. For one thing, it involves the externalization of nature, that is its analogical representation *as* something. For Kant, then, art making has a material dimension in that the artist acts upon nature with an imaginative, transformative aim. Wayne quotes Kant to this effect: 'its producing cause has conceived a purpose to which [the artwork] owes its form' (Kant 1951: 146).

Here, then, Kant prefigures Marx in a striking way. We can see this most clearly in the parallels between a famous section in *Capital*, and a less well-known passage in Kant. The former is found at the start of chapter seven, where Marx is introducing the problem of the labour process and contrasts the work of an architect to that of a bee making honeycomb. Unlike the bee, the architect 'builds the cell in his mind before he constructs it in wax' (Marx 1976: 284). This is very close to Kant's consideration 'Of art in general', where he argues that bees don't make art because, unlike artists, their work 'is based on no proper rational deliberation' (Kant 1951: 147).

Wayne argues that the similarities between the two passages, and indeed between Marx's whole discussion of the nature of labour in *Capital* and Kant's account of art making in the third *Critique*, suggest the basis of the former in the latter. This is a significant contribution to the history of ideas in relation to questions of provenance and influence, but what matters for the present argument, and for Wayne too, is the suggestion that at the heart of Marx's theory of labour is a notion of the essential creativeness of work. Just as with art making for Kant, so too with work for Marx, reason, autonomy and purposive, transformative action are the defining characteristics. In making this argument, then, Wayne is suggesting that cultural work is very much like the thing that work in general really is anthropologically speaking. In effect, he reverses the specialness claim so that the ostensibly peculiar dimensions of art making come to define the core of work in general, namely its creative, transformative and purposive qualities.

Yet, as we know so well from Marx's writing (and from experience), this core has as its corollary the denial of creativity in the form of the capitalist labour process and the intense control and division of labour that it brings. We might say, therefore, that work under capitalism has *constitutively* a normative dimension. In the context of the subsumption of labour, its essentially free nature leads to a state of constant struggle against alienation on the part of workers, which is then compounded with the much more frequently discussed struggle against exploitation (but see Benyon (1973) for a classic account of workers' experiences of *both* kinds of oppression and their resistance to it). In the next section, we will explore some political implications of the foregoing.

Contradictions of cultural work

The first point to make is comparative – namely that the contradiction between actual lack of freedom and the promise of labour's autonomy is much deeper in non-cultural than in cultural work. Work for the many is highly routinized and involves intense supervision and control by management. Yet struggles over autonomy are more frequent and explicit in the cultural sector where actual autonomy is much greater. Why is this and what are we to make of it?

Previously, I have described the tendency of record companies, publishers and so on to grant a good deal of control over the labour process to symbol makers as 'institutional autonomy' (Toynbee 2000). The key factors here are that cultural production tends toward 'infinite variety' (Caves 2002), and every artefact is a prototype such that detailed supervision of production is difficult to achieve (Hirsch 1972). As a result, for pragmatic reasons, the cultural industries have to recognize, to some extent at least, the specialness claim. However, the institutional autonomy that results is also unstable (and varies between different roles and areas of cultural production). Above all, the 'building in' of autonomy to the labour process in cultural industries means that it is a constant focus for dispute. Cultural workers want to claim more autonomy, knowing that their aspirations are quasi-legitimate within the cultural industries system, while managers invoke their better business knowledge to justify more control of creative decision making. It is unsurprising, then, that struggles over autonomy should be acute in this sector. They may also become internalized by workers and refracted in significant ways, as David Hesmondhalgh and Sarah Baker point out in their perceptive study of media work (Hesmondhalgh and Baker 2011: especially 86–112).

At the same time, cultural work tends to be precarious. A combination of labour supply 'push' and demand uncertainty for cultural goods means that the cultural industries are able to impose short-term contracts on workers. As we saw above, the cultural industries are also able to insist on the transfer of copyright from creative artists for these same reasons. Control of copyright is combined with a royalty system whereby payment to artists earned from rights is deferred and depends on the degree of market success of the products one creates. In sum, creative workers are generally in a weak bargaining position and their careers are precarious. Only the extremely successful winners in 'winner takes all' cultural markets can expect to get substantial rewards. As Ruth Towse explains, in the case of musicians and their copyright collection societies, 'the top few receive highly disproportionate shares of the total revenues, while many members (sometimes 50% or so) [of copyright collection and distribution societies] earn less than the minimum that is distributed' (Towse 2006: 578).

Cultural work is thus characterized by a combination of insecurity, inequality and resentment over the way that the relatively large amounts of autonomy that workers have are nevertheless constrained. A common response is for symbol makers to assert their special, elevated status as a way of coping with these conditions. For instance, they may attempt to *convert* a pragmatic autonomy claim into a claim for status, or, related to this, they may invoke special artistic status as a way of *reinforcing* an autonomy claim. These are effectively the strategies adopted by young artists vying for position in the 'field of cultural production' identified by Bourdieu (1990). As we have just seen, there are clearly mitigating circumstances for such tactics. Ultimately, however, they are illegitimate. If you have an innate capacity to create, or else are endowed with the sort of cultural capital that enables you to become a symbol maker, then little more than 'brute luck' is involved (Callinicos 2000: 72–73). In either case, your ability to work in your chosen occupation is an accident of birth. Therefore, to claim special status in respect of that work is illicit; it cannot be a just reward. Even if we agree that merit lies with symbol makers in their own right, that they have 'deserved' their vocation, or have 'paid their dues', the corollary of this is their ability to work in a relatively autonomous way, a benefit that is denied to most workers. This is arguably sufficient reward, absent the conferment of high status.

In important ways, then, it seems that cultural work under a market regime takes on a distinctively pathological form. Conditions and rewards are organized in contradictory ways which give rise to significant troubles, including a hyper-competitive work environment where the relative autonomy of workers is often used by them as the basis for a claim to higher status. If it can be achieved, that status may in turn be invoked as grounds for claiming greater autonomy, so yielding a vicious cycle of distinction in which internal goods – autonomy and creativity – are used to secure an external good – status – which in turn supports the case for more autonomy.

Of course, it would be wrong simply to blame cultural workers for this. The cultural industries for their part foster the notion of specialness in order to legitimate copyright as we have seen. Just as importantly, it also provides a kind of mythological backdrop for the performance of cultural work. Artists, authors, actors and musicians tolerate insecurity and impecuniousness which would not be accepted in other sectors in part because the aura of specialness that surrounds them provides a certain compensation. In other words, the attribution of special status helps the cultural industries to dominate and exploit workers in this insecure and unequal corner of the labour market.

Now, in an important sense, all these contradictions represent further evidence of the way in which the specialness claim is ideological. Creativity and autonomy, rather than being enjoyed by all workers, are granted in a limited and distorted way to a particular fraction. This division of labour may indeed bring a certain 'efficiency' under capitalism – as noted above, cultural artefacts tend towards variety and so to some extent production has to be controlled at arm's length. However, it is also properly ideological in that it keeps *workers* divided, and poses a separate and containable sphere in which the perfectibility of life and work is still offered as a possibility (on this, see Habermas 1976: 78–79, 84–86).

One obvious solution would then be to abolish the capitalist system and socialize the economy as a whole. Under socialism, the pathologies of cultural work could be dealt with as part of the larger process of the transformation of work itself. Specifically, the democratic and public control of the economy pro-mised by socialism would include control over the nature of work, including the just distribution of internal goods such as autonomy and creativity. In other words, under socialism, there would be an egalitarian labour regime such that the agonism of cultural work, its claims for special status and its actual abasement would be transcended. Yet socialist politics, as traditionally conceived, has not addressed issues to do with the nature of labour at all comprehensively. In particular, it has focused on distributive justice rather than 'contributive' questions to do with the quality of work (Sayer 2009).

I would argue, then, that socialism is a necessary, but not sufficient condition for dealing with these issues. What's more, at the time of writing at least, the advent of socialism does not seem imminent. So it seems there is a strong case for making some transitional demands that show how cultural work might be changed for the better, demands that challenge the status quo here and now, but also point towards a socialist future where ultimately the probems of work in general will be confronted in a root and branch way. This is what we turn to in the last section.

Conclusion: towards a new regime of (cultural) work

It seems to me that in the foregoing discussion a fundamental question has been rumbling in the background. That question is: how far cultural production should be paid work at all. As things stand, much culture making goes on in 'proto-markets' at the margins of the cultural industries (Toynbee 2000), and many cultural workers, when considered as workers, are underemployed. The generally precarious, low-wage conditions in the sector are of course a direct result of the organization of the cultural market, its winner-takes-all profile and dependency on copyright, as we saw in the last section. If copyright were radically curtailed in relation to length of term and scope, then cultural industry revenue, and with it number of jobs, would certainly shrink. No doubt emergent forms of cultural commodity, or new 'business models', would also arise. Nevertheless, cultural capitalism would be much smaller. Now there is a strong argument to be made for reducing copyright on other grounds such as improving public access to culture, and increasing possibilities of creative re-use of existing symbolic resources (Toynbee 2010), but I want to suggest that what is often presented as a cost of this, namely fewer creative jobs, would actually be a benefit.

Not only would more culture making take place in amateur or semi-professional contexts where there are fewer barriers to entry, but also creative activity would be less strongly associated with the need for consecration through the market. Proto-markets (both virtual and geographically local ones) would tend to become 'quasi-markets', with a degree of low-level economic exchange as now, but less orientation towards the fully commodified cultural industries. In this 'low copyright' scenario, financial incentives would undoubtedly be lower, but evidence from cultural economics on how far artists are motivated by financial reward as opposed to the internal goods of creative practice is thin (Towse 2006), and we have no good reason to suppose that levels of production are correlated with extensiveness of copyright (Boldrin and Levine 2002). Crucially, decent social security provision, or even a full state living wage, could provide a basic income for those who wanted to devote themselves to cultural production full time.

On the question of distribution, which has traditionally been the capital-intensive bottleneck in cultural production, the Internet has made this relatively cheap and easy, so that artists can potentially reach large international audiences. If the 'production of acclaim' still remains to a significant extent in the hands of the traditional content industries like record companies and publishers, then stripping back the scale of copyright will undermine this function. The production of acclaim will probably still follow existing trends towards its concentration in traditional broadcasting as well as new Internet platforms. This is unlikely to be worse than existing arrangements in terms of aesthetic outcomes. It may be better in that, in principle at least, the Internet enables socialized means of selection and acclaim.

There remains the question of the high capital cost of some forms of cultural production, for instance cinema and much broadcasting. Reduced rights revenues could threaten these forms. However, they could be funded through a combination of public service arrangements (e.g. an enlarged BBC without dependency on rights derived, secondary income) and grants from para-state arts councils. There are alternative funding possibilities too (see, for instance, the suggestions made by Nicholas Garnham (1990) in a report to the Greater London Council on public policy and the cultural industries from 1983 – most of these remain just as relevant today).

All in all, then, the radical cutting back of copyright (perhaps to a one-year term with strong fair use exceptions) would reduce the size of the cultural industries sector and the number of 'jobs' that go with it, but it should not damage cultural production – and might even enhance it. For the present argument, a key benefit of such a regime is the way it could assist the reconfiguration of cultural work: encouraging access and enabling more people to engage in it (as with pre-capitalist societies), as well as reducing the entanglement of status claims with demands for autonomy and strategies for coping with the cultural labour process. Generally, it would mean the freeing up and decommodification of cultural production. This would still be 'special' in its aesthetic and world disclosing dimensions, but it would lose many of its pathological aspects.

Beyond their significance for cultural work, though, all these changes would enable reflection upon, and ground clearing for, the more general transformation of work. If it is indeed the case that autonomy and creativity are at the ontological heart of labour, as argued above, then the question of how to actualize these dimensions takes on a much less mystical hue when specifically cultural work has been toppled from its plinth. By enabling the production of culture to flourish outside the realm of paid-for work, it becomes much easier to confront the problem of how to share out creative and routine tasks in the economy as a whole, and create a new division of labour based on principles of contributive justice. Work should indeed be re-designed and made as satisfying as possible in actuality. However, a key step on the road to achieving this goal will surely be to cut cultural work, and commodification, down to size.

8 Logistics of cultural work

Brett Neilson

A persistent problem in theorizations of cultural work is definition. Drawing the borders between cultural work and other kinds of work is a vexed business. Sectoral definitions confine cultural work to contexts where the production of texts, symbolic creativity and expressive value are paramount. Anthropological approaches open out the field, arguing that all economic activity has cultural relevance. Between these poles we find a host of typologies and schemes that segment cultural work into core and peripheral areas of production (Hesmondhalgh 2007) or nest it in a series of concentric circles that slowly open to the wider economy (Work Foundation 2007). One thing is sure. Cultural work exists within wider networks or chains of supply and demand, production and consumption, which sustain and in turn are sustained by it. Patterns of continuity and change in the evolution and prominence of cultural work are often measured by analysing its position in these networks. Theorizing cultural work with attention to these shifts offers a new perspective on debates that usually pervade discussions of labour in the cultural and creative industries, for instance those that position it as the innovative motor of contemporary capitalism (Cunningham 2006), or those that emphasize the precarious or flexible forms of labour that invest it (Terranova 2004; Rossiter 2006; Ross 2009). This chapter seeks to open such a perspective by drawing on empirical investigations conducted in the cities of Shanghai and Kolkata. The aim is not to resolve the definitional dilemmas outlined above. Rather, by tracking how cultural work relates to other labour processes and experiences, the hope is to delineate a field of debate in which to assess claims for its political potentialities.

In his important book *Intellectual and Manual Labour*, Alfred Sohn-Rethel argues that 'social forms develop and change ... together with the multiplicity of links operating between them according to the division of labour' (Sohn-Rethel 1978: 4). Sohn-Rethel's analysis is interesting because its focus on the 'network of relations' that enable what he calls 'societisation' (ibid.: 4) anticipates contemporary network or assemblage approaches to the social (Castells 1996; Latour 2005; DeLanda 2006) without losing attention to the workings of capital and labour, as many of the latter threaten to do. It is in this spirit that I undertake the work of tracking the 'multiplicity of links' that join cultural work to other economic processes and forms of labour. To give a conceptual name to the economic arrangements and technological routines that enable such linkage, I mobilize the notion of logistics. This describes a series of social practices and technical operations that provide the organizational conditions for current systems of production. By bringing the question of logistics to the analysis of cultural work, I join an emergent field of cultural and social analysis that understands these practices as central to the social form of contemporary capitalism (Thrift 2005; Neilson and Rossiter 2010; Cowen 2010; Holmes 2011).

Originally a military practice, logistics specified those measures that were necessary to assemble a fighting force: recruitment, training, supply, clothing, eating, drinking and marching – in short, everything required so that an army might be in the right place at the right time. In its more recent civilian guises, it has come to name a mode of governance that manages the mobility of people and things in the name of communication, transport and economic efficiencies. No longer seen as secondary to the manufacture of commodities or irrelevant in terms of value added, logistics is now an integral part of globalized trade and production. Yet its material operations have gone under-analysed in the profuse literature on capitalist globalization, transnational flows, spatial rescaling and other topics relevant to recent economic and cultural transformations. One effect of this is a lack of attention to how these processes contribute to the production of labour forces and subjectivities. The analysis of global commodity chains (Gereffi and Korzeniewicz 1994; Bair 2009), for instance, traces how global production processes materially connect economies, firms, workers and households in the contemporary world. However, as Taylor (2008: 18) explains, it tends to treat labour forces 'as an *a priori* factor in the spatial disbursement of productive processes within chains'. By investigating logistical processes that link cultural labour to the wider economy, my intention is the opposite. I seek to highlight the subjective elements that contribute to the production and reproduction of the cultural workforce.

To do this, I draw on research experiences in the cities of Shanghai and Kolkata. These involved visits to sites variously connected to cultural production in the context of a project named Transit Labour: Circuits, Regions, Borders (transitlabour.asia). Apart from aiming to move the debate on cultural work away from a focus on Western metropolitan contexts, this project deployed a 'research platform' method (Kanngieser *et al.* 2010), which brought visiting researchers, activists and artists into collaborative relations with their local counterparts. Deploying Internet technologies as a means of organizing as well as inter-referencing research activities across globally dispersed locations, this method sought to develop collective efforts of research design that move beyond both the model of the individual scholar who writes theory and that of the lone researcher who conducts field work. Crucial was the combination of sustained investigations (interviews, digital documentation, archival research, identification of sites for group visits and people to meet) by locally based researchers with the perspectives brought by participants from other parts of the world. Also important was an openness to contingency and accident that allowed the research to take unexpected directions. This was counterpointed by the wider orchestration of the research process through workshops, mailing lists, blogging, visual design and publishing activities. What emerged from this collaboration was less an attention to cultural work understood as the labour of symbolic expression and more an interest in patterns of exploitation and dispossession that support and supply differently positioned cultural workforces in these Chinese and Indian cities. In other words, the project began to focus on the logistics of cultural work.

That such an interest emerged in the context of a project that itself crossed the cultural and economic divides that separate China and India from the West (if such geopolitical distinctions can be maintained) is significant. It points to the need for new concepts and methods to allow a critical analysis of how the differentiation of labour across spaces, times and scales matches current rearrangements in the geo-economic configuration of the world. It also suggests that the material and theoretical grappling with global inequalities and divisions of labour prompted a concern with the production of subjectivities in areas of the economy that provide the enabling conditions for cultural work. The stories and analytical reflections that follow show how such inequalities and divisions tend to reproduce themselves locally wherever there are attempts to kick-start metropolitan economies through cultural production. These tales from the front line are personal and impressionistic negotiations of complex and collective encounters. They should not be read as definitive pronouncements on the evolution of cultural work outside the metropolitan West.

In the circuit

It is no secret that the Chinese party-state has promoted the expansion of what it calls 'creative cultural industries' (O'Connor and Xin 2006; Keane 2007; Rossiter *et al.* 2008). In Shanghai, as in other major metropolitan centres, this has coincided with the growth of non-manufacturing and service sectors, the development of publicly supported commercial creative industry clusters, diffuse entrepreneurial ventures, and a burgeoning of creatively focused higher education in fields such as animation, advertising and game design. Participants in the Transit Labour project addressed these developments in different ways. One of the researchers, Kanngieser (2010a), visited the Xin Danwei creative co-working space and probed the tense relations between creative labour, political expression and state surveillance in this context. Together with Zechner, she also conducted interviews with cultural workers, asking questions about their 'desires, possible futures, labour conditions, bodies, psyches and mobilities'. These investigations searched for 'different ways of looking at narratives around knowledge, experience and work', challenging the perception that the 'aspiration and idealism' of young Chinese cultural workers can be 'dismissed as a de-politicisation' (Zechner and Kanngieser 2010). Other researchers focused on the consequences of the cultural economy for the city's urban form. O'Connor and Xin (2010) argued that the renovation of 'junk spaces' has been driven less by cultural workers than by 'real estate agencies and local government officials', while Greenspan (2010), through a series of visits to Shanghai's urban edge, showed how migrants supply the 'essential underpinning to China's new cities', constructing a 'shadowy realm – intensely vibrant and dynamic – that exists outside all urban plans'. Another series of investigations focused on the borders between cultural and other kinds of work. These included Sarda's (2010) account of a visit to Baoshan market for recycled electronic goods, Chen's (2010) documentation of labour practices in a provincial village that produces Christmas decorations, and Rossiter's (2009) research on the electronic waste disposal that follows downstream from cultural industries.

It is with these latter investigations into the relations between cultural work and other kinds of labour that I link the following reflections on a group visit to a Hong Kong-owned printed circuit board factory in the Songjiang Industrial Zone to Shanghai's south-west. The use of computers and other hardware items is by now ubiquitous for cultural workers. Across the cultural industries, there has been a remaking of management models to accord with the logistical protocols implicit in the notion of a 'digital supply chain' (Turba 2011; Renard 2010; Yoon and Malecki 2010; Graham 2005). Even small 'craft labour' situations are susceptible to such logistical management styles, with consequences for speed and standardization (Banks 2010). There is also the widespread use of personal computers for design and publicity of all kinds, as well as the deployment of wireless mobile devices for communication and the distribution of cultural products. There can be no doubt that the printed circuit board is an indispensable item in the networks of logistical and infrastructural supply that enable cultural industries. The opportunity of visiting a printed circuit board factory in Shanghai's outskirts thus presented itself as a strategic means of gaining insight into the labour practices that undergird and allow cultural work.

If logistics and supply chains have been an under-researched area in the burgeoning critical discourse on cultural industries in the Anglosphere countries, they have been a central concern in China. Chinese universities frequently offer courses on 'cultural creative industries' and logistics under the same departmental banner. As management scholars Zhiguo Fan and Xiaoliang Zhang (2010) write, the 'ability to form a complete industrial chain, value chain, supply chain are the keys to increase the added value of cultural industries'. They add: 'the various sectors of cultural industries also need to connect seamlessly to achieve real logistics, information flow, capital flow of a smooth operation'. However, for these Chinese researchers, writing in a broken English, the concept of a creative supply chain is really much wider than this: 'Supply chain is starting from the purchase of raw materials, intermediate products and final products made of the final product by the sales network into the hands of consumers will be sent to suppliers, manufacturers, distributors, retailers, until the end-users together into a whole functional network chain structure' (Zhiguo and Xiaoliang 2010: 3).

In this scheme, the printed circuit board would be an intermediary product. As such, it fits into another supply chain that intersects the creative supply chain discussed above. In the case of the factory in the Songjiang Industrial Zone, the production of circuit boards is fed into from, and feeds into, an assembly and supply chain that stretches across multiple locations in China, Hong Kong and Japan, but also Europe with respect to the machinery used in the plant (sourced from Italy and Germany, though also Japan). The relationship between this network and the creative supply chain is neither linear nor teleological. Indeed, the very metaphor of the chain struggles to capture the complexity involved. As Pratt (2008: 99) comments, there is a need for 'more attention to iterative feedback, networks, and webs to better conceptualize' the linkages involved in such cases. The ubiquity of computers and other electronic devices in the cultural workplace is only part of this picture. One could equally focus on the spatial distribution of economic activities across the city, the patterns of interchange that join and separate them, and their implications for the social production of labour power as a commodity. Cultural enterprises tend to cluster in the city centre or in post-industrial spaces, often ironically playing with a sense of industrial heritage – like Xin Danwei (new work unit, recalling the 'work units' of pre-Deng socialism). By contrast, factory production is concentrated in areas like Songjiang Industrial Zone on the urban fringe, an Export Processing Zone established in 1992 and since re-zoned several times. Limiting the investigation to the local connections between such sites, however, would mean shifting attention away from their global extensions. Indeed, the fact that printed circuit boards made in Shanghai find their way into commodities that are distributed around the world means that they supply the conditions of possibility for many more industries than those that support cultural work in the same city. The point of the factory visit was thus not to trace actual connections between particular circuit boards manufactured on this site and pieces of hardware used by workers in Shanghai's cultural industries. Rather, it was strategically to enlarge the terms of investigation into cultural work, remaining aware of the definitional boundaries drawn by scholarly and policy discourses but at the same time deliberately violating them with the knowledge that cultural work always fits into wider social and economic contexts.

From the start, the factory visit was controversial. The factory's management offered to guide the Transit Labour researchers through the production site and then to allow us to eat lunch with some of the workers on condition that we did not ask questions about pay rates. Many of the researchers felt that the situation was rigged, that we were visiting a 'model factory' where the conditions of labour could not possibly match those prevalent in many other such Chinese workplaces. In other words, the very fact that we had been invited to enter the factory made many suspicious. For others, it was the decision to attend the visit that left them doubting. In a dialogue with Isaac Leung posted to the Transit Labour mailing list some months later, the Singapore-based researcher David Teh worried that the researchers visited the factory in search of exploitative labour conditions and projected onto the workers 'the whole armature of the subject, of worker and migrant and migrant-worker, of creative labourer – not to mention all the supposedly transformative subjectivities implied therein'. Leung, a Hong Kong-based art critic who participated in the visit, felt uncomfortable with his role as an unwilling translator: 'I found myself ... constantly placed in between two expectations: "tell the foreigner that I'm happy" and "ask the workers whether they're treated fairly"; subject and object were constantly disconnected, through my very presence' (Leung and Teh 2011). These are fraught and complex cultural dynamics, which register the unease that many of the researchers felt during the visit. I mention them to convey a sense of the anxiety that invested this factory tour, which was clearly engineered by management but also offered the opportunity to observe first-hand the manufacture of a commodity that lies at the material heart of contemporary forms of informatic and creative production: the printed circuit board.

If, as Teh suggests, the visit was conducted with the hope of observing or encountering exploitation, that desire was frustrated. In any case, it is debatable how exploitation might be identified in such a situation, where information about pay rates is deliberately obscured, apart from the observation of harsh conditions, child labour, overtired workers or other such factors. In the classical political economic sense, at least, the presence of exploitation is not gleaned from experience. It requires rather a calculation based on the proportion of unpaid surplus labour a worker performs for their employer to the necessary labour required to produce the value equivalent of the wage. How exploitation might be understood in cases where the labour relationship is not mediated by the wage is an important and pressing question, particularly in the cultural industries where self-employment and precarity are rife. The multiplicity of devices that bind workers to their jobs, aside from the wage, has been emphasized by labour historian Marcel van der Linden (2008), who stresses that the wage relation is not (as Marx tended to assume) a capitalist norm. In the contemporary global context, this remains a relevant issue, particularly in the case of migrant workers who may be bound by conditions of deportability or debt, among others. For cultural workers, the love of the job is often mentioned as a binding mechanism (Gill 2006). In the case of the circuit board factory, however, it was difficult to ascertain the extent of non-wage conditions binding workers to their jobs. Clearly, the workers were housed in dormitories. According to Smith and Ngai (2006: 1456), this arrangement points to a situation in which 'workers' lives are dominated by employers, and working time is more closely under the control of employers than in systems where working life and home are separated'. However, the dormitories were off-limits to the Transit Labour researchers. What we observed, as we were guided around a narrow pathway from which it was possible to see workers operating machinery through glass windows, was the manufacturing process of cutting, printing, laminating, etching, drilling, deburring, washing, stacking and controlling the circuit boards. Some of the rooms were lined with plants so workers could rest their eyes by gazing at them. As Kanngieser (2010b) comments, these workers looked neither 'happy' nor 'extinguished'. From this experience, as with the more tested one of dining with some of the workers who had been selected by management, it was impossible to discern the exact nature of labour relations in this factory.

More interesting, and certainly more relevant for the theme of this chapter, was the brief presentation delivered by the management before they guided us into the factory. They were eager to explain that the printed circuit boards they manufacture are supplied to original equipment manufacturers (OEM) with globally recognizable brand names such as Pioneer, Ericsson, NEC, Fujitsu, Sony, Apple, Alcatel, Sanyo, Canon and Foxconn. They were also keen to show us a series of certificates attesting the factory's adherence to industry- and client-determined protocols for environmental practice and quality management. These were of interest because they gave some indication of how relations are governed within the supply chain of which the factory forms a part. The certificates shown to us demonstrated compliance with standards such as ISO14001 for the promotion of 'effective and efficient environmental management', RoHS (Restriction of Hazardous Substances Directive) and WEEE (Waste Electrical and Electronic Equipment Directive). Some of these were issued by organizations such as the Hong Kong Quality Assurance Agency or the Business Standards Institute (BSI). Others were awarded by the OEMs to which the factory supplies circuit boards. Among these, for instance, was the Sony Green Partner Certificate demonstrating compliance to SS-00259, a Sony Corporation Technical Standard pertaining to environment-related controlled substances.

The presentation of these certificates is an instance of what Pun (2008) describes as the 'reorganized moralism' of foreign corporations operating in China. Writing of the politics of transnational labour codes, Pun claims that such devices provide a 'moral façade for capital' (Pun 2008: 89). 'The principle of reorganized moralism', she contends, 'involves reworking neoliberal principles operating at the micro-workplace level not only to rearticulate labour rights practices from the corporate point of view but also to move into the sphere of labor rights and labor protection, a domain supposedly belonging to the role of the state and civil society' (ibid.: 88). Although Pun writes specifically of labour codes, her observations can be extended to an analysis of the environment-related certificates we were shown. There are two conclusions I want to draw from this episode. First, the certificates show that production in this factory does not occur in some kind of normative vacuum. Contrary to the claim that economic zones materialize a 'neoliberal exception' (Ong 2006), there is a multiplication of discrepant and possibly conflicting norms in this space. Standards such as ISO14001, RoHS and WEEE, whatever their rigour, are not enough. There must also be SS-00259, directly mandated and controlled by Sony. The German legal theorist Gunther Teubner (2009: 263) remarks that, 'unlike when they were first spawned', corporate codes 'are no longer mere public relations strategies; instead they have matured into genuine civil constitutions'. For him, these charters and standards 'beg the same question as *lex mercatoria*, Internet law and other global regimes in which private actors make rules, the binding nature of which is not guaranteed by state power, yet which display a high normative efficacy' (ibid.: 263). In the space of the printed circuit board factory in Songjiang Industrial Zone, such private governance regimes come into contact with ones mandated by sovereign entities more directly subject to political control. What needs to be investigated is the framing of these multiple regimes and the way their orchestration makes possible the productivity of capital. This has implications for labour conditions in the factory space.

With this, I come to the second point I want to draw from the display of the certificates. Once introduced into the logistical operation of supply chains, such codes and standards become instrumental in the production of value. The moral and environmental vigilance attested by these certificates as well as the logos and other branding devices that mark consumer products containing circuit boards manufactured in the factory mean that OEMs can demand a higher price for these commodities. The Sony standard SS-00259, for instance, is accompanied by a host of other protocols, routines and labels such as the Sony Green Partner Quality Approval Program and the eco-product mark. Aside from the actual environmental benefits such programmes may have, which is a matter on which I am unable to comment, they also offer reassuring messages to consumers who are conscious of sustainability issues and are often prepared to pay more for commodities that adhere to such standards. These are specific devices of governance that operate within supply chains and are directly productive of value. In this case, an OEM downstream from the factory mandates a series of measures that resonate back up the chain. As Tsing observes, however, 'the diversity of supply chains cannot be fully disciplined from inside the chain' and 'this makes supply chains unpredictable and intriguing as frames for understanding capitalism'. Under these circumstances, 'the exclusions and hierarchies that discipline the workforce emerge as much from *outside* the chain as from internal governance standards' (Tsing 2009: 151). Thus, the presence of certificates, no matter what they say about the emerging face of green capitalism, tells us little about labour conditions in the factory. On the basis of the Transit Labour visit, it is difficult to say for certain what the labour conditions are like at this site, although from what the management was keen to communicate to us they certainly seemed more amenable than those documented by Pun and other witnesses to the dormitory labour regime. We could only discern through observation and the subtle economy of gesture and eye contact the experiences of workers who were contractually gagged from telling us about their lives, their pay packets, or even their knowledge about labour unrest elsewhere in China. It is precisely in such moments that we sense the traces of another, more disciplinary power intervening amid the logistical governance measures of the supply chain.

Doubtless this factory provides only one quite arbitrarily chosen link in the wider network of relations that connect the manufacture of circuit boards to the conduct of cultural work. However, this chapter does not aim to provide a comprehensive map of such connections. Indeed, this would be an exhaustive task and possibly also an analytically quite useless one. Clearly, such links do exist. Equally, the circuit boards produced in this factory feed into products and contexts that extend well beyond the cultural sector and its specific forms of labour. The point is not to hunt down and analyse direct connections between this factory and Shanghai sites of cultural work or even places of cultural work on a wider global scale. Rather, it is to show how such connections are carried by shifting constellations of indirect social relations, which are mediated by abstract third agents, e.g. logistical calculations, corporate protocols or high-scale moral and environmental narratives that channel the circulation of goods, capital and labour. Such indirect social relations, in which people are linked through abstract mediating agents and may be alienated from each other, cannot necessarily be discerned through techniques of participant observation or read off the surface of culturally fraught encounters (Feldman 2011). Like the relation of exploitation discussed by Marx, they require an attention to norms, logics and technical processes that are inconsistently localized. How such fragmented, particular and material operations make up our view of the global becomes even more obvious in the discussion that follows, which considers another station of research in the Transit Labour journey: the special economic zones set up for high-tech industry in the New Town of Rajarhat on Kolkata's north-eastern fringe.

From the global village to the service village

'It is not the "actual" inter-connections of "things"', wrote Max Weber, 'but the *conceptual* inter-connection of *problems* that define the scope of the various sciences' (Weber 1949: 68). Weber's provocation provides something of a motto for the Transit Labour research, which sought not to trace actual connections between instances of cultural work and other forms of labour that border upon it and sustain it, but to examine the underlying infrastructural and logistical processes that enable such relations even in circumstances where they appear empirically disconnected. The case of Indian Information Technology and Information Technology Enabled Services (IT/ITES) is perhaps a paradigmatic instance of such disconnection, since workers in these industries are subject to outsourcing arrangements that create a scenario of 'virtual migration' (Aneesh 2006). Their labour is mediated by transnational digital networks that bring them into contact with data generated in distant places and set up relations with co-workers or managers whom they never meet directly. Whether in the notorious case of call centre work or in fields such as software research and development, engineering and design, the processing of insurance claims, data entry, transcription or customer service, these jobs are conducted at a distance without ever requiring cross-border movement in physical space. The Kolkata leg of the Transit Labour research focused on this kind of labour within the frame of a wider investigation of the establishment of the New Town of Rajarhat on the city's north-eastern limits.

Initiated by the West Bengal government in the 1990s to relieve the city's housing problems, the development of Rajarhat has now been stalled by the global economic crisis. Empty land is spotted with apartment blocks, shopping malls and office buildings, some of them occupied or slated for occupation by IT/ITES firms such as Accenture, Infosys, Tata Consultancy Services and Wipro. Once a lush and biodiverse area of peasant farming and sharecropping, the agricultural workers who tilled the land have been compelled by government to sell their holdings at rock-bottom prices. Those who refused were intimidated by riot squads or local goons until they decided to walk away from their properties. Some of these dispossessed populations have been gathered into so-called 'service villages', with the view that they will eventually find employment servicing the middle-class communities who are supposed to move into the district. However, the apartment blocks are sparse and without basic infrastructure such as water and electricity. Many of them have been sold as investment opportunities to non-resident Indians (NRIs). It seems clear that the bulk of Rajarhat's former peasants will not be absorbed into the urban or industrial workforces. It is a situation of primitive accumulation without transition.

Amid this scenario, special economic zones for the IT/ITES industries are already appearing. Transit Labour made a visit to a row of makeshift tea and tiffin shops that line the edge of the Unitech Special Economic Zone, where the consulting firm Accenture set up a 'global delivery centre' in February 2011. The company's website describes the outsourced business processing operations (BPO) that take place at this site with the following umbrella statement:

> Our environment of continuous improvement matches the culture of our clients, and helps us attain ever-higher levels of productivity, precision and predictability. Supported by deep industry, technology and business acumen, and by an unmatched breadth of industrialized capabilities – including methods, tools, architectures, analytics and metrics – Accenture helps our clients generate next-generation innovations that can help them achieve high performance.
>
> (Accenture 2012)

Although the labour that takes place in this global delivery centre is not cultural work by the narrow sectoral definition of the term, Accenture emphasizes that it occurs in an 'environment' that 'matches the culture of our clients'. Such an orientation accords with the sense in which Muthyala (2011) characterizes call centre work in India as cultural work. He describes how call centre workers tailor accents, names and locations in 'transnationalizing affective labor by creating home-like atmospheres for their clientele'. 'Culture', Muthyala writes, 'as idea, difference, and value is structurally interwoven into the entire field of worker and management relations, business arrangements, and call center infrastructure'. In the case of the Accenture Global Delivery Centre in Rajarhat's Unitech Special Economic Zone, as in many similar BPO outfits in India, this also implies a tailoring of work hours to match the rhythms of daily life in another time zone. Essential to this arrangement are the logistical elements – the 'methods, tools, architectures, analytics and metrics' – that enable such coordination at a distance. These technologies, standards and protocols materialize abstractions such as 'the economy' and 'the firm' in ways that allow the ideologies of 'productivity, predictability and precision' to touch ground in places like Rajarhat.

The ramshackle tea shops that line the Unitech Special Economic Zone provide a startling contrast to the gleaming futurism of this IT/ITES development. During the Transit Labour visit to one of these makeshift businesses, the proprietor, a former peasant, explained that he keeps the shop open at odd hours due to the fact that the young, English-speaking professionals who work across the road follow the hours of distant time zones. He also indicated that he had diversified his product range beyond the ubiquitous Indian *chai* to include items such as green tea favoured by the BPO workers. Here we see the 'long tail' of informal labour that enables the cultural work performed in the IT/ITES industries, in this instance through the obligatory supply of caffeine. Apart from the indirect social relations created between this particular pocket of Rajarhat and other parts of the globe by large-scale logistical processes, there remain direct encounters that occur on the edge of the spaces set up to accommodate such technologically mediated labour. Who is to say that the tea store and the special economic zone exist at different developmental stages when both are constrained to operate at the rhythms of another time zone? It is certainly necessary to analyse the discourse that presents the BPO workplace as 'yet another campus' (Remesh 2004: 292), the attempts of trade unions and labour groups to organize in these contexts (Stevens and Mosco 2010), and the precarious work conditions and sociocultural adjustments of the graduates who are absorbed into this sector (Upadhyay and Vasavi 2008). However, such an analysis cannot ignore how the developments that have enabled such work processes have devastated the surrounding communities and ecosystems.

The debate on cultural work thus becomes necessarily mixed up with the discussion of peasant struggles, logics of extraction and capitalist developments that have made 'land more valuable to the global market than the people on it' (Sassen 2010: 23). David Harvey's (2005) argument that contemporary capitalism functions according to a logic of 'accumulation by dispossession' is probably the best known of the claims in this regard, but in Kolkata there is a local and highly politicized discussion of land acquisitions, peasant displacement and the ongoing forms of primitive accumulation. This has partly been spurred by successful peasant resistance to industrial developments in the West Bengal towns of Singur and Nandigram – events that were pivotal to the fall of the state's long-standing Left Front government in 2011. In Rajarhat, however, the story has been different, despite the presence of peasant activist groups. Figures such as Kalyan Sanyal (2007) and Partha Chatterjee (2011) argue that primitive accumulation can continue in sites like Rajarhat because governmental mechanisms exist to reverse it. When national or local governments do not intervene, they suggest, there are other states, international agencies or non-governmental organizations (NGOs) that step in with governmental programmes and measures that seek to meet the livelihood means of the dispossessed, and, in so doing, enable the very continuation of primitive accumulation. For Chatterjee, this governmental enablement of primitive accumulation is a process played out in what he calls 'political society', where peasants play an active role in agitating for their livelihood needs. In such negotiations, which often involve a 'calculative, almost utilitarian use of violence', what the dispossessed frequently invite 'is for the state to declare their case an exception to the universally applicable rule'. This makes 'the governmental response to demands in political society ... irreducibly political rather than merely administrative' (Chatterjee 2011: 229–31).

In so far as it treats the governmental response to peasant agitations as exceptional, this argument posits that normative arrangements exist to enable primitive accumulation. To this extent, it runs counter to claims for 'neoliberalism as exception', pointing to normative mechanisms such as India's Land Acquisition Act, a colonial remnant from 1894, and the Special Economic Zone Act (2005) that legitimate processes of accumulation by dispossession. What remain under-emphasized in this approach are the spatial strategies employed in such accumulation and the conflictual and overlapping relations between normative regimes that not only crystallize in economic zones *but also exceed them*. Indeed, this is precisely what is at stake in Rajarhat. The displacement effected by the development of a space like the Unitech Special Economic Zone has to be analysed in relation to the forms of exploitation it allows both within and beyond its borders, whether or not governmental initiatives that seek to assuage the effects of primitive accumulation are effective. In other words, peasant dispossession and the precarious state of IT/ITES workers must be understood with reference to each other. As Jamie Cross recognizes, the 'most significant achievement of India's new economic zones ... is to render visible and legitimize the conditions under which most economic activity in India already takes place' (Cross 2010: 370). By this, he means that the absence of regulation and lack of protection for labour in the wider informal economy is laid bare in the special economic zone, where it is rendered as deregulation and flexibility. Seen in this perspective, processes of accumulation by dispossession must be analysed in relation to processes of accumulation by exploitation. This also implies attention to the normative governmental arrangements that link these accumulation strategies and to the processes of the production of subjectivity they entail. Or, to put it in more figurative terms, the analysis must move between the global village of the economic zone and the service village where former peasants eke out a more-than-precarious existence.

Conclusion

The above sketches of the relationship of cultural work to the forms of labour that support and enable it are rough and provisional, rooted in the peculiarity of circumstances and encounters in China and India. I have undertaken these discussions as a means of tracing the 'network of relations' that articulate cultural labour to other economic processes and forms of work. Recalling Sohn-Rethel's conviction that the 'multiplicity of links' that compose the social mutate together with the global division of labour, this provides a means of examining how cultural work is positioned in wider assemblages of knowledge and power without losing attention to relations of capital and labour. Such an analysis is a necessary prelude to any investigation that asks how the production of subjectivity accompanies the positioning of labour forces within global production, assembly and value chains. Whether it is the Chinese factory worker, the Indian BPO operator or the displaced tea-shop proprietor, these figures are constantly made and remade not only through large-scale economic and social processes but also through a production of subjectivity that perpetuates and sometimes renders vulnerable forms of life, cultures and ways of being. The same can be said of the cultural worker, who may exist at empirical proximity to or mediated distance from such figures but nonetheless is capable of entering into indirect social relations with them. Tracing how such relations change with the global division of labour casts new light on the political potentialities of cultural work. Rather than posing the problem of the precariat (Standing 2011) or of the capacity for cultural workers to unite as a class, it places the political moment of precarity within a wider network of relations. The politics of cultural work begins to turn on the possibilities for issues of precarity to link with those of dispossession, those of the 'reorganized moralism' of foreign corporations in China or those of any number of disciplinary measures imposed from the *outside* of supply chains. Indeed, this becomes the very precondition for the making of a precarious class. Cultural workers, if they are to be political, cannot afford to look inward or fraternize only with their own type.

Inevitably, this approach also implies a testing of the boundaries of what counts as cultural work. My interventions aim to take the debate about cultural work beyond the limits imposed by sectoral definitions that emphasize symbolic creativity, the production and consumption of texts, expressive value and so forth. It is not only that these boundaries shift and blur in cultural and economic contexts such as India and China. It is also, as Lawrence Grossberg (2010: 112) writes, that such a confinement of cultural labour to the cultural industries tends to encourage 'the weakest work, not merely because it often takes "culture" as an economic sector for granted and treats it as isolated or autonomous, but because much of the work is built upon fairly traditional economic and political economic concepts, methods and assumptions'. Extending the debate on cultural work to confront issues such as the claim that capitalism now functions primarily through accumulation by dispossession is a way of breaking this bind. This does not imply a rejection of research that remains within the prevalent definitional boundaries but rather seeks to provide a context to complexify this work and to draw out its insights in more global ways. Recent discussions of cultural work have been replete with claims about the subjective and political potential of precarity and calls to rethink the notion of exploitation under changing capitalist and global conditions. These are certainly urgent theoretical and political tasks, but to ask how accumulation by exploitation articulates to accumulation by dispossession is to resituate cultural work at the very edges where capital works the differences between accumulation strategies. It is to break cultural work out of the ghetto of the cultural industries and to position it in a way that allows us to ask how struggles against the new forms of exploitation might be joined to struggles against dispossession.

In different ways, the research in China and India that I have recounted situates cultural work on this boundary. Transit Labour is not the only project that seeks to join an understanding of the complexity of spatial economic networks with an ongoing concern with labour issues. There is an expanding interest in the informational and infrastructural strata of the global economy and the way they interact with the production of labouring subjects. By titling this chapter 'Logistics of cultural work', I have tried to signal one such line of inquiry. Thrift (2007: 95) describes logistics as 'perhaps the central discipline of the contemporary world'. Not only does logistics organize production and trade but it also structures life in adaptive ways that constantly shift in response to the environment and feedback into prevailing material conditions. Tracking these mutating relations across spaces and scales is a task that cannot be fulfilled by any single essay. It will take time and resources to understand more fully how labour processes and relations are structured by logistical systems and the software routines that enable them. This piece is only a start in putting together a wider jigsaw puzzle.

9 Learning from Luddites

Media labour, technology and life below the line

Richard Maxwell and Toby Miller

The central event of the 20th century is the overthrow of matter. In technology, economics, and the politics of nations, wealth – in the form of physical resources – has been losing value and significance. The powers of mind are everywhere ascendant over the brute force of things – *A Magna Carta for the Information Age.*

(Dyson *et al.* 1994)

A focus on media labour may seem odd given the dominant discourse on culture, which elevates it above monetary exchange and employment. On this account, making culture is so universal yet special, so human yet exciting, so inevitable yet pleasurable, that it transcends worldly issues of alienation or reward. Culture is inalienable and semi-sacred in both the amateur Arnoldian anthropology of the 19th century and the credulous chorine cybertarianism of today.

The supposed universality of culture is being augmented by the comparatively cheap and easy access to making and distributing meaning afforded by contemporary technologies and genres. They are thought to have eroded the one-way hold on culture that saw a small segment of the world as producers and the larger segment as audiences. The result is said to be a democratized media, higher skill levels, more sovereign consumers, and powerful challenges to old patterns of expertise and institutional authority. Traditional relationships are reversed as innovative technologies and norms of communication formalize what was always the case informally – that readers matter to authors and ultimately determine semiosis. The term 'disintermediation' describes the impact of technologies that putatively allow us all to become simultaneously cultural consumers and producers ('prosumers') without the approval of gatekeepers (Banks and Humphreys 2008; Banks and Deuze 2009; Graham 2008; Ritzer and Jurgenson 2010).

This chapter steps away from such heady fantasies. Preferring the mundane world of the everyday to spectacular utopias of transcendence, we analyse life for workers 'below the line' – i.e. people who are categorized underneath writers, producers, executives, directors, actors and managers in the accounting hierarchies of the *bourgeois* media, specifically Hollywood (the term refers to the likes of drivers, caterers, electricians, carpenters, secretaries and interns).

However, we extend the concept beyond the film industry. Doing so takes us both backwards and forwards in the life cycle of the media to include work that literally makes and unmakes media technologies as material entities: mining metals, assembling parts and disposing of detritus. The workers involved in these processes are barely visible in the double-entry bookkeeping that decides profit and loss for a major motion picture studio or mobile (cell) phone corporation. Before undertaking this project, though, we should ask why these people are absent from the discourse of the media.

The cognitariat and consciousness

Today's world of disorganized capitalism or post-Fordism includes a cognitariat of highly educated, occupationally insecure media producers. Classified above the line, they are voluble and newsworthy. The cognitariat was identified and named a quarter of a century ago by the lapsed-leftist Reaganite Alvin Toffler (1983), author of numerous technocentric works and signatory to the cybertarian *Magna Carta* of the mid-1990s cited above. Toffler wandered the same conceptual Cold War corridors of futurism as former National Security Advisor Zbigniew Brzezinski (1969), American Academy of Arts and Sciences prelate Daniel Bell (1977) and professional anti-Marxist Ithiel de Sola Pool (1983). They predicted that information and communication technologies would remove grubby manufacturing from the global North to the South and consolidate US cultural and technical power, provided that the blandishments of socialism and negative reactions to global business did not create class struggle at home or abroad.

The concept of the cognitariat has since been redisposed on the left by Antonio Negri (2007) and his *appassionati*. Negri uses it to describe people mired in casualized labour with heady qualifications who live at the complex interstices of capital, education and government. This college-trained cognitariat plays key roles in the production and circulation of goods and services, creating and coordinating culture as musicians, directors, writers, journalists, sound engineers, editors, cinematographers, graphic designers and so on. The cognitariat also features audiences and consumers, who pay for content, interpret it and elide barriers of entry to media production through their anointment as prosumers. These groups operate within institutional contexts: private bureaucracies, controlling investment, production and distribution across the media; public bureaucracies, offering what capitalism cannot while comporting themselves in an ever-more commercial manner; small businesses, run by charismatic individuals; non-governmental organizations, of whatever political stripe; and networks, fluid associations formed to undertake specific projects. Cognitarians typically engage in dreamy self-exploitation and autonomous identity formation. They announce themselves as autotelic subjects: joining a gentrified poor dedicated to the life of the mind fulfils them and may even proffer a labour market of plenty (Gorz 2004; Ross 2009; Neff *et al.* 2005).

The prevailing ideology of capitalist futurism that underpins this cognitariat requires correction. As Marcuse (1941) predicted 70 years ago, far from liberating all and sundry, innovations in communication technology have intensified managerial coordination. Writing in this neo-Marxist tradition, Herbert I. Schiller recast futurism as an 'infrastructure of socialization' that synchronizes 'business cultures', organizational models, 'institutional networks', and modes of communication and cultural production in the interests of capital (Schiller 1976: 8–9, 16).

Such critical analyses are far from dominant. Marketers, censors, critics, pundits, cognitarians, psychologists and activists obscure the view by focusing on consciousness. The latest merchants of this trade include Negri and his *anglo-parlante* amanuensis Michael Hardt. Mirroring the Cold War futurists, they developed the idea of immaterial labour to describe the tendency to exchange information, knowledge and emotion through computers in ways that are abstracted from physical work (Hardt and Negri 2001: 290–92).

Such an approach excludes crucial cultural occupations. Consider the all-too-material health-and-safety risks endured by camera operators, stunt people, models, singers, transport captains, set carpenters, mobile phone testers, caterers and computer *habitués*. Beyond social and cultural critique, more important discourses fall prey to similar limits and temptations. For example, the Entertainment & Leisure Software Publishers Association (2004) celebrates women and video games, ignoring women's part in their manufacture and disposal. Britain's report on harm to children from games (Department for Children, Schools and Families and Department for Culture, Media and Sport 2008) neglects children whose forced labour makes and deconstructs them. A study prepared for capital and the state entitled *Working in Australia's Digital Games Industry* does not refer to mining rare earth metals, making games or handling electronic waste – all of which should fall under 'working in Australia's digital games industry' (Australian Research Council Centre of Excellence for Creative Industries and Innovation *et al.* 2011). Such research privileges the consciousness of play and the productivity of industry. Materiality is forgotten, as if it were not part of feelings, thoughts, experiences, careers – or money, oddly. By and large, the people who actually make media technologies are therefore excluded from the dominant discourses of high technology. It is as if telecommunications, mobile phones, tablets, televisions, cameras, computers and so on sprang magically from a green meritocracy of creativity, with by-products of code, not smoke.

The dirty division of labour

The disappearance of physical labour from such myths is an illusionist effect of the kind that Marx noted 150 years ago: a 'Fetishism which attaches itself to the products of labour' once they are in the hands of consumers, who lust after objects as if they were 'independent beings' (Marx 1987: 77). Dirty work is secreted within the clean machines that others use to relax. Consumers are preoccupied with peripherals, power and pace, but unaware of the conditions of existence of these possessions and pleasures. Their peculiar enchantment has a totemic, quasi-sacred power: a technological sublime of virtuality, volume and novelty (Nye 1994, 2006, 2007; Edgerton 2007; Winston 2007). To disrupt that technological sublime, we emphasize media technology's life cycle, from production to disposal.

The failure to address life below the line is a consequence of the fetishization of consciousness as the core of culture. For consciousness is merely one phase in a lengthy material process which, thankfully, has been investigated by political economists, workers, journalists and environmental scientists (Mayer 2011; Grossman 2006; Reygadas 2002; Cowie 2001; Clark 1997; Kalm 2001; Nnorom and Osibanjo 2008). Consider the British trade union Unite's path-breaking *How Green is My Workplace? A Guide for Unite Members and Representatives in the Electrical Engineering, Electronics and IT Sector* (2008). We find these approaches challenging and innovative. Among the workers they address who labour below the line, we are exercised by people who are neither classed as the cognitariat nor identified with the Zeitgeist, but on whom the cognitariat silently and ignorantly depend.

Unite's report helps us to resist the cybertarian technological sublime, whose blandishments animate chorines and advocates of the creative indus-tries, the newer media, prosumption and the like. It nudges us in the direction of less fashionable, more venerable ideas: ideas that are sceptical and resistive rather than credulous and adoring. This recalls C.P. Snow's insistence that, in accounting for the 'scientific revolution', we concentrate on people 'lost in the great anonymous sludge of history', where life, he said (troping Hobbes), 'has always been nasty, brutish and short' (Snow 1987: 26–27, 42).

Our approach is predicated on a deep regard for workers and the Earth and a profound disregard for technological hype. Drawing on supply-chain research to comprehend the global scale and inter-sectoral linkages of work, we examine the media's ecological context. Where better to do so than in the company of the much-maligned Luddites, who have passed into technophilic lore as mindless opponents of progress? Their name is used today to disparage workers who are suspicious of technology's capacity to induce job losses and deskilling, but it signifies something much more interesting and compelling than such shibboleths admit.

The Luddites were a social movement of textile labourers in the early 19th century who fought against the machinery and social relations of the emergent Industrial Revolution. They drew on the example of Snow's fellow-Leicesterian Ned Ludd from the previous century (and anticipated the antics of Pete Townshend, Jimi Hendrix and hackers in the next). They recognized that capitalists, who did nothing productive, owned machines that controlled workers. However, the Luddites were also protesting well-established technology, because it had led to disemployment over two centuries. (*À propos*, Lord Byron sought the death penalty for opponents of new machinery in his maiden speech in the Lords, just months after summering with the Shelleys while Mary was writing *Frankenstein*, the first Luddite piece of science fiction.) These workers realized that technology could control their labour, spy on them or shift their jobs elsewhere (Pynchon 1984). We'll examine very-far-below-the-line media labour as per their analyses and protests.

We are also animated by research done over the last three decades under the rubrics of the New International Division of Labour (NIDL) and the New International Division of Cultural Labour (NICL). The original international division of labour kept costs down through the formal and informal slavery of imperialism and colonialism, importing raw materials and manufacturing objects from them in the metropole. Action by the working class at the centre redistributed income via the emergence of a labour aristocracy that benefited from exploitation of the periphery. In response to such redistribution, capital inaugurated a new division of labour. It exported production to the global South, where young women workers were deemed more pliant than their masculine and metropolitan competitors. Developing markets and the shift from the spatial *sen*sitivities of electrics to the spatial *in*sensitivities of electronics further encouraged businesses to go beyond treating countries in the global South as suppliers of raw materials to look on them as shadow-setters of the price of work, competing for employment among themselves and with the global North. As production split across continents, the prior division of the globe into a small number of empires and satellites and a majority of underdeveloped countries was compromised. Folker Fröbel and his collaborators christened this trend the NIDL (Fröbel *et al.* 1980; Anderson *et al.* 1987). This model now applies to culture. The NICL, more specific than the NIDL in its focus on the production of meaning, has been elucidated in numerous research projects covering sport, cinema, television drama and technology (Miller *et al.* 2001; Miller *et al.* 2005; Conor 2011; Lobato 2008; Deuze 2007; Day 2005; Elmer and Gasher 2005; Christopherson 2006).

Culture involves manufacturing as well as art, text and performance. Ever since the development of print, the media have drawn upon, created and emitted dangerous substances, generating multi-generational risks for ecosystems and workers. For example, print labour past and present must contend with poisonous solvents, inks, fumes, dust and tainted wastewater. Similar conditions have affected workers in film-stock manufacture, where cotton dust adds the additional risk of contracting brown lung or byssinosis. Manufacturing and installing batteries exposes employees to lead and other pathogens, fatally damaging the lungs, skin and nervous system. Such illnesses have made battery workers the group most at risk of lead poisoning in the USA. The use of plastics to create media technologies can cause brain, liver, kidney and stomach cancer, while disposing of them releases carcinogenic dioxin and hydrochloric acid into the environment. There is growing concern about low-level radiation emitted by televisions, computers, electronic games, mobile phones, laptops, telecommunication and electrical towers, and power lines. Bio-thermal risks confront workers exposed to media and telecommunications equipment as well as high-rise office workers close to transmission antennae (Maxwell and Miller 2012).

In the late 1970s, big media firms departed factories in the global North for sweatshops in developing countries; by the 1990s, electronic waste from their overhyped, badly engineered products was streaming into salvage yards, a new terminus in the life cycle of high-tech wonders. The NIDL has globalized such problems, and not only for those directly involved: the habitats, flight paths and lives of the world's original and most able globalizers – birds – are endangered by telecommunications towers, and plastic flotsam accumulating in the open waters of the North Pacific, the North Atlantic and the Indian Oceans threatens aquatic life because it breaks down into fragments but cannot be absorbed into the Earth (ocean.si.edu/ocean-news/ocean-trash-plaguing-our-sea; Maxwell and Miller 2012).

Media brands

Such major media brands as Apple, Dell, Hewlett Packard (HP), IBM, Kodak and Sony are core players in the NIDL. These firms are original equipment manufacturers, or OEMs (Lüthje 2006). Before media technologies appear as OEM brands in stores near you (whether physically or virtually), they travel along supply chains to sub-contractors. Mines supply metals to the foundries and factories that make parts for assembly, packaging and so on. In 2008, the proportion of the world's metals going into media technologies was 36% of tin, 25% of cobalt, 15% of palladium, 15% of silver, 9% of gold, 2% of copper and 1% of aluminium (Grossman 2006: 29–33; GeSI and EICC 2008: iii, 24–26, 34–36).

Tracking the metals supply chain is complicated. Many workers are in artisanal and small-scale mining (ASM), a notoriously harsh, low-tech, informal and poverty-driven sector. The International Labour Organization (2010) estimates that, while there are upwards of 13 million workers in ASM worldwide, the number involved is closer to 200 million if we include a large population whose jobs depend on it (porters, buyers, transporters, smugglers, officials, exporters and so on).

ASM is concentrated in Africa, Asia and Latin America, where perhaps 1 million children labour in mines (GeSI and EICC 2008: 56). In the Democratic Republic of Congo, which has one-third of the world's columbite-tantalite (coltan), over 90% of eastern mines are controlled by militia which buy weapons with the profits. They threaten, intimidate, murder, rape and mutilate enslaved women and children who work for them. More than 5 million people have perished in the country's civil war over the past decade. Congolese 'conflict' minerals such as coltan are smelted in China, then sold on the international commodities market as tantalum, a core component in the capacitors of telephones, computers, games and media-production equipment. Responding to this state of affairs, the United Nations (UN) Security Council set up a Panel of Experts and the US Senate passed the S.891 Congo Conflict Minerals Act of 2009 (Global Witness 2009; Montague 2002; Ma 2009; United Nations 2002).

Obtaining information about making the media is notoriously difficult even when OEMs claim to be evaluating occupational health and safety and wages among their sub-contractors. OEM audits frequently fail to assess segments of the supply chain where thousands of labour-intensive firms create resistors, capacitors, cables, switches, microchips, unfinished circuit boards, wires, connectors, power supplies, clips, screws and so on. Part of this activity is internalized within large factories, where it can potentially be monitored, but a significant amount is done in private homes as piece work (Good Electronics *et al.* 2009: 51). Inconsistencies in OEM audits couple with a lack of sociological and historical understanding of contract manufacturing to leave the public misinformed. For example, internal audits disclose the names of HP's suppliers, but not that Apple petitioned the US Federal Communications Commission to hide a governmental review of the iPad, which would have revealed how the company exploits multinational labour (see Apple's letter to the Commission BCG-E2381A).

Apple produces annual *Supplier Responsibility* reports (such as Apple 2009, 2010, 2011, 2012a), but does not name sub-contractors that break the law or ignore its guidelines. The first time the corporation even listed suppliers was in a supplement to its 2012 *Supplier Responsibility* report (Apple 2012b). Investigations into Apple's Chinese suppliers show that it is well aware of their harmful and illegal practices. Examples include chemical (n-hexane) poisoning of 137 workers at Lian Jian Technology Company (owned by the Taiwan-based firm Wintek, Lian Jian is an iPhone supplier with a factory in the eastern Chinese city of Suzhou). N-hexane damages the peripheral nervous system, which numbs the limbs and induces chronic weakness, fatigue and hypersensitivity to heat and cold. In 2010, workers were poisoned while degreasing the Apple logo with n-hexane at the Yuhan Photoelectric Technology (Suzhuo) Company and the Yun Heng Hardware & Electrical factory. Neither firm appears on Apple's list of suppliers, but they are among dozens of suspected Apple contractors harming workers and surrounding communities in China, according to the Beijing-based Institute of Public and Environmental Affairs (2011: 8–18).

Until 2009, Apple had no plans to protect workers (who work in at least four different countries) from mercury, lead and flame retardants. The company began to green its business model after sustained pressure from Greenpeace and other non-governmental watchdogs (Nimpuno *et al.* 2009). However, it barely commented on revelations about the searing conditions behind 15 suicides in 2010–11 at the Taiwan-headquartered Foxconn's Chinese factory, which makes iPhones and iPads. Foxconn boasts close to 1 million employees across China and undertakes almost half the world's electronics manufacturing. It uses military-style discipline, characterized by verbal and physical abuse (many line supervisors are former Taiwanese army officers). When the iPad was launched, protestors in Hong Kong responded to the deaths by burning photographs of iPhones (Maxwell and Miller 2012).

For 'image-conscious companies with which Foxconn does business ... the suicides were a public-relations nightmare and a challenge to offshoring strategies essential to their bottom lines' (Balfour and Culpan 2010). Apple finally responded to the crisis in its 2011 supply-chain audit. Admitting to the poisonings at the Lian Jian factory and assorted violations of codes of conduct, including employment of underage girls by other sub-contractors, it welcomed changes at Foxconn (improved wages, safety measures and counselling). However, while Apple ordered some firms to halt dangerous and illegal practices, its representatives did not meet affected workers or rehabilitate them. The 2012 report on suppliers' compliance again showcases Apple's anxiety about violations (audits allegedly increased 80% over the previous year) and its remediation efforts (terminating contracts of repeat offenders, hiring new oversight staff and consultants, undertaking more clean-ups, improving worker education, adding protective gear, etc.). Nevertheless, the report suffers from corporate *politesse*, refusing to name more than a few well-known offenders across the company's supply chain (Barboza 2011; Apple 2011, 2012a, 2012b).

The Foxconn suicides index the brutality of combining modern means of production with the mass mobilization of rural Chinese youth (by some measures, the largest internal migration in history). They are also tragic reminders of the malicious managerialism that characterizes the global supply chain and follow a pattern of suicide clusters at moments of industrial takeoff that was first noted 200 years ago in Europe (Balfour and Culpan 2010; Institute of Public and Environmental Affairs 2011). This is the dark side of an NIDL that typically contributes 15% to China's gross domestic product (GDP) (Nagy and Qiang 2010: 137), when post-Fordist factory systems meet OEM demands for rapid innovation and just-in-time production. They reveal 'the human cost that can come with the low-cost manufacturing US tech companies demand' (Wong *et al.* 2010: 36).

This inhumane system removes young people from the fun, family, friendship and free association that might help them adjust to high-tech, high-speed, high-security compounds. They are not even permitted to talk to one another on the assembly line (Balfour and Culpan 2010; Institute of Public and Environmental Affairs 2011). Before the suicide era, one of us sought, unsuccessfully, to visit media-technology factories in south-eastern China. He was able to spend time with young women on a rare excursion beyond the gated communities where they were sequestered. Obliged to live where they worked (not exactly as per the cognitariat's live–work downtown lofts), they were permitted half a day of leisure each week outside the compounds. Much of that time was spent walking several kilometres to meet friends from their north-western regions of origin. They had been separated to prevent worker solidarity.

This supply chain manufactures media technologies, brings them to the desks and palms of eager cognitarians, and removes them once their built-in obsolescence has been reached (Cox 2009: 21; Maxwell and Miller 2012). Ned Ludd and his followers have much to offer us in understanding it. Concepts such as knowledge workers, immaterial labour, creative industries or cognitarians do not explain the lives of Foxconn workers and millions more like them. Their wages are at or below the minimum allowed by law, their overtime exceeds legal limits (and is often not paid), and their lives are managed by a totalitarian polity and company. The pressure to manufacture the first iPads was so great that for six months employees were required to work twelve hours a day, seven days a week, with no weekend overtime premium and a rest day every thirteen (Students & Scholars Against Corporate Misbehaviour 2010: 7).

There is some spontaneous labour solidarity and agitation – such as Foxconn employees in Mexico supporting their Chinese counterparts – and Foxconn's Indian facility in Chennai, which creates phones for Nokia, saw the government suspend operations at the plant after workers were overcome by nausea and giddiness. Then the company and the state of Tamil Nadu imprisoned trade union leaders following a major demonstration: over 1,000 workers picketed for the right to negotiate with management through a union (Maxwell and Miller 2012).

However, low levels of unionization in the global supply chain of media technology severely hamper action that could empower labour organizers, environmental activists and industry auditors to improve working conditions and eliminate environmental hazards (Ferus-Comelo 2008: 157; CEREAL 2009; Cheng *et al.* 2011). The political-economic arrangements that militate against unionization also make it difficult to undertake reliable and representative epidemiological and qualitative analyses of workers' exposure to toxic materials and other occupational hazards (McKercher and Mosco 2007; Mosco and McKercher 2009; Mosco *et al.* 2010).

Conclusion

The NIDL is constantly changing. The late 20th century saw poor regions making 'low-value' parts of a device and richer regions producing 'high-value' research and development. That imbalance is largely intact, but the rapid pace and expansion of sub-contracting, and China's desire to emerge from a dirty, demanding dependence on mass manufacturing to a clean, lazy reliance on intellectual property, make stark distinctions of this kind increasingly unreliable as guides to research and activism (Bottini *et al.* 2007; van Liemt 2007: 8; Carrillo and Zárate 2009: 14).

An informed approach to cultural labour must encompass these transformations in the context of environmental and social justice, the labour process and a global appreciation of the life of commodities. Being stuck on questions of consciousness – whether the impact on children of watching television or the experience of cognitarians designing games – can imperil this focus. Media effects and exploitation are important issues, but they must be redefined and remapped to address manufacturing and disposal of the media as well as consuming them. Otherwise, the technological sublime of capitalist futurists, cybertarian fellow travellers, cunning corporations and credulous cognitarians will disparage Luddism and overdetermine our analysis.

10 Presence bleed

Performing professionalism online

Melissa Gregg

Theorizing contemporary cultural work inevitably involves understanding the impact of mobile communication technologies. The diffusion of web-enabled devices in both public and private spheres has been a significant development in the past decade, raising new questions about the appropriate time, location and rewards for labour. If work in creative industries has often involved a degree of flexibility and availability – as jobs appear in unpredictable patterns, with little ongoing security – the added component in today's work context is how always-on connectivity accelerates these features. This chapter draws on empirical evidence and theories of affect to make sense of this online landscape for labour. I use the creative, communication and information industries as a case study to unpack notions of workplace subjectivity and agency premised on 'separate spheres' and 'clock time' – assessing their usefulness in biomediated work worlds (Adkins 2009; Clough 2010). While the evidence used is based on a modest study of professionals in Brisbane, Australia, the discussion bears relevance for workers in a range of industries, due to the growing 'ubiquity' of mobile computing (Dourish and Bell 2011). If modernist notions of labour hinged on a set number of hours for work, often conducted at a set physical location, the fact that labour now escapes spatial and temporal measures poses obvious problems for defining work limits.

For a number of years now, new media technology has been marketed as giving us the freedom to work where we want, when we want, in so-called 'flexible' arrangements that apparently suit the conditions of the modern office (Gregg 2008). At the same time, concern has been mounting as to the consequences of this development, in which work breaks out of the office, downstairs to the café, into the street, onto the train – and later still to the living room, dining room, even bedroom (Turkle 2011; Powers 2010). Online connectivity allows constant monitoring of professional communication channels, whether it is an overflowing email inbox or the plethora of social networking sites. Technology of this kind changes our sense of availability, whether in cultural industries jobs or elsewhere. It heralds a sliding scale of attentiveness, or what we might call a *continuum of professionalism*, as work oscillates between multiple mobile locations on a home/work axis.

Communication platforms and devices allow work to invade, permeate or simply nag at spaces and times that were once less susceptible to its presence – although it matters which workers we are talking about in making this kind of claim. Originally designed and marketed as liberating tools for the frequent flyer (Humphry 2009; Gregg 2007), mobile technologies are having significant side-effects as their take-up extends to a larger group of professionals. As I show shortly, mobile technologies have brought with them new monitoring skills of anticipation, checking and filing for workers at different levels of the workplace hierarchy. Adding to what are already demanding jobs, these practices take place in a range of unpaid locations. They are skills that are deemed necessary to manage what one of my study's participants has identified as the 'Sisyphean' nature of contemporary work life, where 'you never get to the bottom of your email and you never get to the bottom of the tasks you have to complete, and you never have the sense of completion in any way' (male professor, personal interview).

The study summarized in this chapter followed the work lives of 27 employees in 4 large organizations across the information and communication sector in Brisbane, Australia (Gregg 2011). Ranging in age from early 20s to early 60s, the participants included academics, public servants, policy officers, librarians, branding and marketing strategists, senior directors, infrastructure and assets managers, online journalists, television producers and web developers. Employees were chosen based on whether they admitted to doing 'some' work from home – although the amount of work was up to the individual to measure. By focusing on large organizations, I aimed to provide a contrast to accounts of new economy working conditions emerging in the past decade that favoured the creative, entrepreneurial end of the private sector (e.g. Ross 2003). It is important to recognize the many employees whose work facilitates and disseminates the creative ideas of others, and which is similarly dependent on communication technology for its success. So the focus was on back-room, support positions in large cultural organizations, as much as it was the on-air or creative talent.

Consistent across these public- and private-sector workers, whether librarians, publicists or radio producers, was a willingness to use home networks to catch up on work that couldn't be finished or conducted in regular office hours. With the increased reliance on digital technology within the workplace, and the assumption that the stakeholders serviced by each organization in fact preferred online communication, workloads accumulated further expectations over time. These additional responsibilities and obligations were seen as natural extensions to jobs that necessarily required the adoption of new platforms. Yet the anticipatory and affective dimensions that came with the constant imposition of presence performance were the unacknowledged by-products of such technological dissemination.

Workers in my study experienced the 'presence bleed' of contemporary work life, where firm boundaries between personal and professional identities no longer apply. Presence bleed explains the familiar experience whereby the location and time of work become secondary considerations faced with a 'to do' list that seems forever out of control. It manifests as the variable degree of willingness workers feel in letting work seep into and coexist alongside other spheres of life activity. Features contributing to the condition include seemingly incidental practices: taking work home to 'catch up' on what cannot be finished in the office, and checking email outside paid work hours. Together, these apparently individual choices add up to a structural shift in work practices that is exacerbated by online technology's extensive reach. As I will argue, this is an ontological as much as a political problem for labour in the digital era – part of the broader transformation to empiricism, measure and value taking place in response to technological change (Adkins and Lury 2012).

Home/work

Of course, taking work home is hardly an invention of the past decade, let alone the computer age. In the popular classic of white-collar sociology *The Organization Man*, William H. Whyte describes the 'neuroses' of the company executive, for whom home is anything but a sanctuary:

> it's a branch office. While only a few go so far as to have a room equipped with dictating machines, calculators, and other appurtenances of their real life, most executives make a regular practice of doing the bulk of their business reading at home and some find it the best time to do their most serious business phone work.
>
> (Whyte 1963: 136)

Whyte's description predates the BlackBerry or iPhone by 50 years, but it is a fascinating portent of today's flexible office cultures:

> In one company, the top executives have set up a pool of Dictaphones to service executives who want to take them home, the better to do more night and week-end work. In almost all companies the five-day week is pure fiction.
>
> (ibid.: 136)

These details allow us to appreciate that technology has long facilitated particular work styles and preferences, especially for a business demographic, but Whyte's evocative illustration also suggests a set number of coordinates for work. The male executive of the 1950s abides in a commuter landscape in which work generally takes place in one of two places. Today's pervasive and ambient computing devices unsettle this experience considerably. Indeed, advertising campaigns for mobiles and tablets celebrate the freedom to be gained when work can be delivered to locations as diverse as the bus, the hairdresser, even the beach (Gregg 2007). The value systems implied in such images reinforce the pleasures to be felt in maintaining productivity.

As professional practices take place in these increasingly varied and public locations, workers grapple with a loss of established props and cues for conduct. Presence bleed is in this sense a contemporary example of what Erving Goffman called 'region conflict'. For Goffman, the middle class relies upon staging devices – understood modes of dress, permissible sound levels, acceptable affective expressions, in short, manners – to establish how a role is to be performed (Goffman 1973: 110). In the 'front region', where public self-presentations take place, individuals are aware of an audience for their actions, which in turn guides decisions about appropriate conduct. The trouble comes when we can no longer distinguish what behaviour is required of us in a given time/space configuration. Workers now have an infinite range of places in which to perform professionalism. Wireless technology, coupled with a growing suite of online platforms, contributes to work's displacement from a fixed office structure. For participants in my study, these difficulties were clearest in on-call workers, caught dealing with clients on the way to the supermarket, the gym, at children's school events, or first thing in the morning upon waking. However, the experience of region conflict – the bleed between professional and personal roles – also manifested in more routine ways.

For telco marketer Claire, wireless Internet meant that she could work anywhere in her house on Thursdays and Fridays, the days 'when I'm not properly at work' and 'I just want to do a bit'. On her days off, she explained, 'if we are out the front playing cars with my two year old on the driveway I can still be doing a bit of work as well'. Claire improvised strategies to limit her contact with the office on days she spent at home. For instance, 'quite often on a Friday I will actually just turn off the laptop and it will still sit there but it will be turned off so I am not tempted to go and check it'. The convenience of the device contributed to her readiness to engage with work so easily. Claire needed concerted measures to withstand the 'temptation' of her laptop connection, knowing that the potential for work is ever present. Communications technologies underscore Claire's ongoing psychological connection to the job, just as the convenience of the device brings the idea of work to more and more places. Whether or not she in fact does decide to work on her laptop, its presence in the home is a material and visceral reminder of her obligations elsewhere. These obligations had apparently crept into some of the most intimate spaces possible. 'I don't do a lot of work from the bed', Claire later explained, but she had enough experience of doing so to acknowledge that sometimes 'you suddenly realize you've been sitting there for three hours and gosh my back hurts'.

Other study participants spoke of the effects of online technology as a convenient means to stay in touch with work: 'I'm a bit obsessive about it', said university lecturer, Susan, estimating that she would check her email roughly every half hour. 'Even if I'm cooking I'll go and check if I've got another email come through. Is that bad? That is bad.' Susan is one of several employees who adopted pathologizing language in explaining the impact of mediated job demands, chastising herself for 'bad' behaviour. However, another way of putting this is that, in an age of presence bleed, workers learn to embody responsibility for their job role at all hours, crafting a professional habitus fitting the always-on networks of communication. The practice of incidental home work was epitomized during the recruitment phase of the study. When participants were asked if they worked from home, they would often say no to begin with, but, when further prompted as to whether this included reading email, they would admit that, yes, they did do that. The very fact that people discounted the amount of time they spent reading email was an index of the problem I sought to investigate. Even though workers acknowledged that managing high volumes of email was a perpetual drag on their time, they hesitated to assign it the category or status of 'real' work. It is work that dare not identify itself as such: 'It's not even work; it's bullshit work; it's deleting email!' said journalist Patrick. Wendy, a television producer, agreed: 'A lot of it's crap – it's like "yes", "no", "thank you", "I've done that – thank you" or "thank you for thanking me". I hate it – I actually hate email.' This email maintenance continued into all kinds of domestic and leisure practices, like watching television, talking with children and eating dinner with partners.

Workers in mid-level roles showed a particular willingness to engage in extensive regimes of preparation and recovery online before and after the physical hours spent in the office. These anticipatory practices seemed an effort to smooth the way for the formal working day. Susan, for instance, outlined her routine as:

> I start at about half past six in the morning and do an hour or so before I leave to go to work and that's mainly just clearing emails and things like that so I can start the day ready to do 'work'.

Tanya, a part-time project officer, had arrived to 100 emails in her inbox on the morning of our interview. She admitted that:

> Sometimes I'll get into that habit of checking my emails before I come into work. You can spend ages doing that ... It's often checking to remind myself to see if I've got a meeting or something early Monday, to make sure I get here on time.

Tanya's library colleague Donna also acknowledged, 'it's probably more out of habit now ... and I guess being prepared for my week, yeah it's more of a habit ... than a necessity, so yeah. It's my own fault'. Meanwhile, Clive, a senior university professor, felt compelled to diagnose his email problem in the following way:

> I think I'm a bit too either addicted or compulsive about it or obsessive about it ... I worry that I'm going to miss something that I ought to be attending to, and I worry that if I leave it for a day, then I'm going to

come back and then I'll just have 60 or 70 emails at the end of the day ...
So to that extent my emails are completely Sisiphusian [sic]. It's just never
ending. It's like my To Do list. I'm down from 70 things to do on my To
Do list, to 30, but that 30 keeps on – it's a perpetual 30.

Clive checked email at home because 'otherwise it would just get on top of
me ... I don't want email to swamp me. If I have a weekend off the Internet,
then on Monday, I have just a huge mailbox'. This practice was also clear in
part-time workers, who checked email on the evening of days off 'just to see'
what had been missed. After her regular Thursday off, Laura, a part-time
instructional designer, said that 'There is usually a lot of emails that I have to
deal with when I get back on that Friday morning and they take up work
time'. At the end of her day off, she would 'have a little whiz through and
check so I know what to expect the next day'. Asked what would happen if
she didn't check the email and actually took the full day off, Laura reasoned:

> Well, I would just be surprised when I got to work on Friday morning
> and found out all the things that had been going on. I would just be a bit
> less prepared I think, for what I have to do.

The importance of being 'prepared beforehand' for the work 'missed' during
her day off meant that Laura took individual responsibility for her part-time
hours. It also eased the possibility that anything surprising might occur in
between appearances at the office. The flexible workplace here allows changes
to the scheduling of work, but has little effect on the amount of work to be
completed. What seems vital about the home space is its capacity to allow
workers to feel connected and competent before arriving at the office for a
normal day.

Anticipatory affect

In these examples, the emotional labour of professional performance includes
the development of psychic strategies that will allow some sense of control
over what feels like an always unpredictable situation. Opening their inbox
each day, workers can't be sure just what it is they can expect to find. The
anxiety that comes from anticipating the highs and lows in an infinite number
of potential messages is a key dimension of the affective labour of contemporary
knowledge work. Here it is not hours spent on the job that occasions workers'
sense of security and accomplishment. Instead, it is the sense of being 'in
control' and 'on top of' persistently pressing online obligations. A particular
combination of anxiety and attunement develops in workers whose jobs are
perceived to involve a never-ending schedule of tasks that must be fulfilled –
especially since there are rarely enough workers to carry the load. Management trends that decentralize power structures – encouraging 'team work'
between colleagues – contribute to the sense that the actions of the individual

play a vital role in the smooth operation of the entire company. Perversely, this commitment to work beyond stated expectations came across as empowering for several workers. Claire, a part-time marketing professional put it this way:

> Management would never expect me to be online, you know. But it's more just if I don't, like if I've had a really crazy day of meetings, like yesterday, and there were so many back-to-back meetings, and I just knew my email was out of control and I had things that I needed to get done, I will sleep better if I spend an hour or an hour and a half at night just getting on top of that, otherwise I will wake up at 4am in the morning and I'll be just spinning around my head. Got to do this, got to do that. So yeah, for my own sanity.

Claire insists that it is a personal choice to work the way she does – 'for her own sanity'. She downplays relations with other workers that may make her feel obliged to do extra work for which she is not paid. Rather, 'she will sleep better' if she spends just a small amount of time taming her out-of-control workload. Such a perspective fails to appreciate that online networks regularly carry more information than it is possible for workers to absorb, process and action in the limits of a regular day. Indeed, Claire's body signals that she continues to process tasks beyond standard work hours, whether or not she acts upon these symptoms.

Another colleague in the same telecommunications company admitted that impending work communication interrupted her sleep. Jodi was a junior marketing manager who was temporarily charged with an extra on-call dimension to her job. She spoke of the difficulty she and her partner faced during this transition period for the company:

> I had to keep my mobile on last night because they told me at the 8.30 bridge they were going to call one at 6 o'clock in the morning. So normally I would have my phone on silent and only turn it on when I woke up, but because I knew this one was coming, I had to have my phone on ... I didn't sleep very well, actually, and I had this by my bedside and I was just thinking about this stuff I had at work and I had to get up, about 3 o'clock in the morning, and write down the things that were running through my head that I had to do for work because my head was racing with all the stuff I have to do and I couldn't relax until I'd written it down and my mind could forget about it.

Claire and Jodi's descriptions of work eerily echo one another. They both find it hard to wind down and rest easily at day's end without a lot of work-related issues continuing to circulate subconsciously. Awareness of the phone as the conduit for work – much like the presence of Claire's laptop on her days off – makes it hard to resist the job's invasion into the home and the mind.

Professional presence bleed means that there are fewer opportunities for them to feel completely free of their employment commitments. In Goffman's terms:

> Incapacity to maintain [front region] control leaves the performer in a position of not knowing what character he will have to project from one moment to the next, making it difficult for him to effect a dramaturgical success in any one of them.
>
> (Goffman 1973: 137)

What's also fundamental to these experiences of work is that employees face these anxieties alone. To the extent that their personal attunement to work rhythms colours the experience of home life, the families of these women are unable to offer enough solace from the driving imperatives of the office. Moreover, in spite of Claire and Jodi's shared workplace, and presumably shared sources of anxiety, they appear to have little sense of the drama unfolding in each other's home outside office hours.

Performing presence

Presence bleed is an appreciable response to fashionable management dictates encouraging workers to 'do more with less' and maintain 'work/life balance' through personalized relationships to their workload. In this sense, the attitudes workers adopt to online presence performance speak of some of the broader anxieties affecting the very notion of professionalism. Such a suggestion is evident in the thoughts of policy officer Jenny, who combines notions of competence, diligence and assertiveness in her approach to answering email:

> I feel that if I don't answer an email someone thinks I'm purposely ignoring them instead of I haven't read it yet … It's a concern and it's also just how I see myself as a professional. I want people to know I am looking after things, and I think sometimes when you send an email out, if you don't get anything back, you don't know whether they're ignoring it, dealing with it, thinking about it, pending a response – and I want people to know that if they send an email to me, I'm actioning it.

A defining feature of Jenny's sense of professionalism is her approach to email monitoring. Here she provides an intricate interpretation of how she perceives her own and others' time as a precious resource that must be treated with care. Too much time passing is taken to signal a lack of attention and ultimately a form of negligence that must be avoided. It is both a personal slight and a professional gaffe to take too long to answer an email. As other responses in the study showed, a platform that was first designed to overcome the asynchronous schedules of co-workers has by now transformed into its opposite. Email is now used regularly in workplaces as a means to demonstrate *co-presence* with colleagues and enhance the pace and immediacy of busy office schedules. It is a way of signalling intimacy and connection when the practical and physical context of office culture and its lived experience have changed. (With the phasing in of platforms like G-chat, Facebook and Twitter over the course of my study, colleagues who may have once worked agreeably in neighbouring desks and offices also used social media to stay abreast of work and non-work gossip, as restructures, flexible attendance patterns and trends in office design conspired against face-to-face sociality.)

In the passage above, complicity between always-on technologies and emerging forms of workplace subjectivity are powerful disciplinary incitements for Jenny to engage in what might otherwise appear as compulsive behaviour. She admits: 'I think that the anxiety I have with emails is absolutely ridiculous. I just think it's stupid; I should get over it. I don't think it's something that's placed upon me; I think it's truly a personal manifestation.' Whether a personal choice, an addiction or simply a sensible response to new norms in the workplace, Jenny is one of a growing number of workers engaged in a punishing and solitary habit of performing presence. While her comments are evidence of dedication to her job, they also indicate that her workload is a transaction to be managed alone. Another study participant, an online content producer, conceded that her online performance was based on her sensitivity to others' perceptions, sensing that, 'unless I reply instantly, they'll think that I'm baking a chocolate cake or at the coffee shop or something'. Lisa responded to email as soon as possible, 'partly because I'm conscious that if I don't, then it may be perceived that I'm slacking off somehow'. Working from home full time led Lisa to adopt corrective measures to compensate for her lack of physical presence – whether or not her colleagues were themselves located in the office. Indeed, with the mainstream adoption of mobile computing devices, the office is less a place (a noun) than it is an idea to be enacted (a verb): there are now any number of locations where workers perform 'officing' (Humphry 2009).

Presence performance is part of a broader context in which workers believe expectations for processing and turning around information have accelerated over time. An associate professor expressed this plainly during an interview that happened to take place on a day that he had come into work early to clear a backlog of email. Peter admitted that he often felt compelled to 'reply that I will reply later' to colleagues' emails because of the sense of pressure he felt about turnaround times:

> And that's the thing I hate about email I have to say – this feel[ing] that there's an instant need for an instant response, and … some people, if you don't reply within an hour or two, they wonder whether you've got it or not. So I do actually dislike that. I hate it to be honest. I really truly do, and I hate the fact that you can't get away from it. Like I was at a conference for a week just recently, and then you come in and there's 5 million emails, and it's sorting out what do you need to do, what can you delete, what is

out of date now, and I've actually become very good at putting on an email message saying I'm out.

This interview, it should be said, took place prior to the widespread penetration of smartphones, a stand-out feature of which is, of course, enhanced email delivery. Even prior to this latest tool taking hold in the mass market, workers spoke of a diminished capacity to claim uncontactability, with breaks in the feed of online communication less and less permissible. With his out-of-office message on, it was clear that Peter still read his email away from the office, just as he would read it at night and weekends. He had worked out that leaving his away message on 'for a few days extra' after returning from travel gave him 'a bit more space' to catch up on everything.

The considerations of professional etiquette that guide the actions of Jenny and Peter have an important historical lineage. In *The Laws of Cool: Knowledge Work and the Culture of Information* (2004), Alan Liu describes the office as the embodiment of modern manners, arguing that, to gauge 'the tone of modern emotional experience', we must look not to the sphere of private life but to 'the great impersonal organizations of modernity – above all, the workplace' (Liu 2004: 89). Email and online social networking are just the latest tools necessary to master for professional success, which for Liu entails an intricate performance of emotional suppression that he describes as corporate 'cool'. Liu's idea of professional cool draws on a history of feminist scholarship establishing the significance of 'emotion work' in a range of occupations. As is well documented, Arlie Russell Hochschild (2003) pioneered efforts to demonstrate the 'affective' labour in service industry jobs, which can be physically tiring in the same way as apparently more physical, 'manual' work. Hochschild's early research studying airline hostesses and parking infringement officers showed the traumatic impact of working with the general public in emotionally volatile situations. Workers in these service industries become accustomed to 'deep acting' so that the needs of the job and their own desires are ultimately aligned. Liu explains how the flexible office persona today is a further development from these previous formations of capitalism. While the service worker controls her outwardly directed emotions for business profit, the knowledge worker's affective labour operates as much in the opposite direction. Inward-facing, it is devoted to developing reserves of emotional resilience to withstand the ontological challenges of the typical work day – to ensure the façade of professional cool remains unblemished (see Gregg 2010). Liu's writing is thus useful for noting the particular combination of affect regulation and emotional distance required of workers dependent on communications technology for daily interaction. In the course of this study, performing an affable online persona became one of a growing number of requirements expected of cultural workers increasingly charged with spreading the organization's message in web-based forums, from instant messaging (IM) to Twitter, MySpace to Facebook. Professional presence bleed means there is no easy distinction between the corporate space of the office cube and the branded platform dialogue box, as more and more organizations seek to utilize social networking sites for profit.

Feeling productive

As a key feature of online connectivity, presence bleed emerges in a period when management techniques have responded to the desires of workers at all levels to exercise autonomy, giving rise to the feelings of enterprise and esteem central to cultural work's psychological appeal (Weeks 2011; Banks 2007). As Luc Boltanski and Eve Chiapello argue, the 'new spirit of capitalism' revolutionizes past models of employment because it 'guarantees the workers' commitment without recourse to compulsion, by making everyone's work meaningful' (Boltanski and Chiapello 2005: 76). The fulfilling nature of contemporary jobs, at least at the level of institutional rhetoric, rewards employees for being self-motivated agents, ready and willing to work: 'everyone knows what they must do without having to be told. Firm direction is given without resorting to orders, and employees can continue to organize themselves. Nothing is imposed on them since they subscribe to the project' (ibid.). Like Liu, Boltanski and Chiapello show how appropriate affect is the route to employee complicity with these new demands of the workplace. Workers can be relied upon 'to control themselves, which involves transferring constraints from external organizational mechanisms to people's internal dispositions' (ibid.: 79). The performance of professionalism in online communication is one of the principal disciplinary techniques through which employees engage in the 'deep acting' required to maintain pleasantries and employability in a competitive job market.

Throughout history, a notable feature of white-collar work has been the affective labour involved in developing emotional and psychological capacity (Haigh 2012; Illouz 2007). This includes the ability to project confidence and productivity while occupying positions and workloads with no definitive beginning or end. For Paolo Virno, this 'dramatic lack of foundation' in the modern workplace has a sinister edge:

> Fears of particular dangers, if only virtual ones, haunt the workday like a mood that cannot be escaped. This fear, however, is transformed into an operational requirement, a special tool of the trade. Insecurity about one's place during periodic innovation, fear of losing recently gained privileges, and anxiety about being 'left behind' translate into flexibility, adaptability, and a readiness to reconfigure oneself.
>
> (Virno 1996: 17)

Virno's reference to 'virtual dangers' has a useful double meaning for this chapter's discussion of online labour. Communications technologies play a key role in the reconfiguration of modern work, as online platforms create new avenues of availability (or its flipside, surveillance) for busy professionals.

This in itself is a cultural shift in what we consider measurable labour, as social networking sites, calendar scheduling devices, chat programmes and above all email bring a raft of opportunities and requirements for work-related contact. What remains puzzling is the extent to which employees have embraced the use of these communication platforms in the name of organizational productivity. Like the mobile devices facilitating task loads, jobs have themselves become subject to 'function creep' with the adoption of new media.

The idea of labour politics has always rested on the notion that limits must be placed on the work day, but, in an era of presence bleed, the possibility of asserting absence from the workplace becomes a matter of newfound concern. If the office exists in your phone, how is it possible to claim the need to be away from it for any length of time? Indeed, how do employees assert the right to avoid work-related contact if the bulk of their colleagues are friends? Labour activism is powerless to meet these challenges with its current vocabulary. Like never before, communications technologies grant access to the workplace beyond physical constraints, just as workplace intimacies trouble the sense of what is coerced or freely chosen labour. When the work day is no longer contained by space, the importance of time becomes paramount. Yet existing measures for labour continue to be based on 'clock time' (Adkins 2011, 2009), whether of the factory floor or the daily commute. While this framework has served the salaried class well to a point, it has been less successful in delivering benefits to the precarious contract-to-contract employment that is by now a feature of the employment landscape, especially in cultural industries. Indeed, today's white-collar workplaces often lack the basic infrastructure of the office, preferring cost-saving measures like 'hot desks' and 'hubs', lest employees remain too wedded to outdated entitlements.

The experience of presence bleed therefore points to some of the long-term inadequacies of theorizing labour politics through the separate spheres of home and work. The impasse that resulted from the exhaustive 'separate spheres' debates in Marxist feminism shows how women's exclusion from paid work and differential access to technology in private and public space have been structuring influences on widely held notions of modernity. As women entered the workforce in substantial numbers, and organizations aspired to create so-called 'flexible' solutions to suit their needs, the weaknesses of previous models for industrial representation have been rendered apparent. We are now at the precipice of a new chapter in understanding work, one in which the multi-sited labour of women is regarded as the paradigm for work in the information age (Morini 2007; Hardt and Negri 2001).

The gender make-up of the contemporary workplace is thus one of the defining differences between the professional world of the 'organization man' and the present, although some things remain familiar. The pace of workplace productivity evident in the comments of workers in this chapter puts a contemporary spin on C. Wright Mills's famous definition of the white-collar professional, who gave his life over to work because he had 'no firm roots, no sure loyalties to sustain his life and give it a centre'. Mills wondered: 'perhaps because he does not know where he is going, he is in a frantic hurry; perhaps because he does not know what frightens him, he is paralysed with fear' (Mills 1951: xvi). Workers in cultural organizations interviewed for this project engaged in online work beyond the formal work day for a range of reasons. For some, it was to 'keep sane' amidst a constant tide of communication requests that a hectic schedule could not accommodate. For others, it was to maintain perceptions of competence surpassing the call of duty – to reassure clients of their importance, or to keep the rest of 'the team' happy. In the absence of formal policies regarding new media use, these experiences revealed online devices to be part of an armoury of psychological preparedness that workers bring to their jobs even before the work day begins. In a mutually reinforcing cycle, online technology allowed workers to carve out strategies to cope with conditions that were highly intensified because they were taken to be individual rather than structural in nature.

Part III

Futures

11 Feminist futures of cultural work?

Creativity, gender and difference in the digital media sector

Sarah B. Proctor-Thomson

Policy makers and commentators have claimed that recent economic trends have created new opportunities in cultural work domains for a diverse group of workers (e.g. DCMS 2001; Culture North West 2006). In the digital media sector specifically, a widening recognition and valuing of worker 'difference' and workforce diversity as essential to creativity is seen to offer an increasingly open and attractive work domain for women workers (e.g. DTI 2005a). Nevertheless, recent statistics show that women (and others) continue to be excluded from this cultural work domain. Feminist theory can help to understand better disjunctive continuities and transformations of cultural work by opening up notions of creativity, difference, diversity and gender. Drawing on Judith Butler's theory of performativity (Butler 1990, 1993), this chapter will argue that, while ostensibly supporting the opening of new opportunities for women, much of the current rhetoric around the creative industries, and women cultural workers specifically, is in fact constraining in its assumptions and implications. It further contends that the concept of 'difference'[1] is the fulcrum around which discursive practices of both gender and creativity are performed and as such lies at the centre of advancing the theorization of cultural work.

This chapter begins by setting out what has been identified as a continuing problem of low female participation in the cultural workforce of the digital media sector (DTI 2005a). The chapter then goes on to introduce empirical research that explores gender performativity in the creative and digital industries through an analysis of popular and political commentary and practitioner interviews drawn from in and around the North-West digital media sector in the UK. The domain of digital media production provides a fruitful focus for theorizing the transformation of cultural work and gender inequalities because it sits at the nexus of technical professions, which have demonstrated long-standing marginalization of women workers (Wajcman 2011), and the reputedly more open and emergent spheres of creative and cultural work (e.g. Florida 2002; Leadbeater 1999). A discussion of how feminist theory helps to tease out the relations of power and inequality in this domain is then advanced.

A continuing problem

Women have for a long time been under-represented in the digital industries. For over a decade, the response in the UK has been an explicit political commitment to redressing gender imbalances of participation (e.g. DTI 2005a, 2005b; Haines 2004a, 2004b; Greenfield *et al.* 2002; Millar and Jagger 2001; Phillip and Trinh 2001). Early policy work in this area focused on push factors (the geeky image of the sector, incompatible career pathways) and pull factors to support women entering the digital industries (better training, mentoring, and building capacity and skills of women) (e.g. Phillip and Trinh 2001; Greenfield *et al.* 2002). Increasingly, though, political and public responses to gender inequality in this domain have been framed in terms of the value of women's contribution to workforce diversity (e.g. DTI 2005a; Skillset 2011). This approach has developed in parallel with popular and governmental claims emergent since 1998 that the future of the British economy will be determined by individual workers' capacity to think creatively and 'differently', and, furthermore, that workforce diversity drives creativity (e.g. DCMS 2001).

The notion that difference of thinking and diversity is essential for creativity is not new, but the pairing of this idea with social goals of inclusion and equal opportunities in economic domains is. The 'dual agenda' in UK government policy constitutes a re-framing of equal opportunity (EO) debates for women and ethnic minorities (Oakley 2006). Participation rates of women workers are reported as primary indicators of a diverse workforce (e.g. Skillset 2011). Similarly, in some government policy accounts, women are presented as 'diverse workers' who are therefore potential contributors to creativity in this domain (e.g. DTI 2005a). In these accounts, women's assumed 'difference' from the norm is identified as a potential competitive edge for individual workers and for the UK sector as a whole.

This chapter will argue that, despite the dominance of such positive rhetoric, there is little evidence that the identification of women's diversity and assumed creative potential actually positions them favourably in cultural work domains. Certainly, there have been some important shifts for women in contemporary work and employment in the UK: participation rates of women in higher education are now higher than those of men (Broecke and Hamed 2008), the overall participation rate of women in the UK labour market has increased to over 72% (Jaumotte 2003), and industries traditionally employing greater numbers of women, including the service and communications sectors, have continued to expand in the last two decades (Castells 1997; Hampson and Junor 2010).

However, the most recent evidence available demonstrates that representation of women workers, in addition to workers from Black Asian or minority ethnic backgrounds (BAME), older workers and disabled workers, remains lower in the creative industries than across the UK economy as a whole (Skillset 2011). Moreover, contrary to the UK labour market more broadly, women's participation in these industries has been found to be declining in recent years, from 38% to 27% (Skillset 2009, 2011). Similar patterns of participation are found in the digital industries and are particularly stark in technical and creative roles. While it is difficult to obtain comparable and accurate statistics, the most recent UK policy research has found that only 4%–6% of workers in interactive media and digital games production are women, including design and development of websites and applications, offline multimedia, mobile applications and interactive television (Skillset 2009, 2011). This demonstrates the greatest decline in female participation of all creative industries in the UK since the early 2000s (Skillset 2009, 2011).

These statistics raise a paradox, since it is at once implied that there has never been a better time for women in the digital media sector, but at the same time that inequalities are continuous. The identification of a gap between the rhetoric and reality of cultural work is hardly novel (e.g. see Banks and Milestone 2011; Gill 2002); however, this chapter aims to go further, to explore the possibility that the rhetoric employed to frame cultural and digital work may itself be performative of the 'reality' of inequality.

Researching the rhetoric of difference and diversity

The following analysis is informed by feminist theories of gender, work and organization, which have argued that, rather than trying to understand gender in terms of how to promote women's participation in the workplace, it would be preferable to investigate how workplaces, organizational hier-archies and imagined ideal workers become gendered (e.g. Acker 1990; Puwar 2004). Here, gender is seen to be 'a constitutive element in organizational logic' (Acker 1990: 147) at the same time as being constituted by that logic.

Specifically, a feminist poststructuralist approach to discourse analysis based on Judith Butler's theory of gender performativity is employed. The theory of gender performativity suggests that gender relations embedded in the material practices, processes and structures of cultural work are produced through the sedimentation of repeated discursive practices (Butler 1990, 1993, 2000, 2004). For example, such an approach would see the recognition of skill and the identification of creativity in self and others (and the material follow-on decisions to recruit specific workers and how to organize work) as neither true nor false, but as produced as truth through constant reiteration and repetition in discourse (Butler 1990). In order to understand the specific gender relations of a given domain, then, there is a need to interrogate the shared and repeated articulations that populate that domain.

In these terms, public policy interventions that seek to promote the expansion of the creative industries, or redress gender imbalance through discourses of diversity, are relevant as temporally embedded moments in the constitution of gender relations. The following analysis tracks discursive practices across two sets of data gathered during fieldwork for a broader project in the digital media sector of the North-West of the UK. These consist of governmental policy documents related to the creative and digital industries published during 2004–08 and in-depth interviews with 23 men and women working in the digital media sector.[2] The analysis draws out recited discursive practices in this data and extant critical and mainstream organizational research literature. By bringing a feminist analysis to bear on the network of discursive practices working within and across these discursive sites, taken-for-granted conceptualizations of 'difference', 'diversity' and gender are interrogated and challenged.

Valorizing difference and diversity

Since the time of the first Creative Industries Mapping Document in the UK (DCMS 1998), government policy makers and commentators have declared that the future of the British economy is dependent on individual workers and their ability to think 'differently' and creatively (e.g. Robinson *et al.* 1999). Creative thought is seen to lie not only at the heart of cultural activity but also 'increasingly at the centre of successful economic life in an advanced knowledge-based economy' (DCMS 2001: 5). Government policy documents define creative thought as thinking that deviates from the norm. Individuals are deemed creative if they 'think laterally', behave differently, demonstrate 'original thinking', and are challenging, abrasive or contradictory to established norms (e.g. DCMS 2001; Hutton 2007). In these documents, attributions of 'inner attitudes', differences of thinking, behaviour and deviation from social norms are valorized and held as proxies for creativity.

Furthermore, creativity is seen to be bred by, and even dependent on, workforce diversity (e.g. DCMS 2001). Government policy makers have exclaimed that 'the diversity of an open society stimulates creativity' (Culture North West 2006: 14), that diversity is 'a creative and business imperative' (DCMS *et al.* 2008: 22), and that 'the creative industries depend on diversity for their success' (Hutton 2007: 138). At the launch of the UK Creative Economy Programme (CEP) in 2005, diversity was identified as a 'key driver' in the productivity and growth of the creative economy (Purnell 2005; see also DCMS 2005, 2006). In summary, it is claimed that individual difference and workforce diversity are significant factors which may contribute to creativity in cultural work and thus bring a range of business benefits.

Like the government policy, an emphasis on individual difference as an indicator of creativity was advanced by all of the participants who described their own creative work as different from that of others in their industry. The phrases that participants used to describe their work included 'it's different, definitely', 'un-typical', 'pretty individual', 'not following on from what's been done before', and 'alternative and non-conventional'. In each case, participants sought to highlight the distinctiveness of their work in comparison with that of their colleagues and competitors, and through such characterizations to distinguish themselves as creative. The valorization of difference is exemplified in the following quotation:

The creative industries are really, if you are any good, you might get ideas off other people but it has to be different from other people if you're really going to be any good, if people think you are good.

Another participant remarked:

Unless you find something that makes you stand out, you'll just be along with everyone else [laugh]. You need to find something that's gonna make you different.

These accounts indicate that the recognition of one's ideas as novel and different becomes integral to creative identity; however, it is not simply an individual's ideas or work that must stand out, but the worker themselves (see Deuze *et al.* 2007 for related discussion).

The digital media workers interviewed presented thinking differently and creatively as requiring active effort, strategies and techniques. Participants identified a number of strategies for 'coming up with something different' and keeping 'creativity on the surface', including practices of consuming a mass amount and range of media, engaging in personal art practice and collaborating with a range of people. The creativity of their work and thus their identity requires investment of long hours and extensive effort (e.g. Jarvis and Pratt 2006; Gill 2009). For example, one participant remarked that he was the most creative 'two hours before my eyes water shut, when I start getting tired', and another suggested that his is no longer 'a nine-to-five job. It's a twelve–twelve, soaks up all your time'.

Running alongside accounts of creative practice, highly creative individuals were also described by the participants as being naturally talented, if a bit insane. For example, participants described a creative director, an organizational director and a superstar programmer 'as off his head', 'head on another planet' and 'the stereotypical mad professor', respectively. These accounts drew attention not only to the unconventional nature of creative workers' thinking, but also to the way in which their creativity is performed. Differences in thinking are manifest in behaviour; one 'highly creative' individual was known to talk and even argue aloud when he was alone in his room, and, as another participant describes below, the 'most creative person' he had ever known was demonstrably playful:

I've never met anyone who viewed the world in the way he did and I've never met anyone who was off his head you know as much. I mean when I was a member, there was a load of balloons on the office floor one day, and I mean he was a director of a company and he just runs and dives and jumps on them, you know.

The behaviour of the colleague was particularly notable given his position of authority as organizational director.

Difference and gender

While participants did not themselves initiate discussions of gender in regard to creative difference, their responses above indicate the potential relevance of a gender frame for understanding the creativity/difference relationship. For example, it was noticeable that each of the highly creative colleagues described above were white, male, between 40 and 50 years old, and at senior levels of their respective organizations. Perhaps *because* these individuals were in high-status positions and conformed to worker norms in the industry (white, male), their deviant behaviour could be read as *minor* or slight creative difference, rather than being dismissed as outrageous, unacceptable or irrelevant.

In contrast, in discussions in which gender was explicitly made salient (either through researcher questioning or the given context), it was suggested that the simple difference of being a woman could in itself be an advantage in creative occupations. For example, in a notably celebratory discussion during a field observation of a creative industries seminar for women, the argument was advanced that, because music, design, digital media and film were generally dominated by men, to be a woman working in these fields 'is an asset because you are something different'. A number of successful women (in terms of reputation, financial success and their position at top levels of organizational hierarchies) at the seminar and within later interviews endorsed this assessment. They described the advantages of being a woman in the creative industries because they were identifiably and visibly different from the normalized male worker and therefore stood out as distinctive.

Some male participants also identified potential advantages for women in the digital media sector. One commented that a woman worker might 'have her womanly instincts to help her along, if she's doing something that she wants to appeal to her fellow women kind'. Another suggested that creative and highly skilled designers tended to be very good at multi-tasking, working on multiple screens and quickly shifting from one to another. He observed, 'they're doing like ten things, which for a man is hard but women can do it really easily'. Across these and other comments, both female and male workers therefore identified advantages for women in the creative industries on the basis of innate qualities rather than performed or expressed difference.

Public agency initiatives to promote women's participation in the digital industries similarly describe the creative potential of populating the digital media sector with greater numbers of women (e.g. DTI 2005a, 2005b; Greenfield *et al.* 2002; Haines 2004a, 2004b). In these, there is a clear linked chain of discursive practices, which, rather than emphasize women's individual differences, articulate women's contribution to workforce diversity:

1 Workforce diversity contributes to creativity in the digital and creative industries, and
2 Women 'bring' workforce diversity into the digital media sector, thus
3 Women are valuable workers because they contribute to creativity through their diversity.

These three linked arguments are recited as part of a coherent and logical business case for increasing women's participation in the digital industries. The business case for diversity is said to be an *essential* component to increase the quality and quantity of women's participation in the digital industries by '[convincing] companies to consider investments in mostly intangible human capital assets' (DTI 2005a: 23). As Haines (2004b: 14) states, 'companies will only change in order to improve the bottom line'. In this policy context, women offer an 'added bonus' for creative businesses (Haines 2004a; DTI 2005a). Despite the statistical evidence of their continuing under-representation in the creative workforce, it is even contended that, because women offer the crucial contribution of diversity, they are potentially at an advantage in the digital media labour market (Haines 2004b).

The approach taken in these policy documents suggests that women can contribute because they have a 'different view of things', 'different preferences' and a 'different way of communicating', and that these are valuable as a contribution to diversity (Haines 2004a: 6–12), for example:

The Benefits of Diversity ...

ii.iii.iii Improved creativity, innovation and problem solving

Women can contribute because of their broader life experiences and responsibilities and provide a different 'voice'. Enhanced creativity, new viewpoints, challenging accepted views, learning, flexibility, organizational and individual growth and the ability to adjust rapidly and successfully to market changes are some of the benefits women bring.

Women's presence in the boardroom is said to lead to more civilized behaviour and sensitivity to other perspectives as well as a more interactive management style.

(DTI 2005a: 25)

Women workers, cast as Other to the norm, are seen here to constitute difference and, through this, add to the diversity of the digital media sector. Again, notions of individual (creative) difference are conflated with claims of the benefits of diversity. However, here women are not simply seen to contribute their ideas or 'different voice', but also to *balance, tame* and *civilize* the workplace.

Consistent with the policy documents, a number of the participants also discussed the contributions to diversity that women make to the creative work process in the digital media sector. In response to a statement about the comparatively high number of women in his digital design firm (almost 40%), one participant described the added benefits of diversity:

because we have a lot of women here as well it's, you know, quite different to a lot of new media companies that are all blokes. So, I think the end result of our products is different.

And that:

> The more diverse it is [the workforce] the more it just helps with the creative vision at the end of the day. Just different views you get, the better it is.

Similarly, another participant stated·

> The sort of ideas as well that you get off blokes can be very, very different from what you get from women. Having that diversity is much better for getting creative ideas.

In these accounts, because women are different to, and fewer in number than, male workers, they are presented as valuable and feeding into creative vision and ideas. However, when participants discussed the specific creative contributions of women's 'difference', they tended to emphasize facilitative, rather than creative, roles for women in digital media work. One participant shifted from describing women workers as providing creative difference broadly to emphasizing women's potential to bring balance and a pleasant atmosphere to an a priori masculine space. As evidence of how women can contribute to creative work, this participant remarked that, when his freelancer wife worked with their all-male firm, 'the atmosphere is much, much, nicer' and 'so much more pleasant'. Other participants described their women colleagues as balancing the workplace because they are 'more serious', 'just [get] on with the job, they don't mess around', they are 'calmer' and 'more chilled'.

Interestingly, although, for the male participants, women workers constituted 'the Other' and contributed to diversity, in contrast, none of the female participants presented parallel discussions about the value of male workers for diversity in their organization. Where female participants did describe the benefits of engaging with a variety of other people, it was, without exception, in reference to working with people with different skills or interests. Thus, the relationship between discourses of diversity and creativity is peculiarly feminized.

Discussion: the gendering of 'creative difference'

The valorization of difference and diversity as a creative good in contemporary economies has not gone unnoticed by academic researchers. A number of critical organizational researchers have identified the premium accorded to individual difference in contemporary and cultural work domains. Some have argued that the ability of workers in these domains to demonstrate even 'slight different-ness' (Negus 1998) is crucial for their success (see also Nixon 2006). As in the data above, workers have been found to reiterate and over-emphasize very minor differences as a means to mark themselves out as creative individuals (ibid.). Indeed, the demand for workers to perform individual difference is so strong in some contemporary organizations that scholars have identified a 'norm of difference' in which the expression of individual difference is openly encouraged and even expected so that it might be used by organizations in their services, operations or development (Fleming and Sturdy 2006). While workforce diversity (including workers of different ethnicities, genders and sexualities) is generally celebrated in such organizations, attention is primarily turned to the workers' individual expression of their inner selves, to just be themselves, to 'have fun' and 'be playful' (ibid.).

Academic research on organizational creativity has also argued that not all 'modes of diversity' will contribute positively to creativity (e.g. Milliken and Martins 1996). In this literature, creativity is considered to be produced in the tension, dissonance and 'abrasion' arising in groups of workers who have 'in-depth', 'intellectual', 'task-oriented' and 'informational' diversity based on individual differences of function, background and beliefs (see meta-reviews by Joshi and Roh 2009; and Mannix and Neale 2005). In contrast, 'immutable', 'readily detectable', 'visible' and 'surface-level' diversity on the basis of social demographic groupings (gender, race, age, disability) is regarded as less job-related and has been associated with 'negative attitudes toward dissimilar others and negative performance consequences' for teams (Joshi and Roh 2009: 600). Leonard and Swap (1999: 28), prominent creativity theorists, explain: 'visible cues of difference among group members (gender, race, age) frequently merely add abrasion without creativity'.

Such discussions, however, fail to theorize adequately how notions of gender come to play in accounts of creative difference in cultural work spheres. Feminist theories offer a better understanding of the implications of the kind of conflating of diversity, difference, gender and creativity that is at play in the discursive practices discussed in the previous section. Feminist theorists have argued both for and against the strategic use of 'difference' in combating gender inequality and these debates shed light on the emancipatory potential for women workers of recent political and practitioner rhetoric regarding notions of creative diversity.

Since the publication of Simone de Beauvoir's *The Second Sex* (1949), the idea that gender is a process of 'making difference' and the implications of this idea have been hotly debated. Some, including de Beauvoir herself, have argued that the positioning of woman as the 'second sex', as different and Other to the normative male figure, is the root cause of gender inequality. In this light, an egalitarian concept of difference is a contradiction in terms (Delphy 1996) and any appeal to 'difference' is seen as problematic and potentially 'useful to the oppressing group' (Trinh 1987: 101). Here, inequalities are taken as socially constructed and can be addressed by the reduction of difference between the sexes.

By contrast, feminist scholars taking a more radical perspective have disputed what they see as a liberal feminist desire to eradicate difference and tendency to overlook the gendered nature of structures and institutions. Feminists including Luce Irigaray (1995) have rather argued for the strategic deployment of sexual difference, in which the feminine might be re-written on women's own terms. For Irigaray, it is precisely the prospect of constructing feminism around women's sexual difference that offers the promise of liberation (Kaufmann 1986).

Rather than posing a dilemma, these 'difference debates' in feminism highlight a productive tension that might be applied for a better understanding of inequality in the digital and creative industries. If, as Trinh (1987) argues, the very theme of difference is always useful to the oppressing group, then it is crucial to consider the formulation of difference in regard to cultural work. However, it is also necessary to consider the potential for the valorization of difference and diversity in popular and policy rhetoric to act as a mechanism for greater equality between men and women in these work domains. Melissa Tyler (2005) has argued that there may be two levels of difference and 'Otherness' in positive diversity discourse: one in which there is relative equality across the Otherness; and one in which Otherness is produced through inequality, where mutual recognition is not made and the relationship is one of submission. She states: 'It is not then merely woman's Otherness but her subjection – the nonreciprocal objectification of what it means to be a woman – that de Beauvoir is concerned with' (Tyler 2005: 565–66).

In the discursive sites discussed in this chapter, difference is associated positively with creativity. Creativity is defined across these sites as requiring thinking that is expressive of the inner self, deviates from others, but which also requires work and active effort. 'Being different' is assumed to manifest through conscious creative work techniques, strategies of presentation and self-expression. However, across this discursive network, there is a failure to theorize adequately how power is exercised through the making of specific forms of difference, particularly in regard to minoritized and differentiated groups of workers including women. Notably, some of the most creative workers identified by those interviewed were individuals with high organizational status and who met normalized notions of digital media workers as white males.

In addition, 'women's difference' was repeatedly described as innate rather than as something performed or worked at. However, if differences associated with women are not recognized as performances, they are unlikely to be identifiable as workplace resources (see Adkins 2001 for related discussion). While women may stand out from the male norm, their difference is less likely to be taken as evidence of creativity. Instead, the differences are interpreted in other terms. For example, accounts that seek to promote the participation of women in the digital industries specifically emphasize women's superior communication skills and ability to civilize, bring balance, and ease potential 'conflict' or 'communication breakdown' (DTI 2005a). Other scholars have noted the gendered roles of facilitation and balancing that women are expected to play in team and creative work (e.g. Ollilainen and Calasanti 2007; Banks and Milestone 2011). In the sites discussed in this chapter, women were not marginalized from the creative process through active denial of their expertise by male workers (as Banks and Milestone (2011) found in their research), but through their repeated association with narrow and traditionally feminized facilitating roles which support the creativity of others.

The association of men with the cultivation of creative skills and women with innate difference therefore has implications for the ways women are potentially valued as creative workers in cultural work domains. The application of a feminist poststructuralist analysis reveals that apparently progressive statements of the creative benefits of women's difference and diversity in cultural work potentially entrench gender inequalities, rather than disrupt them. This occurs because unproblematized claims to 'difference' place women in an apparent position of power but simultaneously keep them permanently at the margins of cultural work in the digital industries. It is as if, by 'bringing' difference to their cultural work, women are not seen to bring anything else of creative worth. The conclusion must be that business case approaches in governmental policy which integrate business aims with the political objective of redressing gender inequality (e.g. DTI 2005a; Haines 2004a, 2004b) co-opt feminist concerns in the pursuit of a broader neo-liberal agenda for creative economic development, and in doing so they constitute, at the very best, a precarious approach with uncertain benefit for women.

Conclusion

The importance of considering gender power relations in spheres of cultural work becomes clear as we move between public policy documents, organizational research literature and interviews within the discursive field of the digital media sector. There is a network of inclusion and exclusions performed in this field in which difference is depoliticized and is reified as a valuable form of human capital, a resource or an individual creative quality that is produced through relationships of mutual recognition. Here, all workers are included as contributing to creativity through their difference. However, such inclusionary accounts also exclude particular forms of difference and diversity from those considered to hold creative potential. In contrast to the valorization of individual creative difference across the sector broadly, claims that women are 'different' kinds of workers and can contribute to diversity are made on the basis of their immutable membership of a naturalized gender group. Women are positioned as supportive but marginal to the creative work processes of others and, at the same time, apparently gender-neutral 'creative' attributes of difference such as unconventionality, playfulness and insanity become associated with normalized masculine subjects. While women are seen to bring difference and diversity into the digital media sector, they also bring gender and its sedimented practices of power and inequality.

Notes

1 Scare quotes around the concept of 'difference' are used to indicate that throughout this chapter a cautionary approach is taken when using the term such that it is

assumed that notions of 'individual difference' or 'women's difference' are performed through discursive practices rather than relating to any essential or immutable characteristic (quotation marks dropped in successive references).

2 Participants were recruited through a snowballing method and included digital training providers, organizational directors, creative directors, designers and programmers working across 19 organizations, the majority of whom were based in Liverpool or Manchester. Eight women and fifteen men were interviewed. In addition to the interviews and government documents, the broader project included discursive data from participant observation of a North-West digital industries training course and a set of recruitment advertisements for the digital industries published in 2003–05. Ethical principles were followed closely throughout the development of this research (see Proctor-Thomson 2009 for more detail).

12 Creativity, biography and the time of individualization

Lisa Adkins

Drawing on interviews with web designers in the North-West of England,[1] this chapter is concerned with the work biographies of creative workers. Much has been made of such biographies, not least because they are routinely located as paradigmatic of new forms of the ordering of life, and especially economic life, in post-Fordism. Thus, portfolio and/or precarious patterns of work, a lack of discernible boundaries between working life and home life, life-world detraditionalization, continuous patterns of skilling and re-skilling, as well as the positioning of work as a self-managed, self-directed, unfolding event, have all been taken to indicate the decline of the proprietary skilled worker and corresponding culture of training and lifestyle (or the decline of the standardized collective work biography) and the emergence of do-it-yourself biographies. In short, creative biographies have been taken to be exemplary of processes of individualization in regard to economic life, including its contradictions and exclusions. In this chapter, however, I raise a number of questions regarding this assumption. I do so by enquiring as to the status and relevance of biography for the study of work and working lives in the context of individualization and the decline of the proprietary skilled worker and I do so despite the widespread use of biography as a methodological device for tracking, mapping and describing creative working lives. More specifically, I raise questions regarding the methodological efficacy of biography for the study of creative workers and cultural work not least because biography orders events in a fashion that is more akin to the rhythms of industrial society than those of post-Fordism. In short, this chapter locates biography as an anachronistic methodological device for the study of creative labour, one which not only eschews the restructuring of time paradigmatic of post-Fordist production but also consistently confuses this time with evidence of pervasive individualization. In this chapter, I therefore also question the widely held assumption that creative labour is paradigmatically individualized labour.

Creative biographies

It is by now a truism that creative work and creative workers are routinely located – albeit often problematically – at the cutting edge of socio-cultural change. This is no more clearly so than for the case of post-Fordist capitalism where, prior to the recent financial crisis and subsequent recession, creative labour and the creative industries were habitually positioned in a range of policy measures (including in economic, social and educational policy measures) and in academic and popular writings as central to economic growth and prosperity (including urban and regional regeneration), as well as to transformations in work, working lives and modes of living (see e.g. Leadbeater and Oakley 1999; Florida 2002; Hartley 2005). Indeed, while located as central to wealth creation prior to the global financial crisis, in the subsequent and ongoing recession, the creative sector is now being considered central to economic recovery and, in particular, to job creation. In the UK, for example, Arts Council England have proposed that 'the cultural and creative sector is vital to national economic recovery', not least because it is a sector that can 'get people back to work' (Arts Council England 2009). Thus, and even in the context of sovereign debt crisis, rising unemployment and recession, creative work has maintained its exceptional status.

While such policy and writings have been subject to much critique, not least for their utopianism and over-reliance on and recuperation of romantic notions of the autonomous, norms-transgressing creative artist (see e.g. Banks and O'Connor 2009), nonetheless the significance of creative labour and the creative industries cannot be denied for post-Fordist accumulation. This significance is expressed not only in the positioning of cultural work as key to innovation, accumulation and recovery strategies, but also – at least prior to the current recession – in an expansion of employment in the creative industries. Thus, and for the case of the UK, Banks and Hesmondhalgh (2009: 415) note that between 1997 and 2006 employment in the creative industries grew by an average of 2% per annum. Such employment growth, together with a more general increase in the significance of the cultural content of commodities, signalled a changing relationship between culture and economy – or, as it is sometimes termed, the art–commerce relationship (see e.g. Lash and Urry 1994). For some, this latter shift amounted to the emergence of a cultural economy, an economy in which culture was put to work in the service of value creation in all manner of novel ways (see e.g. du Gay and Pryke 2002; Thrift 2005).

Given this significance, not surprisingly, from the mid-1990s onwards, creative labour and the creative industries have been the subject of sustained critical academic attention, both empirical and conceptual. This has included, but has not been limited to, analyses of policy (see e.g. Garnham 2005; Hesmondhalgh and Pratt 2005); empirical studies of the working lives and working practices of creative workers, including the conditions of cultural production (see e.g. Kotamraju 2002; McRobbie 2002; Ross 2003; Wittel 2001); investigations into the shifting intensive properties of cultural products (see e.g. Lash and Lury 2007); analyses of how creative labour is contributing to new forms of value creation (see e.g. Adkins 2008); analyses of the changing politics of cultural work, including its links to broad shifts in governmentality (see e.g. Banks 2007); and analyses of how creative labour is both entangled in and is exemplary of a range of processes and phenomena specific to, or at least prevalent within, post-Fordism. The latter include the rise of insecurity and precariousness as a generalized state of existence (see e.g. de Peuter 2011; Gill and Pratt 2008; Morini 2007; Ross 2008); the process of economization, that is, the process of the dispersal of value creation across the social body (see e.g. Terranova 2004), and the emergence of immaterial labour as the hegemonic labouring form (see e.g. Hardt and Negri 2001; Lazzarato 1996).

Of this large and complex body of research, it is that concerning the working lives and working practices of creative workers which is of concern in this chapter. Of particular interest are the ways in which this research has documented such lives as characterized by a particular set of qualities and features. Specifically, creative labour has been found to be characterized by and associated with irregular and short-term patterns of work; chronic job insecurity; long working hours; little job protection; a lack of a discernible boundary between work and home, with working practices often looking more like social practices; passionate and sometimes excessive attachments to work; rapid patterns of skilling and deskilling, with skill sets often updated in a do-it-yourself, informal fashion; life-world detraditionalization; and (paradoxically in the light of the latter) the constitution and inscription of new axes of inclusion and exclusion (see e.g. Adkins 1999, 2002; Banks 2007; Banks and Hesmondhalgh 2009; Banks and Milestone 2011; Gill 2002, 2009; Gill and Pratt 2008; Kotamraju 2002; McRobbie 2002; Morini 2007; Ross 2003, 2008; Wittel 2001).

Given these features of creative working lives and working practices, it is perhaps of little surprise that they have been taken to be exemplars of the general claim found in recent social theory that in conditions of post-Fordism a political economy of insecurity prevails (see e.g. Castells 1996; Beck 2000; Boltanski and Chiapello 2005; Bourdieu 1998; Sennett 2006). Elaborating this political economy, Ulrich Beck suggests that it is one characterized by a process of the spread of temporary and insecure employment, discontinuity and loose informality, and this is particularly so for those societies that were hitherto strongholds of full employment. Hence, in the political economy of insecurity well-paid, full-time and highly skilled employment is on the wane and a nomadic, 'multi-activity' paradigm of work takes its place (a paradigm which Beck suggests until now has mainly been associated with female labour in the West).[2] A further feature of this political economy, Beck maintains, is the redistribution of risks away from the state and the economy towards the individual. Thus, a compulsion to individualization prevails, a compulsion that means standardized 'life-stories are breaking up into fragments' (Beck 2000: 3). In the political economy of insecurity, the standard biography, therefore, becomes a chosen biography where pervasive processes of individualization compel subjects to construct not only their own life stories, but also their own futures.

As workers whose work and working lives are characterized by insecurity, discontinuity and informality, and whose working biographies are therefore necessarily broken into fragments, creative labourers can readily be cast as exemplars of the multi-activity paradigm of work. Indeed, within the literature on creative working lives, we find precisely such a casting. Thus, and often drawing explicitly if circumspectly on the conceptual language of Beck, creative labour is repeatedly described as individualized labour (with all the complexity that inheres in this process), a process assumed to be evidenced by the do-it-yourself, non-standard biographies of such workers. Indeed, in much of the literature on creative workers not only are non-standard biographies assumed to evidence individualization, but also the method used to elicit such evidence is very often biography itself.

I will return to the issue of the use of biographical method and the relationship of this method to individualization, but before I do so it is important to note that Beck is not alone in his view that standardized biographies are increasingly breaking into fragments. Richard Sennett (2006), for example, understands the political economy of insecurity to mean that the resources required to build a narrative account of one's life and, in particular, the resources that would enable the making of a seamless, linear biography – a biography in which one event leads to another and where events are cumulative in time – are no longer present. Paramount in the decline of the narrativized biography for Sennett is the replacement of long-term and often life-long jobs by short-term projects and contracts; the replacement of strong organizational ties by weak ties (involving the replacement of commitment and loyalty by short-termism, detachment and ambivalence); and the restructuring of organizational forms away from large-scale, relatively stable hierarchical forms towards constantly moving networks. Paramount, in other words, is the destruction of the socio-economic conditions that allow for shared and linear biographical narratives to be made, and their replacement by resources (if they can be understood as resources at all) which allow not for linearity – where experience concerns events linked in time – but for experiences of fragments and drift. In the political economy of insecurity, events are therefore divorced from context, a separation that not only means that a linear biography becomes an impossibility, but also that the future cannot be anticipated and is a constant unknown. Indeed, for Sennett, the demise of what he terms 'social capitalism' witnesses the emergence of workers who do not require, aspire towards or indeed can construct a sustaining or sustainable life and/or work narrative, but instead the worker who has to 'improvise his or her life-narrative, or even do without any sustained sense of self' (Sennett 2006: 4). Thus, and much as Beck proposes that in the political economy of insecurity individuals are compelled to make their own futures, Sennett also understands that, in a context of the collapse or undercutting of resources that secure a predictable future, workers must increasingly invent their own prospects.

Creative futures

Certainly, data from my own interviews with creative workers – in this instance with web designers – regarding their working lives appear to give support to the claims of both Beck and Sennett in regard to the decline of a standardized, narrative biography and knowable and predictable futures. These data also apparently shore up findings of existing studies of such working lives, especially in as much as they highlight similar characteristics and features of creative work. Consider, for example, James, a 25-year-old graduate in design whose work history is one of moving from small company to small company and of constant skills updating on a self-taught basis. James described his working patterns in the small web design company in Manchester in which he was employed at the time of interview in the following terms:

> It's fairly flexible. There is a lot of give and take in that we will work evenings and weekends when deadlines are looming ... I think that is something that is common in the industry that people are asked to work outside normal hours. But it is manageable if you have got a vested interest in it, if it is something you are passionate about, if it is something that you want to do.

James's working pattern appears typical of that associated with creative labour. More specifically, and in line with existing studies, James's working hours are non-standard, flexible and often long. There is also little distinction between work and non-working time. In addition, his description demonstrates the entanglement of passion and flexibility so often found to be characteristic of creative work (see e.g. McRobbie 2002).

Or consider the response of 28-year-old Tom when asked to describe the process by which he got into web design, a response which, because of its richness, is worth quoting here at length:

> I don't think it's the traditional one that most people have done because when I was studying at college, I didn't go to university, my background is in graphic design, in print ... I started to get into web design through an application called Flash[3] which was something a friend of mine had started to learn and showed me. I had always had quite an interest in animation and that kind of thing right back from days when I had Amiga,[4] you could paint, you could do animation on it. So I started to learn Flash at home on my own before I actually even got a job in design. So I guess that was my first steps into web design although at the time I didn't consider it web design, I just considered it an animation tool that I used to play with. So not long after that I got my first job which was basically designing small adverts for support advertising for charities and things. Very boring but it was a step in the door to design and basically there they didn't have much web experience and there wasn't much going on at that time really in that company anyway, and I brought in a few Flash samples that I had done and from there on it just developed. From there I had shown them I could do a few things in Flash and they sort of

gave me the role of developing their website then. So then I had to learn HTML[5] which was quite tricky at first, there is quite a lot to get your head around when you have been used to being able to move things around on the screen. It is quite a different discipline. So that is basically where I started.

Tom's process of becoming a web designer, and especially his skilling and re-skilling on a do-it-yourself, often experimental basis, and the blurring of work and play also at issue in this process, resonates strongly with existing accounts of creative work. In particular, it resonates with accounts that stress the intersection of work and leisure in the creative and cultural sectors and the often informal character of the creative labour market (see e.g. Gill 2002). It also underscores the constant process of skills upgrading characteristic of web design in particular (Kotamraju 2002).

After describing how he became a web designer, Tom then went on to discuss how, while he was working at the company in which he initially became a designer, the internal department in which he worked 'sort of set up a separate company while still remaining [at] the design department for the larger company, a little complex but it was almost like we were setting up our own company there'. He went on:

> from there I became the web design manager of that company so it was basically wearing two hats. It was doing half a day working for the original company and then half a day working on other projects. And then from there I moved on to another job which was basically web design ... I didn't stay there very long for various reasons but then I started here [a small Manchester-based web design company].

Tom's work history is therefore one that combines movements from small company to small company with entrepreneurship. It is also one in which different kinds of labour, including waged labour, short-term project work and contract work, are entangled. As such, Tom's story bears all the hallmarks of the political economy of insecurity, particularly inasmuch as it involves multi-activity, discontinuity and informality. Indeed, and inasmuch as Tom's work history comprises fragments and bits, it might be taken to be emblematic not only of Beck's do-it-yourself individualized worker, but also of Sennett's drifting worker, one who is denied a standardized linear biography by short-term projects and contracts, weak ties and short-termism.

Both the accounts of James and Tom therefore appear to give support to the view found in the literature on creative working lives that these lives are characterized by non-standard work biographies, biographies which in turn evidence pervasive individualization. This view also appears to be shored up by the final data I will present here. These are data from an interview with Peter who is 37 and is self-employed. Peter owns a small web-design company, works from home and describes himself as a 'workaholic'. He graduated in

1992 with an MSc in Data Telecommunications and Networks and immediately on graduation went to work at Ericsson (a telecommunications company) as a programmer.

Peter described to me how he was a:

> programmer for a good number of years and in 1999 I became an external contractor, I resigned and the market was such ... in the late 1990s there was a huge demand for this skill and I could basically just pick where in the world I wanted to go for a job on £40 an hour or something. So I actually went to live in Italy for three years ... I was in this strange environment in Italy and in the evenings you have got two choices, you have got the pub or club or sit at home ... So I just taught myself web design at the age of 31 ... I just got a book and with my laptop, just started making a website for the guy who ran the local club ... it was just something I taught myself which is obviously not typical of what other people are going to be saying.

Peter then went on to elaborate how he taught himself web design in the context of a declining demand for his existing programming skills and how he decided to 'really have a go at this web-design business'. Peter returned to Britain from Italy in 2002 and 'decided to try to make it as a web designer'. He describes how he 'did a website for an estate agency and basically just did this dummy website for properties and I just wrote to dozens and dozens of estate agencies in the North-West and I managed to sell one or two. So from a very small beginning, things picked up from there'. He then describes a process whereby over four years his business both grew and diversified in terms of clients, to the point where one company became, in his words, so 'reliant' on him that he was offered a part-time job for three days a week. So now, he says, 'I've got the best of both worlds really because I am self-employed and I am also employed so I can just cherry pick the jobs I want to do for the self-employed part and I've got the steady income'.

In many ways, Peter's account of his working life might be regarded as archetypal of the do-it-yourself, individualized biography, for not only does his account involve an excessive attachment to work and multi-activity (with a shuttling back and forth between different fields of activity including employment and self-employment, and formal and informal training), but it also evidences a distribution of risks towards the individual, a process which Beck, of course, locates as central to individualization. Thus, and in the context of a declining demand for his programming skills, Peter took charge of reinventing himself as a web designer and of becoming the author of his own work story. Indeed, and in as much as Peter's account is one of overcoming adversity and triumphing, his account bears a heroic quality, a quality which has often been found to be associated with creative labour (Thrift 2005). Yet Peter has done more than simply overcome potential insecurity and risk through his own self-mastery, for in adopting a do-it-yourself work biography he also controls his own future, a future which is of his own making. On the future he commented:

> I have to keep trying to learn new things ... in some ways I can knock a job out very quickly by just calling on things that I've done in the past but I can't do that indefinitely because I'm going to lose my skills if I'm going to do that. Or I can do some things that are outside my own comfort zone when I've got to learn something new but that will take me three times longer than I would like. So there is a balance to being productive and getting the money coming in using the skills I've already got and then actually working and learning new stuff where I know I'm not actually making money doing that but I know that it is for the future.

Via pushing himself outside of his comfort zones and continuously learning new skills, Peter's work future is therefore constituted not by external collective resources which engender a future that is predictable and knowable. Instead, and much as Sennett might predict, Peter crafts his own prospects.

What does biography do?

All three of the working lives I have presented in this chapter might easily be taken as substantiation of the prevalence of do-it-yourself biography in the cultural and creative sectors – that is, of a (non-linear) biography which compels creative workers to manage risk individually and to create their own working futures. Indeed, in existing research on the work and working lives of creative workers, and on the basis of similar interview data, such conclusions are very often drawn. Yet in what follows I want to problematize such a straightforward conclusion by raising a series of questions around the use of biography as a methodological device to understand the work and working lives of creative workers. While, as we have seen, most accounts of the latter precisely stress the do-it-yourself nature of these lives, what is less commented on is the fact that the methodological device commonly used to describe and map these biographies is biography itself. Thus, in empirically based accounts of creative labour, we find a biographical methodology and/or method employed both explicitly and implicitly (see e.g. Gill 2002, 2009; Ravenscroft and Gilchrist 2009; Thiel 2005). Yet, in the take-up of biography as a methodological device, there is a clear slippage between theory and methodology where biography is simply assumed to be an appropriate device for the study of such lives because it is posited theoretically that the biographies of creative workers are non-linear and 'do-it-yourself' in character. In this slippage, questions regarding the methodological relevance of biography for the task in hand are usually not raised. Instead, any such questions tend to be silenced. However, I want to ask, is biography an appropriate method for the task of mapping and describing such lives? More specifically, is this a method that has traction and purchase in a form of capitalism where, and to draw on Sennett once again, events have been cut loose from context?

To address this question, it is necessary to think about biography not simply as a device that social scientists may use to collect data, but also as a device that orders data in a particular fashion. That is, it is necessary to consider what biography as a methodological device *does* rather than dwell on what it is. Consider, for example, that one of the key virtues of the bio-graphical method for the social sciences is understood to concern a particular relationship between events and time. Thus, according to a recent discussion of the use and merits of this method within social research, 'biographical research places people in context' (Merrill and West 2009: 40) and more specifi-cally places people and the events in their lives in the broader 'social, cultural and economic context' (ibid.: 40). As such, the authors continue, biographical method allows researchers to 'weave threads between the detail of [people's] lives ... and the wider ... context' (ibid,: 40).[6] If we focus on the question of what biography as a methodological device does, what is clear in this discus-sion is that biography orders the world in a specific fashion. In particular, it separates out and differentiates events from context – or events from history – and orders the world in this manner, an ordering which, moreover, places context or history as external to the events it seeks to describe. Biography, then, orders the relationship between events and time in a fashion that externalizes socio-historical time even as it seeks to link, connect or thread events to and in that time – that is, to locate events in history.

A number of points are worthy of discussion here. First, and inasmuch as biography as a device organizes events and time in this manner – that is, as differentiated entities, but at the same time allows connections to be made from the former to the (externalized) latter – we might observe that this is the very organization of the social which Sennett understands the political econ-omy of insecurity to have undone. More specifically, this is a social in which experience and events may (and can) be linked to context, be that social, economic and/or political. It is, in other words, a social in and through which a linear biography may be built. It is also a social where, because links may be made between events and time, futures may be anticipated and can be known. In short, this is the model of social formation that Sennett associates with social capitalism.

Yet second, and inasmuch as Sennett posits that this organization of the social has been undercut by short-term projects and contracts, weak ties and unstable networks – that is, by economic forms that work to set events loose from context – surely biography must be declared a method that has little or no purchase in the political economy of insecurity. Indeed, given that this is a political economy in which – as Sennett posits – it is increasingly difficult to link events to context, we might ask: what use is a methodological device that precisely orders data in such a manner to allow attempts to draw connections between the two? My point, of course, is that biography as a methodological device belongs to a different socio-historical time and has questionable relevance in the political economy of insecurity. As such, its use as a method for the study of creative work and creative lives must surely be challenged, particularly if that work and those lives are posited to be characterized by – indeed to be exemplary of – the process of the cutting loose of events from context.

From biography to event

If, as I have argued here, biography as a methodological device is relevant for a particular social formation and has little traction for a multi-activity paradigm of work – that is, for the political economy of insecurity – then this surely begs the question of what method or methods might be relevant to and for such an economy? To address this issue, let me return to the case of Peter, and in particular to Peter's account of the future. It will be recalled that this account appeared to bear all the hallmarks of the do-it-yourself, individualized biography, one in which Peter shoulders risk to craft his own prospects. Thus, Peter's account appears to evidence not only a lack of external collective resources which make predictable and knowable futures, but also – and in the absence of such resources – an improvised working life and future. In this way, Peter's account of his working life appears to evidence the cutting loose of events from context, or the cutting loose of events from socio-historical time.

However, while it might be tempting to understand Peter's account in this way and hence add further fuel to the view that cultural labour is thoroughly individualized, to do so would be to bracket the ways in which Peter's account concerns a particular relationship between events and time. At issue, however, is not the releasing of events from time – that is, the process of individualization. Rather, at issue is a merging of events and time, or a folding of context and events into one another, a folding that I have elsewhere termed 'event time' (Adkins 2009b). Thus, when Peter discusses making his own future via continuous skills updating, such a folding is at issue, not least because time (the future), while certainly not externally present, is folded into events in his work and more specifically into skilling and re-skilling. Hence, Peter talks of a future not as something that he simply has responsibility for making, but he talks of futures that are entangled with events – in this instance, with 'learning new stuff'. Time (the future) and event ('learning new stuff') are here merged together: Peter's time is not individualized time but event time.

As we have seen, while literature and research on creative work and creative workers repeat the mantra that such work and workers are thoroughly individualized, and often reach this conclusion via relying on the methodological device of biography, the case of Peter serves to open vistas to other possibilities. In particular, this case serves to open the possibility that creative labour may not be as thoroughly individualized as is usually assumed; indeed, that a cutting of events from socio-historical time or context has been assumed to be evident in creative work and creative lives, but that this assumption has taken place in the absence of a consideration that socio-historical time – context – does not necessarily take an externalist form. While the latter was certainly the case for industrial capitalism, where events took place under the shadow (and hegemony) of the clock, it is certainly not an assumption that can be taken for granted in post-Fordism, not least because the hegemony of the clock time has been undercut, with events evading external forms of measure. As I have stressed here, this latter does not necessarily concern a cutting loose of events from context or agency from structure, but may also involve a folding of previously differentiated entities – events and time, people and contexts – to create some unpredictable, unfolding and in motion assemblages.

This leads me to return to the question of method, and in particular to the question of what kind of method or methods might be appropriate for the study or creative work and workers. I have already suggested that as a methodological device biography is not appropriate for this task, not least because it assumes a social formation that is out of time with the contemporary present. However, I have also argued that this present is neither one in which socio-historical time or context stands in an external relation to people or events nor one in which such time has necessarily been undercut. Indeed, I have suggested that one feature of this present is the folding together of time and events. As such, and for the study of creative work, it might be suggested that social scientists embrace methods tuned into the event, or event methods – methods that do not seek to contextualize or historicize, but are attuned to phenomena in which time and events are entangled, however unpredictable they may be.

Conclusion

In this chapter, I have sought to shift the ground in regard to how creative work and creative lives are understood, researched and positioned by social scientists. This has comprised two interventions. First, I have suggested that biography is an inappropriate methodological tool for understanding creative labour, not least because biography orders data in a manner that seeks to place events in time. I have suggested that this ordering of events and time is precisely that encountered in industrial capitalism and hence that biography is a device that is ill equipped to engage the political economy of insecurity. It is ill equipped, for example, to engage the cutting loose of events from context, which writers such as Beck and Sennett posit to be characteristic of this economy. However, second, and via engagement with interview data with web designers, I have proposed an alternative understanding of the relationship between time and event in post-Fordism to that of the divorce of events from context. Specifically, I have suggested that creative labour may not be so tightly hinged to the process of individualization as has been imagined. Indeed, rather than straightforwardly individualized, I have suggested that creative work – like other forms of labour in post-Fordism – needs to be understood in terms of more complex shifts in the organization not only of the economy, but also of the social; shifts which in turn demand new orientations to issues and questions of methodology and method.

Notes

1 The research on which this chapter draws was funded by the Centre for Research on Socio-Cultural Change (CRESC), The University of Manchester/The Open University. The research involved 15 semi-structured interviews with web designers working primarily in the Greater Manchester area of England and was carried out in 2006. At the time of interview, by far the majority of the interviewees were primarily employed in small to medium-sized enterprises, although a minority were self-employed. Some combined employment and self-employment. Interviews with participants lasted between one and one and a half hours, and all interviews were recorded and transcribed. In conducting the research, the guidelines set out in the British Sociological Association's (BSA) Statement of Ethical Practice (2002) were adhered to. In line with these guidelines, and to respect 'the anonymity and privacy of those who participate in the research process' (British Sociological Association 2002: 5), the names given to participants throughout this chapter are pseudonyms. For an important discussion of practice of anonymization in social science research, see Gross (2012).

2 For a critique of the view that in post-Fordism work is increasingly taking on characteristics historically associated with women's labour, see Adkins 2009a.

3 A multimedia authoring programme.

4 A personal computer launched by Commodore in 1985 which was distinctive in that it combined multimedia technology with ease of use.

5 HTML is the acronym for Hypertext Markup Language, a language for the creation of web pages.

6 It is of interest to note that this definition of biographical research resonates with C. Wright Mills's (1959) understanding of sociology as that concerning the intersection of biography and history, or the intersection of personal troubles and public issues.

13 Professional identity and media work

Mark Deuze and Nicky Lewis[1]

This chapter examines the particularities and (potential) consequences of labour individualization in the creative industries, with specific reference to the ways in which cultural workers self-define a professional identity. It could very well be argued that there is something special about working in the creative industries. Yet, as models for working and being at work across industrial sectors converge under equivalent conditions of a global creative economy, the distinctive nature of cultural work seems to become more generic for labour across the spectrum. This makes the study and theoretization of cultural work a project uniquely situated in the here and now of rapid technological developments, a global reconfiguration of labour relationships (what Toby Miller and Marie-Claire Leger call a New International Division of Cultural Labour, 2001), and ever-increasing precarity of media work (Deuze 2007). At the same time, many of the trends that can be highlighted about the lived experience of cultural work extend to the nature of work in general, and upon closer scrutiny do not seem to be particular to our time. The economy has been stretching across national and continental boundaries for many years – a process amplified through the development and implementation of information and communication technologies since at least the early 20th century (Beniger 1989). The current popularity among businesses and the political establishment of creativity and a creative economy to some extent is rooted in a shift towards post-material values across Western cultures since at least the early 1970s, signified by a prioritization of life goals such as belonging, esteem, and aesthetic and intellectual satisfaction (Inglehart 2008: 132). Part of this long-term shift is the conflation of labour and work with value priorities such as individual self-expression and self-realization. In other words, it is quite commonplace for (especially younger) workers to think of their job or career as a vehicle to become who they 'really' are rather than – or next to – earning them a paycheque and giving them some control over their financial future. Those engaged in cultural work – which we define in the context of our contribution broadly as anyone engaged in the professional production of culture within the context of the creative industries – can arguably be seen to be at the forefront of these trends.

In our contribution, we argue that a focus on how workers across the creative industries construct and give meaning to their professional identity may reveal a particularity of cultural work. We suggest that the building blocks for modelling professional identity in cultural work – telling stories (content), finding an audience (commerce), establishing relationships with customers as fans (connectivity), and finding ways to remain artistically autonomous in the process (creativity) – are the same for practitioners across the wide range of cultural production. This would include (but is certainly not limited to) journalists, creatives in advertising and marketing communications, film and television workers, digital game developers and leisure software designers, as well as professionals in the music and recording industries. By eliminating the disciplinary boundaries between these fields of cultural work, we articulate a perspective on what it means professionally to produce culture from the point of view of the practitioners involved.

Cultural work generally, and media work particularly, takes place in paid and unpaid contexts, gets validated by for-profit and reputational motives, and attributes creative roles to all actors in its process: producers as well as consumers. Indeed, while not all actors are identified as 'creatives', the creative process itself is no longer left to so-called 'professionals', nor exclusive to particular domains of cultural work. The age-old divisions between 'creatives' and 'suits' or between managers and creators increasingly give way to more hybridized conceptualizations of (media) work. With the rise of convergence culture and Web 2.0, the creative process is furthermore fused with the free labour that consumers do as co-creators of cultural content and experiences. Given the particulars of today's media ecology, everyone – at some point, in some way – does cultural work. Given the worldwide economic shift away from the manufacturing industries to the cultural sectors and creative industries (Flew 2004) and the signalled 'culturalization' of labour more generally (McFall 2004), this problematizes notions of what cultural work is, while at the same time pressures us to articulate more carefully what it can be for those who want to do cultural work for a living and see it as a way of life. In doing so, our approach is informed by the work of David Hesmondhalgh and Sarah Baker, who benchmark their analyses of interviews with media workers across three cultural industries with the deliberate intent 'to take creative workers' accounts seriously' (Hesmondhalgh and Baker 2011: 50). Although it is important to highlight old and new sources of exploitation in a labour market that is premised on people seeing their work primarily in terms of personal fulfilment and a market that is decidedly global and therefore beyond the control of any individual agent, we feel it is of equal value to articulate ways in which professionals 'make it work' (paraphrasing fashion consultant Tim Gunn in his role as mentor on the US television show *Project Runway*[2]). This will be the focus of our chapter, of which the primary takeaway point will be a model for both understanding and explaining the process of identity formation in the everyday decision-making processes of those engaged in cultural work. This model is derived from interviews with a broad range of media workers across different creative industries – notably journalism, film and TV, digital games and advertising – and a review of the literature (see Deuze 2007, 2011 for more details regarding methods).

Context of cultural work: individualized labour

Media companies operating in fields as diverse and interconnected as public relations, marketing, advertising and journalism traditionally have been considered cultural industries, representing those companies and professions primarily responsible for the industrial production and circulation of culture (Hesmondhalgh 2002). In the ongoing academic debate on the definition of culture (or cultural) industries, media production tends to be emphasized as particular to the field of action of the companies and corporations involved. In recent years, policy makers, industry observers and scholars alike have reconceptualized media work as taking place within a broad context of creative industries. The term was introduced by the UK government Department of Culture, Media and Sport (DCMS) in 1998, defining creative industries as:

> those industries which have their origin in individual creativity, skill and talent and which have a potential for wealth and job creation through the generation and exploitation of intellectual property. This includes advertising, architecture, the art and antiques market, crafts, design, designer fashion, film and video, interactive leisure software, music, the performing arts, publishing, software and computer games, television and radio.[3]

The concept of creative industries aims to reconcile the emergence of increasingly individual and small-scale, project-based or collaborative notions of commercial and non-commercial media production with institutionalized notions of cultural production as it exclusively takes place within the cultural industries. John Hartley explicitly defines creative industries as an idea that 'seeks to describe the conceptual and practical convergence of the creative arts (individual talent) with cultural industries (mass scale), in the context of new media technologies (ICTs) within a new knowledge economy, for the use of newly interactive citizen-consumers' (Hartley 2005: 5). Although Hartley's definition suggests an optimistic outcome of the merger between individual creativity and mass cultural production, Neilson and Rossiter (2005: 8) warn against uncritical acceptance of the concept, arguing it consists of 'an oxymoronic disingenuousness that wants to suggest that innovation can coexist with or become subordinated to the status quo. In this context, innovation becomes nothing other than a code word for more of the same – the reduction of creativity to the formal indifference of the market'. The significance of the 'creative turn' in definitional debates about individualized creativity in cultural work is its dislocating effect, effectively divorcing professional identities of media workers from the context of those who pay their salaries or otherwise fund their work. A benevolent reading of this effort would emphasize its empowering potential toward the role of the individual in cultural work, acknowledging how most of the work in media today takes place outside the walls of newsrooms, studios, sets and office buildings that traditionally make up operationalizations of 'the' media industries.

As cultural work becomes individualized in a context of its increasingly non-permanent and contingent character, its 'atypical' structure of employment – as documented for journalists by the International Federation of Journalists (2006) – remains largely invisible, as it effectively prevents media workers from organizing collectively to make themselves or their concerns known. In this context, all kinds of other informal organized networks have emerged, particularly on the Internet (Rossiter 2006; Mosco and McKercher 2009). Early studies on such online networks of, for example, audiovisual media professionals suggest that, beyond the expression and mobilization of interests, their effectiveness to represent workers is limited (Saundry *et al.* 2007). On the other hand, informal networks of media workers have emerged online which contribute to a renewed sense of self among especially younger professionals in such industries. This new kind of self-identification among cultural labourers can be seen as a translocal social movement of precarious workers, emerging beyond the traditional institutional contexts of governments, employers, as well as outside of unions or guilds (Bodnar 2006). Here, a shift of responsibility and accountability for employment and professional identity towards the individual (Munro 2001) coincides with a macro-level move away from institution-based representation to a post-national constellation based on the role of people as individual citizens, consumers and workers 'to shape their own social environment and [to] develop the capacity for action necessary for such interventions to succeed' (Habermas 2001: 60). Bauman correspondingly articulates the post-national project with individualization and globalization, arguing that '[t]he new individualism, the fading of human bonds and the wilting of solidarity, are all engraved on one side of a coin whose other side bears the stamp of globalization' (Bauman 2006: 146).

Bourdieu (1998) has been one of the fiercest critics of the increasing precariousness of work in the digital age, suggesting that living under precarious conditions prevents rational anticipation and, in particular, the basic belief and hope in the future that one needs in order to rebel (individually or collectively) against intolerable working or living conditions.

The shift towards an individualization of labour to some extent counters – and runs parallel to – the historical trend towards socialization and salarization, instead favouring more fluid and flexible notions of work, ushered in through rapid developments in technologies of communication, a decentralization of management practices and the fragmentation of markets (Storey *et al.* 2005). The responsibility for articulating, developing, maintaining and enacting professional identity thus comes to rest solely on the shoulders of individual workers – not just in practice (as it always has been), but also in theory and policy. This is the context for thinking through the creative industries conceptualization of the role of the individual in the context of media organizations. What sets these approaches additionally apart is how creative industries open up ways of thinking about (commercial and non-commercial) cultural work in the media without assuming the exclusivity of the storytelling experience to be resting solely in the hands of the professionals involved: journalists, advertising creatives, public relations officers, games developers and so on. If the process of telling stories, making meaning and sharing mediated experiences becomes both more co-creative and individualized – be it within a multiplayer game, on a news site discussion forum, or through a viral marketing campaign – it becomes crucial to understand the roles of the producer and the consumer as (to some extent) interchangeable and (at the very least) interdependent. Cultural work (and thus the professional identities performed) is produced by all actors involved in the communicative process.

The creative industries approach thus can be seen as opening up a fertile, albeit far from unproblematic area for considering a future of cultural work, where professional identity is increasingly influenced and shaped by the various ways in which professionals interact with and give meaning to their publics as individuals beyond the affordances of social institutions.

Regardless of one's apprehension about the implications of integrating creativity with the market and, in a broader sense, culture with economy, a broad consideration of the social realities in cultural work does offer a number of important and fascinating insights into a more complex society where individualized work styles somehow find ways to retain a sense of what Ulrich Beck considers the zombie categories of modernity, while adapting to the conditions of contemporary liquid life, as articulated by Zygmunt Bauman throughout his work on the human condition. What makes the media as creative industries particular and special is not so much their awesome power to generate revenue and compellingly to entertain, but the ways in which commerce, creativity, content and connectivity as purposes and goals of individuals, organizations and transnational networks come together, blend and produce a wide variety of inputs and outcomes.

A model for cultural work

The ways in which media professionals give meaning to what they do – as documented in the literature, as articulated in the interviews we did, as visible in their expressions in trade magazines and on social media such as Twitter, where cultural workers tend to be quite active – are a primary source for understanding what it is like to work in the creative industries. This does not necessarily mean that people's lived experience of cultural work matches what actually happens, nor does it translate easily across the different industries and areas of production involved. On the other hand, there are striking similarities in these self-expressions. In fact, we find it profoundly useful to construct the discourse of media workers into several categories of values, goals and priorities that feature prominently in their everyday strategies and tactics. Regardless of whether a media worker is (or considers herself to be) successful, or whether the measure of that 'success' conforms to traditional notions of good (or bad) work, the value set she deploys to articulate that struggle (or joyride) remains largely constructed out of the same principal components.

Doing cultural work shows that the market does not rule with an iron fist, that informal networks exist side by side with sedimented structures and routines, that the production process includes as well as excludes both commercial aspiration and creative impulse, and that the democratic nature of convergence culture is both a bottom-up (user-generated content) as well as a top-down (cross-media marketing and franchising) trend. Within this complicated frame of reference, the individual tends to stand alone – both in terms of labour protections (or, rather, the lack thereof) and regarding sense making processes. In terms of cultural (or media) work, what gets produced refers not only to spoken and written words, audio, still or moving images, but (and increasingly) also to providing platforms for people to make, edit and exchange their own content. What makes up one's professional identity within today's creative industries involves four constituent elements: content, connectivity, creativity and commerce. Professionals in media industries in particular and creative industries more generally produce content, yes, but also invest in platforms for connectivity – where fans and audiences provide free labour. Media work is culture creation, yes, but tends to take place within a distinctly commercial context.

Within a context of destabilizing legacy industries and dissolving boundaries between media consumption and production, the media worker may feel individually isolated. However, this isolation can give some creative control to the media professional as well. Arthur (1994) suggests that creating a career without boundaries could be the best, if not only, way to survive in the current work environment. To some extent, individuals can be seen as taking control of their career paths, resulting in a new type of self-directed job security. It is also possible that those who are willing to train themselves become more attractive to management. By being proficient in various methods of media production, workers can use multiple creative talents to their advantage – or are increasingly expected to be doing so.

Whereas for most workers in traditional temporary and contingent settings their employment situation is far from ideal, many in the higher-skilled, knowledge-based areas of the labour market seem to prefer such precarious working conditions, associating this with greater individual autonomy, the acquisition of a wide variety of skills and experiences, and a reduced dependence on a single employer. The portfolio work style of the self-employed information or cultural worker/entrepreneur can be characterized by living in a state of constant change, while at the same time seemingly enjoying a sense of control over one's own career. Zygmunt Bauman warns against overtly optimistic readings of the relative freedom that these prime beneficiaries of inevitably inequitable globalization claim to enjoy: 'We are called to believe today that security is disempowering, disabling, breeding the resented "dependency" and altogether constraining the human agents' freedom. What is passed over in silence is that acrobatics and rope-walking without a safety net are an art that few people can master and a recipe for disaster for all the rest' (quoted in Bauman and Tester 2001: 52). Freedom and security, often seen as mutually exclusive, become ambiguous in the context of how different people from different walks of life deal with, and give meaning to, the consequences of not having either. It is perhaps the perfect paradox: all the trends in today's work life quite clearly suggest a rapid destabilization of social bonds corresponding with increasingly disempowering effects of a fickle and uncertain global high-tech information economy, yet those workers caught in the epicentre of this bewildering shift also express a sense of mastery over their lives, interpreting their professional identity in this context in terms of individual-level control and empowering agency. Melissa Gregg (2011) shows how this interpretative process is part and parcel of being part of a community of peers in cultural work, and sometimes quite willingly includes self-delusions of making it work, while, from an outsider's point of view, the professional involved clearly does not. What explains this element of more or less deliberate negotiation of otherwise debilitating forms of labour exploitation – rampant unpaid ('spec') work, expectations of 24/7 engagement, a mutually enforced always-on mentality, and experiencing no control over one's future under the guise of a 'nobody knows' mantra and the disempowering effects of generally operating in a labour context without traditional lines of feedback and support – is the fact that cultural work tends to be affective. The professional identity of your job in the creative industries tends to have meaning beyond instrumental functionality as something that earns you a living. The fact that people who do cultural work often deeply care about what they do not only opens up more opportunities for exploitation, but can also be seen as raising the stakes for a personalized sense of professional identity as a coping mechanism that can be self-delusional as well as empowering.

In the everyday construction of a sense of self for cultural workers – that which leads to a more or less coherent (or at least imagined) professional identity – it is the interplay between the values of providing content, organizing connectivity, managing creative freedom and being commercially successful (which is not necessarily an expression in monetary terms) that structures one's negotiations. The external factors intervening and complicating these everyday negotiations are many. Key historically continuous elements include the uneven structure of ownership over cultural products and the control of its modes of distribution (where in all industries a handful of major corporations and holding firms operate vis-à-vis many smaller or independently operating enterprises), an overall lack of adequate legal protections for atypically employed workers, as well as a profound age, gender and life phase imbalance throughout the creative industries (featuring a workflow that tends to privilege young men living in unmarried and childless circumstances). These structural elements of the identity equation are not particular to the early 21st century, and are not experienced in the same way by everyone involved in cultural work. However, their omnipresence co-determines deliberations about one's choices and priorities when considering a career in cultural work.

Although the role of technology is a continual one, there can be said to be something quite particular about the current media ecosystem within which cultural work takes place. This primarily has to do with the disruptive potential of increasingly ubiquitous and pervasive information and communication technologies, wrestling control over all aspects of the media value chain – especially production, marketing and distribution – away from gatekeepers such as record labels in the music industry, distributors in the film industry and publishers in the games industry. In a real sense, these trends further contribute to the individualization process in cultural work, as the artist – whether a fashion designer, intrepid reporter or aspiring movie maker – is considered to be individually empowered by relatively cheap and easy-to-use technologies to do 'their own thing' and be successful at that. Celebratory accounts of formerly unknown individuals striking it 'big' through massively popular songs or videos on YouTube obscure the significant investments made by individuals to make it work both within and outside of creative industries, and thus tend to highlight product over process. Notions of long-term affective investment in one's craft or art get sidelined in favour of often one-time oversized success (in turn generally only assessed through rather traditional industrial metrics, such as number of hits/visitors/likes/retweets/copies sold).

It is within this system of variables that the individual media professional can be expected to be outlining his or her sense of professional identity in terms of the stories they want to tell (content), their relationship with audiences and publics (connectivity), their particular perception of what kind of work they aspire to (creativity), and the role that success in whatever shape or form plays in all of this (commerce).

Professional identity in theory

The impact of the key values outlined in our model – content, connectivity, creativity and commerce – on the professional identity of media workers emphasizes the continuous negotiation processes going on regarding the individual media actor – a negotiation between the dynamics of the cultural worker as a person and as a professional, each of which functions with its own characteristics, conditions, perceptions and (thus) factors of influence on creative decision making and media production. In this respect, van Zoonen (1998) and others tend to refer to issues of 'organizational identity' in a media profession such as journalism, which refers to the agency of journalists as shaped by the constant interplay between structural constraints of the media production process on the one hand, and the influence of a wide array of subjective personal aspects that journalists bring to the job. Randy Beam (1990) has argued that the process of professionalism in journalism can be defined by looking at the identity of journalists as an organizational-level concept in terms of the success of journalists in gaining control over the products and production processes within their organization.

The rich literature on social identity, organizational identity and corporate identity in companies tends to draw distinctions between different levels of analysis: the 'individual (relating to people's personal sense of self within the organization), group (relating to the shared identity of teams and sections within an organization), organizational (relating to the identity of the organization as a whole) and cultural (relating to commonalities in identity across organizations and within a society as a whole)' (Cornelissen *et al.* 2007: S2–3).

According to social identity theory (as originally voiced by Henri Tajfel and John Turner in the 1970s), an individual has multiple selves that align to specific membership groups. Indeed, media workers are likely to engage those multiple selves at individual, group, organizational and cultural levels. Their professional identities are directly affected by how much they consider themselves to be a 'part' of cultural work and all levels of categorization that entails. As media actors internalize specific group memberships as part of their identity, they also seek the positive self-esteem that results from those group memberships. Accordingly, how media workers self-identify, behave and adopt shared attitudes has traditionally been largely dependent on their immediate peer group and organization's reputation. Beyond industrial parameters, the norms and constraints that exist in the creative industries influence how media workers place themselves within their environment. The structure of social identification in creative industries can be said to have three more or less distinctive variations. First, through participation in communities of practice that gets determined by co-location, for example working in the same space or workplace: a studio, an office building, an artists' collective. Identification tends to follow patterns of socialization into a relatively well-established set of routines and relationships on the work floor; journalists in particular are good examples of cultural workers being thusly drafted into the professional ideology of journalism as practised in a particular news organization. Second, through similar patterns of professional participation which are, however, much more short lived and temporary, such as within groups or teams of co-workers on a movie set, or among members of a projectized working arrangement at an advertising agency. Professional identity thus follows both collective as well as individualized trajectories, whereby people bring to the new constellation their experiences of previous practices, while at the same time carving out the 'new' rules of the informal hierarchies and ways of doing things of the temporary arrangement in which they find themselves. Third, and increasingly, cultural work takes place in relative isolation – especially in the digital realm of software development and games design, but also in all kinds of other sectors of the creative industries (one could think of film post-production, audio mixing, clothing design, freelance reporting, video production, so on and so forth; see Elefante and Deuze 2012 for a case study).

Working in the creative industries would seem to allow the individual to identify themselves as a single producer of content and as part of a larger whole, whereas the intermediate level of the company or organization seems to disappear. One's peer group gets more established through informal networks – meeting now and then at a local pub to discuss one's working experiences working for disparate employers – and social media (such as Twitter and LinkedIn) than through collegial encounters on a work floor. It is in this context that one could understand the popularity of cultural work co-operatives (offering individual members joint working spaces, organizing workshops, providing equipment and so on) as not just providing professional empowerment to a fragmented workforce, but also allowing one to sustain a sense of collective social identity as a cultural worker.

As individuals in the workforce increasingly either choose to or are forced to build their own support structures, they must do so within the context of a peer group and some kind of organization, creating connections between the individual and the organization that are short term, contingent and rootless. Lack of stability and comfort in the current position one is in present further obstacles to establishing a more or less coherent sense of professional identity, requiring a delicate balance of responsibility and accountability to themselves and within the larger context of the provisional group.

A more singular view of professional identity is warranted when assessing contemporary changes and challenges to media work in general and journalism in particular, since it does not assume that a professional is necessarily situated within a given medium-specific organizational context. Such an assumption is hard to maintain in the current context where media professionals can be seen as having multiple organizational identities – through working for different realms within one or more organization(s), windowing content cross-media, freelancing or producing content independent from organizational constructs (for example, as bloggers or copywriters), and not least by competing for editorial space with consumers as co-creators of cultural content and experiences.

Professional identity in practice

The work of authors in various fields defines media content today as increasingly consumer generated, customer controlled or user directed (see for an overview Deuze 2007: 99). Researchers in different disciplines signal a corresponding industry-wide turn towards seeing the consumer as co-creator in cultural work, particularly where the cultural industries' core commodity is (mediated) information. Online, media participation can be seen as the defining characteristic of the Internet in terms of its hyperlinked, interactive and networked infrastructure and digital culture. None of this is essentially new, nor is it necessarily tied to the Internet. Yet it must be argued that continuous blurring of the real or perceived boundaries between making and using media by professionals as well as amateurs ('pro-ams') has been supercharged in recent years – particularly in terms of its omnipresence and visibility online. Bucy and Gregson (2001), for example, suggest how a growing frustration and scepticism among the public regarding the highly staged, professionalized and exclusionary nature of mediated reality in fact has pushed people towards pursuing alternative – include their own – media formats.

People who make media have collaborated with those who used media in the past. Many of the great works of art came into being because rich patrons commissioned painters and sculptors to make specific portraits, decorations and other representations signifying status and prestige in society. Such works were not just created by single art 'producers', but often through intense collaboration and exchange by dedicated teams of artists, their apprentices, sponsors and visitors. Participation as a value and expectation in journalism was first established through 'letters to the editor' sections in newspapers, and later expanded to include functions like newspaper ombudsmen and reader representatives which became an accepted part of news organizations worldwide. All areas of the creative industries – advertising, marketing communications and public relations, journalism, architecture, (visual and performing) arts and crafts, design, fashion, film, video and photography, software, computer games, music, publishing, television, radio – have historical trajectories that show how the oft-maintained distinction between production and consumption in cultural work is quite artificial, largely serving to sustain discursive structures of power and control within creative hierarchies (seeing the 'artist' as intrinsically more enlightened than the 'audience' or, in the case of a radical democratization theory of digital culture, the other way around; see Benkler 2006).

A consequence of the new media environment is the shift of power to the audience, both in power of resources and power of selection. This presents a double-edged sword to professional media workers. For established professionals, it becomes more difficult to utilize their power in the industry. For up-and-coming newbies, there are more tools and opportunities to break into the field. The lines between production and consumption continue to be drawn, erased and redrawn, all of which takes place within an industrial context offering a fascinating blend of large multinational corporations and grassroots initiatives, predicating an hourglass structure of cultural employment where few networked companies employ thousands of people worldwide, while most of the production of content and experiences in media takes place in thousands of tiny companies often employing less than a handful of people.

Indeed, media participation is a phenomenon at once top-down and bottom-up, involving both elites – such as politicians operating their own profile pages on social networking sites and corporate weblogs often operated by ghostwriters – and the multitude. In this process of amplified interaction and heightened mutual mediated awareness, the process of media production and dissemination also becomes more transparent and open to external intervention, giving users increasing communication power both outside of and within corporate industrial contexts. Henry Jenkins typifies the current media ecology in practical terms as driven by *convergence culture*, defining the trend as:

> … both a top-down corporate-driven process and a bottom-up consumer-driven process. Media companies are learning how to accelerate the flow of media content across delivery channels to expand revenue opportunities,

> broaden markets and reinforce viewer commitments. Consumers are learning how to use these different media technologies to bring the flow of media more fully under their control and to interact with other users.
>
> (Jenkins 2004: 37)

In practical terms, Jenkins's convergence culture highlights the pressure on cultural workers to strike a balance – for every project – between the 'auteur' ideal of creating *content* and compelling user experiences, and the often considered as oppositional value of providing people with platforms for *connectivity* and sharing their own free labour. This precarious balancing act between content and connectivity benchmarks cultural work, and leads journalism scholars such as Jane Singer (1998) to signal the end of the 'gatekeeper' as an appropriate metaphor for a journalist's professional identity – an identity according to Bruns (2005) better described as a 'gatewatcher': monitoring rather than reporting news, managing rather than filtering information.

Participatory media production and individualized media consumption are two different yet co-constituent trends typifying an emerging media ecology determining the direction of cultural workers' professional identities – an environment where consuming media increasingly includes some kind of producing media, and where people's media behaviour always seems to involve some level of participation, co-creation and collaboration, depending on the degree of openness or closedness of the media involved. The concepts of 'open' and 'closed' media in this context refer to the extent to which a given media company or site of cultural work shares some or all of its modes of operation with its target publics. A media organization can, for example, increase the level of transparency of how it works, or can opt to give its customers more control over their user experience. Yet, as McChesney and Schiller (2003) remind us, the same communication technologies that enable interactivity and participation are wielded to foster the entrenchment and growth of a global corporate media system that can be said to be anything but transparent, interactive or participatory. Bagdikian (2004) argues that five corporations – Time Warner, Disney, NewsCorp, Bertelsmann and Viacom – control most of the media industry in the USA and, indeed, across the globe. This control must not be exaggerated, however, and Compaine (2005) among others presents evidence that worldwide media consolidation and increased diversity of choice or genuine competition in the production and distribution of content are not anathema. In the context of the model we propose, these trends must be seen as co-existing and symbiotic. Evidence collected for the media industries by Perren and Holt (2009), the service industries by Flew (2004) and the manufacturing industries by von Hippel (2005) suggests that much of this consumer co-creation is in fact instigated within (or appropriated by) corporations for distinctly commercial purposes. The *creativity* of workers – paid and unpaid alike – throughout the creative industries thus must be always considered within the competing as well as enabling framework of *commerce*.

It is crucial to note that the delicate dance of cultural work in convergence culture is not a phenomenon particular to the contemporary context. All elements of Jenkins's framework have a lineage that traces back well into the earliest days of cultural industries, indeed all forms of cultural production. The stranglehold of the major business entities in most creative industries over financing, organization of labour, mode of distribution, as well as promotion and marketing, is a much more recent phenomenon, and, however optimistic some of the readings of cultural workers' individual agency and cultural productions' convergence may be, uneven and exploitative relationships remain a significant structural factor in how one's professional identity gets shaped and correspondingly shapes the political economy of cultural work. This last point is significant in its suggestion that much of the precarity of media work is in fact maintained by individuals trying to 'make it work' within the system – for example, by not collectively organizing, and by acquiescing to free labour and speculative work. In the same vein, one cannot conclude that 'the corporation' is the source of all constraints on the development of a professional identity in cultural work.

Conclusion

Convergence culture particularly impacts on both sides – structure and subjectivity – of professional identities in cultural work. Elements of structure are: the status and protection (by law) of the profession, ethical guidelines of one's organization (if any), budgets, preferred sources (every media organization has its own range of experts), market characteristics, set routines and rituals on the work floor, ownership and so on. Subjectivities are those things that an individual cultural worker brings to the job at hand: upbringing, life cycle and life phase, motivation and commitment, family situation, current relationships, political views and role models. In terms of subjectivities, convergence culture adds a new type of media worker to the agency equation: the 'produser' (Bruns 2005). This is someone with whom professionals now have to compete for a chance to create content, and to get the attention of consumers, competitor colleagues and advertisers. As the 'produser' is generally someone who does not get paid, and he or she contributes unpredictably (and often using anonymous aliases or avatars), this new entry into the media production sphere is both ubiquitous as well as imperceptible. On the structural side, convergence culture introduces a constantly changing mix of features, contexts, processes and ideas into the work of individual workers as their employers, organizations and working environments get reshuffled under the managerial impetus of integration and expectation of synergy. This, in combination with changes in (international) media law – making it easier for transnational corporations to own, sell or integrate their holdings, while still controlling all copyrights and intellectual property – and a gradual erosion of union or trade association membership and protection, amplifies the precariousness of media work today.

Theorizing professional identities in cultural work needs to take into consideration both the theory and practice of convergence culture as it is articulated with the values that drive the creation of media content and experiences. To some extent, these values – content versus connectivity, creativity versus commerce – are not new, nor are they necessarily specific to cultural work. Within the contemporary media ecology, these values get new articulation and produce new challenges for workers. It is important to note the potential for exploitation, precarity and marginalization of cultural workers that all of this engenders, as well as how the same forces open up new opportunities, can be empowering and give rise to exciting forms of creative production. We are less impressed by the efforts of commercial companies to exploit their workers than the effect laws and policies are having on the work that producers as well as consumers of media do: with the crackdown on copyright violations, the ongoing global criminalization of convergence culture-inspired behaviour (cf. sharing and forwarding content), and the relatively lawless context within which both multinational corporations and individual cultural workers do what they do, it seems that this is a key area for critical analysis and active intervention.

Media workers need to determine their own destiny and create an identity by inventing new institutions on their own terms, perhaps uniting in more informal and international contexts. Seen as such, the deconstruction of union and trade associations can lend power to the individual. Without the barriers of membership, including formal rules and fees, media workers can initiate meaningful, if temporary, connections with a variety of networks. In today's media landscape, these new social, group and organizational connections may be without roots, but perhaps this is just the next step in development of media work. The challenge is to ensure that new connections have value and meaning.

Notes

1 The authors here represent The Janissary Collective – an informal writers' collective based at Indiana University. Established in 2009, the Collective is a writers' group consisting of students (both graduate and undergraduate) and faculty advocating a militant rejection of disciplinary dogma, and an aggressive pursuit of free thinking beyond traditional theories, paradigms and methods. The group consists of people from units across campus, including Telecommunications, Learning Sciences, Journalism, Informatics, and Communication and Culture.
2 See en.wikipedia.org/wiki/Tim_Gunn.
3 See en.wikipedia.org/wiki/Creative_industries.

14 Theorizing cultural work

An interview with the Editors

Andrew Ross

QUESTION FROM THE EDITORS: The cultural and creative industries have always been discussed as a global sector, even though there are undoubted variations and inequalities between and within different countries and regions, and contrasts in specific policy rhetorics. What would you see as the distinctive aspects and issues around cultural work in the US at present?

ANDREW ROSS: In the United States, these industries tend to view themselves as global market leaders, and there are government agencies that promote their positions in the global market through all kinds of trade policy initiatives, most conspicuously in the strong-arming efforts to protect intellectual property and enforce intellectual property licensing overseas. The wave of creative industries policy making in other countries in the 2000s was often presented as a catch-up initiative, especially again in a bid to grab a chunk of the fast-moving economic landscape around IP [intellectual property]. This situation gave rise to the illusory perception that the US does no policy making in this sector, which is complete nonsense. Ever since the US became an IP exporter, government officials have been in the business of looking after, and assisting, the rent-seeking of corporations in the culture business.

From the point of view of employees, the situation is more mixed. The traditional media and entertainment industries are still heavily unionized, or have craft guilds that protect pay scales and workplace standards, though they cannot and have never been able to guarantee steady work. At the other, deregulated, end of the spectrum is the burgeoning urban freelancing sector, where independent employees subsist from project to project, navigating digital pathways to the attention economy. Customarily, this divide reflects whether your work is below or above the talent line. The line is reflected in other ways in adjacent industries, such as telecommunications, where the landline infrastructure is maintained by union employees, while the workforce for mobile telecom is non-union.

Q: Given this variety, how far do you think the idea of 'cultural work' continues to offer an identifiable or appropriate object of intellectual discussion? Has the global financial crisis and economic recession changed the way we should think about cultural and creative industries?

AR: The recession has been so long and its impact so deep that patterns of employment generated by the shortfall in economic activity may well have turned into more permanent shifts or transformations of work mentality. This is perhaps more noticeable in the sector of cultural work, broadly defined, because of the intensification of precarious labour conditions endemic to that sector. In particular, I think we have seen an upsurge in unpaid, or token-wage, work. Indeed, a cynic might well conclude that 'working for nothing' is the latest high-growth jobs sector, and a substantial portion of that economic activity might be classified as cultural in nature.

Some of these forms of unpaid labour are new, and are occurring as part of the ongoing transfer of work to digital platforms. Others seem to be upgrades of existing patterns, or they entail the conversion of formerly paid positions to unpaid ones, as is the case with internships. Still others rest on the industrial uptake of amateurism and volunteerism as the price of entry into the cultural marketplace of rewards for youthful effort.

Q: What is the role of the digital in this particular context?

AR: In the realm of digital labour, I have in mind the following:

a) The establishment of free online media content as an industrial norm. This has taken a predictable toll on the pay scales of professional writers, and we hear a lot about it because these writers have ready access to the platform to broadcast their complaints.

b) The extensive data mining from social media platforms like Facebook, which takes advantage of amateur users' aspirations to build, polish and 'market' their online identities.

c) E-lance programs like Amazon's Mechanical Turk, which allocate micro-tasks that may take no more than a few minutes to perform but which can add up to a minor source of revenue for taskers.

d) Crowdsourcing, especially of creative or interesting work, and the evidence shows that the more creative the request, the more obliging the crowd in coming up with free solutions.

e) A host of other sophisticated digital techniques (involving the use of personalized algorithms) for extracting rents from user/participants.

These are all forms of 'distributed labour' that tap the use of the Internet to mobilize the spare processing power of a widely dispersed crowd of discrete individuals. None of them comes close to any definition of non-standard employment used by the Bureau of Labor Statistics, yet they are sources of sizable revenue and profit to knowledge firms. You need only look at the ratio of earnings to employees of leading information services firms like Google and Facebook to see one very influential model for the future of capitalism – each firm posts billions of dollars of profits, while maintaining a very small paid workforce – their astronomical earnings rest on the unpaid input of users.

Q: Concerns about unpaid internships have begun to receive political attention in the UK. Do you think the trend towards their use has peaked?

AR: Internships have become near-obligatory in the cultural sector, and increasingly they are unpaid positions. My students are more familiar with the ubiquitous phrase 'internship opportunities' than they are with 'job opportunities', and somewhere in the back of my head I am hearing the immortal words of The Clash: 'Career opportunities are the ones that never knock'. Internships are no longer a rite of passage into the professional service sector. For many, they are becoming a terminal limbo, not unlike the time spent by graduate students in teaching, which is no longer a term of apprenticeship, but, practically speaking, the end of their teaching career. In the last few years, unpaid internships have become the norm, and, according to Ross Perlin's estimate from a few years ago, cumulatively provide a $2 billion subsidy to employers in the US alone. As the market for internships develops, these unpaid positions are being openly sold, with the more sought-after placements generating large returns that will surely amplify this subsidy in the near future. Much of this labour activity does not get officially recorded, and a goodly portion of it is illegal. Financing an unpaid internship, or a series of them, is usually only within the reach of families with wealth, and so there is a clear class divide opening up between those who can afford to graduate from the unpaid positions into the prestige institutions of cultural workers and those who cannot. Conservatives are increasingly on solid ground when they carp about the 'cultural elite'.

Q: Class is certainly one issue, but in the UK, at least, the possibility of entering and securing a position in the cultural and creative industries – whether through internships or otherwise – has become more, rather than less, difficult for women and ethnic minorities. What are your thoughts on why this has become such a prominent failing of the sector?

AR: The evidence is that the unpaid internships are disproportionately occupied by females, so that's a significant obstacle, and surely that pattern feeds off the assumption that women are more socialized in the customary ways of doing sacrificial work. Nor is there any labour market without a gender pay gap. The pay gap by race has narrowed because of greater access to college education, but in recent years the mounting student debt burden has complicated that pattern. Minorities, as well as women, are disproportionately impacted by student debt, so, unless they are from prosperous, middle-class families that can see them through the unpaid internships, they are less likely to enter the cultural/creative workforce than white males from the same economic background. To the degree that any livelihood in this sector requires a debt-financed degree as an entry credential, then it will hold back the more indebted. Of course, this applies to many other professions, but none of them draws on the longstanding tradition of feast-and-famine livelihoods that cultural work does.

Q: For those without internships, or the facility to support one, there is always the possibility of one's own talent being recognized and cultivated, but why is this belief so prevalent when the chances of success are so slim?

AR: Contestant volunteering has transformed many sectors of the culture industries into an amateur talent show, with jackpot stakes for a few winners and hard-luck schwag for everyone else. The talent show/reality TV model has rapidly become an industry standard and, given the industry's influence among young people, it is becoming the normative work mentality for a generation of youth, with uncertain economic consequences. It used to be that the stars were in their own orbit, beyond reach. Now youth can see how quickly and easily fame can be achieved – with a little help from YouTube, you could be Justin Bieber too – the pathways are more democratic, and this has made the model of the talent contest all the more glamorous and seductive. For those who are persuaded to play (and it doesn't take much), the wages of industrialization are being replaced by the affective currency of attention and prestige – working for exposure – and their amateur labour buys them the equivalent of a lottery ticket in the livelihood sweepstakes. Is this emergent norm a significant shift beyond the more traditional use of 'auditioning' as a workforce entry model? Has the 'casting call' been industrialized as a more extensive mode of cultural production, relying on a free labour supply?

Q: Thinking in terms of the labour process, and the extent to which it has changed, there is now a well-established academic field that discusses cultural work in terms of its post-industrial 'individualization', 'precarity', 'immateriality' and 'self-exploitation', and so on, often with a strong emphasis on suggesting a profoundly new confluence of forces and effects that is somehow formally distinguishable from earlier periods. Does this emphasis on novelty still seem appropriate to you, or would you see more social precedent in current conditions?

AR: Yes, I do think that new work mentalities emerge under the conditions you are describing. 'Working for nothing', if it is emerging as an industrial norm, is a shift beyond the varieties of 'temping' that have characterized job casualization over the last few decades. It's also different from the fitful, lumpy or spiky income profiles that have long been associated with artists and other self-employed creatives. Precarity, as it was described by many scholars in the years before the financial crash, is being succeeded by an even more tenuous contractual relationship. Many of the new arrangements leave little trace of employment, and certainly nothing to implicate an employer in any legal or regulated network of obligations. Nor is the musicians' profile of 'gigs' any longer adequate as a label writ large for intermittent work. The patterns of expropriation may be more systematic than they are intermittent.

   Yet, even at the core of the new, there are always echoes of earlier ways of making a living. Take, for example, some of the arrangements I have described that are driven by the self-promotion of ordinary, unpaid individuals, attracted toward the entrepreneurial path of securing a niche in the attention economy. In some ways, this kind of conduct is more typical of a pre-industrial era, when the careful nurturing of attention from wealthy and powerful names or institutions were sources of considerable value and social mobility. So, if this is a move beyond temping, it's also a throwback to before the routines and standards of industrialization.

Q: What you seem to be suggesting is that there is some kind of re-traditionalization, even re-feudalization of the workplace – a return to a pre-modern mode before professional, waged artistic and creative labour, and to an economy of patronage and prestige? Is that what you're suggesting, and if so what are the wider implications?

AR: Feudalization might be pushing it, if only because feudal relations require some obligations on the part of the master, but there are pre-modern aspects to the lines of patronage and prestige. The difference, of course, is in the sheer mass of those competing for attention, and also that the patrons who bestow the attention are often quite ordinary audiences, and not executors of elite taste. Boosters will say that this represents a democratization of the process of 'getting ahead', and a more authentic form of talent market than one driven by nepotism and old boy networks. Critics see a debasement of cultural product through pandering, and the degradation of work standards by the ceaseless time and energy required to make useful contacts.

Q: In current conditions, projective talk about the cultural or creative economy is now considerably quieter, though still occasionally audible. What are your own expectations and hopes or fears for the sector, and for the workers of today and tomorrow?

AR: Clearly, the hype, in the 2000s, about creativity was not likely to be sustainable. Urban managers, for example, were very interested in the turnaround economic potential of Richard Florida's creative class paradigm, and rushed to promote their metro areas as creative cities, but much of that wilted along with the housing crash. After all, they were primarily interested in how the presence of creatives would boost rents and land values. Creative industry policy making, also distinctive of that period, has become both more routine and more fractious because of the copyfights over intellectual property. The struggle waged by artists' communities against neoliberal bureaucrats has sharpened – the ham-handed efforts to establish Creative Scotland is a good case study of this – and it continues to generate critical debates about the public function of culture and the livelihoods that culture supports. These debates might not have taken shape in a more complacent environment but they have received a good airing because of the conflict.

One of the outcomes is that cultural workers are much more conscious of their labour conditions and their serviceability to corporate and political elites than they were 10 or 15 years ago. Much more likely to stand up for their rights not to be exploited or showcased without compensation.

In that earlier time, there was more attention to the culture wars, and the conditions of expression as they related to traditions of artistic freedom. When bureaucrats carved out the 'cultural sector' and the 'creative industries', they made creatives more conscious of themselves as workers. There are some virtues to this, in my view. Creatives are less likely to see their labour as exceptional (in line with the legacy of the Romantic cult of the artist), and more inclined to see their livelihood as fully worldly.

Q: One concern for Anglo-American academics recently has been the extent to which cultural and creative work has provided a model for 'good' or 'bad' work, including through the supposed promise of self-actualization. At this point, what are your thoughts on the nature of 'good work' and the range of potential 'goods' available to workers?

AR: On the one hand, we have seen how the gratification that comes with creative work is a double-edged sword. Everyone should have access to passionate, fulfilling work, but we also know that this pleasure is seen as a bonus for which the worker pays through discounted compensation. In some respects, this is a form of wage theft – since employers will factor in workplace gratification as a reward in and of itself, built into any compensation package. For those who are able to get by, the trade-off is acceptable, it's one they can live with, on an individual basis – though let's be clear that the class profile that accompanies this choice is a genteel one, traditionally speaking. When the cultural discount becomes an industrial principle, however, then it is more flatly exploitative, and is often experienced as such. By industrial, I mean the norms that are established throughout a sector, even one with participants that are widely distributed and spatially disaggregated. The 'goods', or advantages, for those who can access and enjoy them fully, are the freedoms of the independent worker, over her schedules, choice of revenue sources, clients, workplace locations, not to mention the recognition that rewards well-turned work. However, we also know that these goods are trapdoors that open onto the vast pools of obligations and responsibilities that come with high-stress, self-directed work, and that those who don't have the 'right stuff' will be underwater for much of the time, with little chance of sharing the spoils equitably. The more free that work is, the less just it is likely to be.

Q: You've referred to the 'goods' associated with cultural work, yet 'ordinary' or non-cultural work has always had its goods too, including, to varying degrees of course, pay, social contact, life-anchoring routine, and the stimulation and satisfaction that can follow from expertise and accomplishment. Why do you think it happened that the goods of ordinary work seemed to fall out of the limelight at a particular historical juncture and cultural work came to seem so desirable by comparison?

AR: Promoters of the good side of post-Fordism always made the case that 'craft' was being reinvented and revalorized as part of the shift toward the provision of value added goods for the high-end consumer market, but you don't have to look very far to see evidence that younger people are learning and, in some cases, resurrecting, artisanal work: skills in farming, for example, and food preparation for the more choosy corners of the food movement; carpentry and metalwork; clothing design and fabrication; not to mention the whole new world of digital know-how and self-application. Most of these areas are 'ordinary', and not usually classed as 'cultural', and they are flourishing, primarily as pursuits of the educated middle class who are making an art out of the production of basics (William Morris would approve!). The masculinist side of this has been celebrated in books like Matthew Crawford's *Shop Class as Soulcraft*, and Richard Sennett's *The Craftsman*, while the wave of domestic craftivism has been embraced by feminists like Betsy Greer around the Etsy network.

As for the continuing production of mass goods, we know how that story is playing out in offshore locations in Central America, Eastern Europe and North Africa, and especially in East Asia, where we have seen industrialization in high Fordist mode, with all the attendant toll on substandard working conditions and alienation of the human spirit.

Q: To return to the present, what kinds of politics are appropriate for intervening in the current moment? Are there connections between the politics of cultural work, the precarity movement and those of Occupy? What kinds of impact are the financial crisis, recession and austerity having on politics in cultural work?

AR: A variety of semi-organized initiatives have sprung up to counteract the erosion of fair labour standards in a few of the areas I mentioned. Some of the remedies are aimed at bringing unpaid labour practices into line with existing laws and workplace regulations. Others are focused on pioneering and setting new standards for independent workers. Few of them fall within the traditional orbit of the trade union movement, though some of them may well spark new forms of worker protection and organization, along the model of workers' centres, or pioneer alternatives such as the Freelancers Union, which is the fastest growing union in New York and Los Angeles, with offshoots beginning to appear in cities like Toronto. Even in the most unlikely sectors we are seeing these initiatives – the Model Alliance here in New York, which is pushing labour standards and protection for vulnerable young women in the fashion industry who are subject to child labour violations, sexual abuse, and who are often paid with only the clothes they model.

Within Occupy, I have been very active with anti-debt organizing initiatives (see www.strikedebt.org), and so I tend to see many things now through the lens of debt. Now that more and more of our basic social needs are being debt-financed, our level of indebtedness has become a major factor in how people prepare for employability, and in how they choose livelihoods. Borrowing, especially of education debt, is increasingly consuming our futures.

In the course of industrialization, the conflict over wages emerged as the central organizing principle for labour. In societies like ours, which are heavily financialized, the struggle over debt is increasingly the front-line conflict. Not because wage conflict is over (it never will be), but because debts, for most people, are quite literally the wages of the future.

For folks going into the cultural work sector, an increasingly larger share of their income is going to servicing the debts incurred simply to prepare themselves for employability and to meet the basic mental and physical requirements demanded for modern work. Debt service, in that regard, is a form of indirect wage theft on the part of the finance industry, and for those who will be paying off their student loans for their entire working lives, it is a form of indenture – going into debt in order to labour is the essential principle of indenture.

Our work has been to encourage debtors to seek relief for themselves – legislators are not going to do this – and we favour debt resistance in the form of organized, public strikes. Many of the people with whom I have been organizing the Strike Debt initiative are drawn from the Arts and Labor working group of Occupy Wall Street. They came into the movement because they see a direct relationship between their cultural work and the politics of debt.

Q: Do these or other initiatives lead you to retain any optimism or positive feeling about the future of cultural work?

AR: Well, it looks like there is going to be more, rather than less, cultural work, so I suppose that's good. If the trends I've outlined are accurate, much of that work will be beyond precarious, which is to say barely compensated, unless the organizing initiatives gain strength and clout, which I also expect to happen. So I am optimistic about the organizing part, notwithstanding how challenging it will be.

Second, just as the mergers and acquisitions continue among multinational corporations, concentrating more and more ownership of culture in fewer hands, we will also see a steady move towards the 'commons' among younger folks involved in arts and culture. If social democracy continues to erode, then the anarchist outlines of an alternative economy, based on mutual aid, will emerge – indeed, that is already the dominant mentality of progressive youth. That doesn't mean the state won't come back into the picture in some form other than its current neoliberal one; it will just have to be reinvented before young people will connect to it.

Bibliography

Accenture (2012) 'Global Delivery: Services Overview', www.accenture.com/za-en/Pages/service-technology-global-delivery-sourcing-overview.aspx (accessed 5 March 2012).

Acker, J. (1990) 'Hierarchies, Jobs, Bodies: A Theory of Gendered Organizations', *Gender and Society* 4: 139–58.

Adkins, L. (1999) 'Community and Economy: A Retraditionalization of Gender?' *Theory, Culture and Society* 16(1): 117–37.

——(2001) 'Cultural Feminisation: "Money, Sex and Power" for Women', *Signs* 26(3): 669–95.

——(2002) *Revisions: Gender and Sexuality in Late Modernity*, Buckingham and Philadelphia: Open University Press.

——(2005) 'The New Economy, Property and Personhood' *Theory, Culture & Society* 10: 323–39.

——(2008) 'From Retroactivation to Futurity: The End of the Sexual Contract', *NORA – Nordic Journal of Feminist and Gender Research* 16(3): 182–201.

——(2009) 'Creative Biographies', Symposium, Open University, UK, April.

——(2009a) 'Feminism After Measure', *Feminist Theory* 10(3): 323–39.

——(2009b) 'Sociological Futures: From Clock Time to Event Time', *Sociological Research Online* 14(4): 8, www.socresonline.org.uk/14/4/8.html (accessed 28 June 2012).

——(2011) 'Money is Time: Temporalisation, Economic Crisis and Bourdieu', *Gender and Cultural Studies Seminar*, University of Sydney, March.

Adkins, L. and Lury, C. (2012) *Measure and Value*, Wiley.

Adorno, T. (2010) 'Functionalism Today', in G. Adamson (ed.) *The Craft Reader*, Oxford: Berg.

Ahlering, B. and Deakin, S. (2007) 'Labour Regulation, Corporate Governance, and Legal Origin: A Case of Institutional Complementarity?' *Law and Society Review* 41: 865–908.

Amabile, T. (1983) *The Social Psychology of Creativity*, New York: Springer-Verlag.

——(1996) *Creativity in Context: Update to 'The Social Psychology of Creativity'*, Boulder, CO: Westview Press.

——(2001) 'Beyond Talent: John Irving and the Passionate Craft of Creativity', *American Psychologist* 56.4: 333–36.

Anderson, P., Folker, F., Jürgen, H. and Kreye, O. (1987) 'On Some Postulates of an Anti-systemic Policy', *Dialectical Anthropology* 12: 1–13.

Aneesh, A. (2006) *Virtual Migration: The Programming of Globalization*, Durham: Duke University Press.

Apple (2009) *Supplier Responsibility: 2009 Progress Report*, images.apple.com/supplierresponsibility/pdf/SR_2009_Progress_Report.pdf.

——(2010) *Supplier Responsibility: 2010 Progress Report*, images.apple.com/supplierresponsibility/pdf/SR_2010_Progress_Report.pdf.

——(2011) *Supplier Responsibility: 2011 Progress Report*, images.apple.com/supplierresponsibility/pdf/Apple_SR_2011_Progress_Report.pdf.

——(2012a) *Supplier Responsibility: 2012 Progress Report*, images.apple.com/supplierresponsibility/pdf/Apple_SR_2012_Progress_Report.pdf.

——(2012b) *Supplier List 2011*, images.apple.com/supplierresponsibility/pdf/Apple_Supplier_List_2011.pdf.

Arendt, H. (1998) *The Human Condition*, 2nd edn, University of Chicago Press.

Arons, M. (1996) 'Frank Barron and the Creativity Revolution', in A. Montuori (ed.) *Unusual Associates: A Festschrift for Frank Barron*, Cresskill, NJ: Hampton.

Arthur, M. (1994) 'The Boundaryless Career: A New Perspective for Organizational Inquiry', *Journal of Organizational Behaviour* 15(4): 295–306.

Arts Council England (2009) 'Do it Yourself: Cultural and Creative Self Employment in Hard Times', www.artscouncil.org.uk/media/uploads/downlloads/ndotm.pdf (accessed 3 January 2012).

Ashton, D. (2011) 'Upgrading the Self: Technology and the Self in the Digital Games Perpetual Innovation Economy', *Convergence* Vol. 17: 307–21

Australian Research Council Centre of Excellence for Creative Industries and Innovation, Queensland University of Technology and Games Developers' Association of Australia (2011) *Working in Australia's Digital Games Industry: Consolidation Report*, Brisbane: Australian Research Council Centre of Excellence for Creative Industries and Innovation, Queensland University of Technology, and Games Developers' Association of Australia.

Bagdikian, B. (2004) *The New Media Monopoly*, Boston: Beacon Press.

Bair, J. (ed.) (2009) *Frontiers of Commodity Chain Research*, Stanford: Stanford University Press.

Baldas, T. (2008) 'Is Booting Up a Computer Work, or a Work Break?' *Law.com*, www.law.com/jsp/nlj/PubArticleNLJ.jsp?id=1202426038668&slreturn=1&hbxlogin=1 (accessed 31 July 2011).

Balfour, F. and Culpan, T. (2010) 'The Man Who Makes your iPhone', *Bloomberg Business Week*, 9 September, www.businessweek.com/magazine/content/10_38/b4195058423479.htm.

Banks, J. and Deuze, M. (2009) 'Co-Creative Labor', *International Journal of Cultural Studies* 12, No. 5: 419–31.

Banks, J. and Humphreys, S. (2008) 'The Labour of User Co-Creators', *Convergence: The International Journal of Research into New Media Technologies* 14, No. 4: 401–18.

Banks, M. (2006) 'Moral Economy and Cultural Work', *Sociology* 40(3): 455–72.

——(2007) *The Politics of Cultural Work*, London: Palgrave Macmillan.

——(2010) 'Craft Labour and Creative Industries', *International Journal of Cultural Policy* 16(3): 305–21.

——(2010a) 'Autonomy Guaranteed? Cultural Work and the "Art-commerce Relation"', *Journal for Cultural Research* 14/3: 251–69.

Banks, M. and Hesmondhalgh, D. (2009) 'Looking for Work in Creative Industries Policy', *International Journal of Cultural Policy* 15 (4): 415–29.

Banks, M. and Milestone, K. (2011) 'Individualisation, Gender and Cultural Work', *Gender, Work and Organization* 18(1): 73–89.

Banks, M. and O'Connor, J. (2009) 'After the Creative Industries', *International Journal of Cultural Policy* 15(4): 365–73.

Barboza, D. (2011) 'Workers Sickened at Apple Supplier Chain in China', *The New York Times*, 23 February, B1.

Barron, F. (1953) 'Complexity-Simplicity as a Personality Dimension', *The Journal of Abnormal and Social Psychology* 48(2): 163–72.

——(1968) *Creativity and Personal Freedom*, Princeton, NJ: D. Van Nostrand.

——(1988) 'Putting Creativity to Work', in R.J. Sternberg (ed.) *The Nature of Creativity: Contemporary Psychological Perspectives*, Cambridge: Cambridge University Press.

Barthes, R. (1993) 'The Death of the Author', *Image/Music/Text*, London: Fontana.

Bauman, Z. (2005) *Liquid Life*, Cambridge: Polity Press.

——(2006) *Liquid Fear*, Cambridge: Polity Press.

Bauman, Z. and Tester, K. (2001) *Conversations with Zygmunt Bauman*, Cambridge: Polity Press.

Beam, R. (1990) 'Journalism Professionalism as an Organizational-level Concept', *Journal Monographs* 121, Columbia: Association for Education in Journalism and Mass Communication.

Beck, U. (2000) *The Brave New World of Work*, Cambridge: Polity.

Becker, H. (1992) *Art Worlds*, University of California Press.

Bell, D. (1977) 'The Future World Disorder: The Structural Context of Crises', *Foreign Policy* 27: 109–35.

Bendix, R. (2001) *Work and Authority in Industry: Managerial Ideologies in the Course of Industrialization*, New Brunswick, NJ: Transaction.

Benhabib, S. (1996) *The Reluctant Modernism of Hannah Arendt*, Thousand Oaks: Sage.

Beniger, J. (1989) *The Control Revolution: Technological and Economic Origins of the Information Society*, Cambridge: Harvard University Press.

Benkler, Y. (2006) *The Wealth of Networks*, New Haven: Yale University Press, www.benkler.org/wealth_of_networks.

Benyon, H. (1973) *Working for Ford*, London: Allen Lane.

Berardi, F. (2009) *Precarious Rhapsody: Semio-capitalism and the Pathologies of the Post-Alpha Generation*, London: Autonomedia.

Berlant, L. (2008) *After the Good Life, the Impasse: Human Resources, Time Out, and the Precarious Present*, public lecture, University of Melbourne, August.

Bevir, M. (2011) *The Making of British Socialism*, New Jersey: Princeton University Press.

Biernacki, R. (1995) *The Fabrication of Labour: Germany and Britain, 1640–1914*, Berkeley: University of California Press.

——(1997) 'Work and Culture in the Reception of Class Ideologies', in J. Hall (ed.) *Reworking Class*, Ithaca, NY: Cornell University Press.

——(2001) 'Labour as an Imagined Commodity', *Politics and Society* 29: 173–206.

Bilton, C. (2010) 'Manageable Creativity', *International Journal of Cultural Policy* 16(3): 255–69.

Blond, P. (2009) *The Ownership State*, London: NESTA.

——(2010) *Red Tory*, London: Faber.

Bodnar, C. (2006) 'Taking it to the Streets: French Cultural Worker Resistance and the Creation of a Precariat Movement', *Canadian Journal of Communication* (online) 31(3), www.cjc-online.ca/viewarticle.php?id=1754.

Boldrin, M. and Levine, D. (2002) 'The Case Against Intellectual Property', *Center for Economic Policy Research Discussion Paper* No. 3273.

Boltanski, L. and Chiapello, E. (2005 [1999]) *The New Spirit of Capitalism*, trans. G. Elliot, London: Verso.

Bonnett, A. (2010) *Left in the Past. Radicalism and the Politics of Nostalgia*, New York: Continuum.

Bottini, N., Ernst, C. and Luebker, M. (2007) *Offshoring and the Labor Market: What are the Issues?* Geneva: International Labor Office.

Bourdieu, P. (1990) *The Field of Cultural Production*, Cambridge: Polity Press.

——(1998) *Acts of Resistance: Against the Tyranny of the Market*, New York: New Press.

British Sociological Association (2002) *Statement of Ethical Practice*, Belmont, Durham: BSA.

Broecke, S. and Hamed, J. (2008) 'Gender Gaps in Higher Education Participation: An Analysis of the Relationship Between Prior Attainment and Young Participation by Gender, Socio-economic Class and Ethnicity', *DIUS Research* Report 08 14, London: Department for Innovation, Universities and Skills.

Bruns, A. (2005) *Gatewatching: Collaborative Online News Production*, New York: Peter Lang.

Brzezinski, Z. (1969) *Between Two Ages: America's Role in the Technotronic Era*, New York: Viking.

Bucy, E. and Gregson, K. (2001) 'Media Participation: A Legitimizing Mechanism of Mass Democracy', *New Media & Society* 3(3): 357–80.

Butler, J. (1990) *Gender Trouble: Feminism and the Subversion of Identity*, New York: Routledge.

——(1993) *Bodies that Matter: On the Discursive Limits of 'Sex'*, New York: Routledge.

——(2000) 'Appearances Aside', *Californian Law Review* 88: 55–63.

——(2004) *Undoing Gender*, New York: Taylor & Francis.

Caldwell, J.T. (2008) *Production Culture: Industrial Reflexivity and Critical Practice in Film and Television*, Durham and London: Duke University Press.

——(2009) 'Hive-sourcing is the New Out-sourcing: Studying Old (Industrial) Labor Habits in New (Consumer) Labor Clothes', *Cinema Journal* 49(1): 160–67.

Callinicos, A. (2000) *Equality*, Cambridge: Polity.

Callus, R. and Cole, M. (2002) *'Live for Art – Just Don't Expect to Make a Living from it*: The Worklife of Australian Visual Artists', *MIA* 102: 77–87.

Carrillo, J. and Zárate, R. (2009) 'The Evolution of Maquiladora Best Practices: 1965–2008', *Journal of Business Ethics* 88, Supplement 2: 335–48.

Castells, M. (1996) *The Rise of the Network Society*, Cambridge: Blackwell Publishers.

——(1997) 'The Power of Identity. The Information Age', *Economy, Society, and Culture* Vol. II, Oxford: Blackwell.

Caves, R. (2002) *Creative Industries: Contracts between Art and Commerce*, Cambridge, MS: Harvard University Press.

CEREAL (Centre for Reflection and Action on Labour Issues) (2009) *Labor Rights in a Time of Crisis: Third Report on Working Conditions in the Mexican Electronics Industry*, sjsocial.org/fomento/proyectos/plantilla.php?texto=cereal_m.

Chatterjee, P. (2011) *Lineages of Political Society*, New Delhi: Permanent Black.

Chen, H. (2010) 'My Trip to Santa's Workshop', Transit Labour: Circuits, Borders, Regions, transitlabour.asia/blogs/my-trip-santas-workshop (accessed 23 January 2012).

Cheng, J.Y., King-lun, N. and Yan, H. (2011) 'Multinational Corporations, Global Civil Society and Chinese Labour: Workers' Solidarity in China in the Era of Globalization', *Economic and Industrial Democracy* DOI: 10.1177/0143831X11411325.

Christopherson, S. (2006) 'Behind the Scenes: How Transnational Firms are Constructing a New International Division of Labor in Media Work', *Geoforum* 37, No. 5: 739–51.

Christopherson, S. and Storper, M. (1989) 'The Effects of Flexible Specialisation on Industrial Relations and the Labour Market: The Motion Picture Industry', *Industrial and Labour Relations Review* 42(3): 331–47.

Clark, C. (1997) *Radium Girls: Women and Industrial Health Reform, 1910–1935*, Chapel Hill: University of North Carolina Press.

Clark, K. (ed.) (1967) *Ruskin Today*, Harmondsworth: Penguin.

Clough, P.T. (2010) 'The Affective Turn: Political Economy, Biomedia, and Bodies', in M. Gregg and G.J. Seigworth (eds) *The Affect Theory Reader*, Durham: Duke University Press.

Compaine, B. (2005) *The Media Monopoly Myth: How New Competition is Expanding Our Sources of Information and Entertainment*, New Millennium Research Council report, www.thenmrc.org/archive/Final_Compaine_Paper_050205.pdf.

Conor, B. (2010) *Screenwriting as Creative Labor: Pedagogies, Practices and Livelihoods in the New Cultural Economy*, unpublished thesis, Goldsmiths College.

——(2011) 'Problems in "Wellywood": Rethinking the Politics of Transnational Cultural Labor', *Flow* 13, No. 7, flowtv.org/2011/05/flow-favorites-problems-in-wellywood-rethinking-the-politics-of-transnational-cultural-labor-bridget-conor-goldsmiths-college-university-of-london.

Cornelissen, J.P., Haslam, S.A. and Balmer, J.M.T. (2007) *Social Identity, Organizational Identity and Corporate Identity: Towards an Integrated Understanding of Processes, Patternings and Products, British Journal of Management* Vol. 18: S1–S16.

Coté, M. and Neilson, B. (2014) 'Are We All Cultural Workers Now?' special issue of *Journal of Cultural Economy* (in press).

Coté, M. and Pybus, J. (2007) 'Learning to Immaterial Labour 2.0: MySpace and Social Networks', Ephemera', *Theory & Politics in Organization* 7(1): 88–106.

Cowen, D. (2010) 'A Geography of Logistics: Market Authority and the Security of Supply Chains', *Annals of the Association of American Geographers* 100(3): 600–20.

Cowie, J. (2001) *Capital Moves: RCA's Seventy-Year Quest for Cheap Labor*, New York: New Press.

Cox, S. (2009) 'Cell Phones Generate Particularly Dangerous E-Waste', in Cynthia A. Bily (ed.) *What is the Impact of E-Waste?* Detroit: Greenhaven Press, 18–26.

Cross, J. (2010) 'Neoliberalism as Unexceptional: Economic Zones and the Everyday Precariousness of Working Life in South India', *Critique of Anthropology* 30(4): 355–73.

Culture North West (2006) *Creative Economy Programme – North West Regional Consultation*, Manchester: Culture North West, in association with the Burns Owens Partnership.

Cumming, E. and Kaplan, W. (1991) *The Arts and Crafts Movement*, London: Thames and Hudson.

Cunningham, S. (2002) 'From Cultural to Creative Industries: Theory, Industry and Policy Implications', *Media Industry Australia, Incorporating Culture and Policy* 102: 54–65.

——(2006) 'What Price a Creative Economy?' *Platform Papers*, Sydney: Currency House.

——(2007) 'Creative Industries as Policy and Discourse Outside the United Kingdom', *Global Media and Communication* 3(3): 347–52.

Davidov, G. (2002) 'The Three Axes of Employment Relationships: A Characterization of Workers in Need of Protection', *University of Toronto Law Journal* 52, No. 4: 357–418.

Davies, W. (2011) *Happiness and Production*, www.opendemocracy.net/ourkingdom/william-davies/happiness-and-production.

Day, W.W. (2005) 'Being Part of Digital Hollywood: Taiwan's Online Gaming & 3D Animation Industry Under the New International Division of Cultural Labor', *International Journal of Comic Art* 7, No. 1: 449–61.

DCMS (1998) *Creative Industries Mapping Document*, London: Department for Culture, Media and Sport (DCMS).

——(2000) *Creative Industries: The Regional Dimension*, London: DCMS.

——(2001) *Culture and Creativity: The Next Ten Years*, London: Department for Culture, Media and Sport (DCMS).

——(2005) *Creative Economy Programme: Diversity Original Hypothesis*, DCMS, headshift.com/DCMS (accessed 25 July 2006).

——(2006) *Diversity Working Group. Final Report*, Department for Culture, Media and Sport (DCMS), headshift.com/DCMS/ (accessed 9 August 2006).

DCMS, DIUS and BERR (2008) *Creative Britain: New Talents for the New Economy*, London: Department for Culture, Media and Sport (DCMS), Department for Innovation, Universities and Skills (DIUS), and the Department for Business Enterprise and Regulatory Reforms (BERR).

de Beauvoir, S. (1949) *The Second Sex*, trans. H.M. Parshley, London: David Campbell Publishers.

Denning, M. (1997) *The Cultural Front. The Laboring of American Culture in the Twentieth Century*, London and New York: Verso.

DeLanda, M. (2006) *A New Philosophy of Society: Assemblage Theory and Social Complexity*, London: Continuum.

Delphy, C. (1996) 'Rethinking Sex and Gender', in D. Leonard and L. Adkins (eds) *Sex in Question: French Materialist Feminism*, London: Taylor and Francis.

Department for Children, Schools and Families and Department for Culture, Media and Sport (2008) *Safer Children in a Digital World: The Report of the Byron Review: Independent Review to British Prime Minister*, Annesley: Department for Children, Schools and Families and Department for Culture, Media and Sport.

de Peuter, Greig (2011) 'Creative Economy and Labor Precarity: A Contested Convergence', *Journal of Communication Inquiry* 35(4): 417–25.

de Peuter, G. and Dyer-Witheford, N. (2005) 'A Playful Multitude? Mobilising and Counter-mobilising Immaterial Game Labour', *Fibreculture* No. 5, five.fibre culturejournal.org/fcj-024-a-playful-multitude-mobilising-and-counter-mobilising-immaterial-game-labour/ (accessed 19 January 2012).

de Sola Pool, I. (1983) *Technologies of Freedom*, Cambridge, Mass.: Harvard University Press.

Deuze, M. (2007) *Mediawork*, Cambridge: Polity Press.

——(ed.) (2011) *Managing Media Work*, London: Sage.

Deuze, M., Martin, C.B. and Allen, C. (2007) 'The Professional Identity of Gameworkers', *Convergence: The International Journal of Research into New Media Technologies* 13(4): 335.

Dorling, D. (2010) *Injustice. Why Social Inequality Persists*, Bristol: Polity.

Dourish, P. and Bell, G. (2011) *Divining a Digital Future: Mess and Mythology in Ubiquitous Computing*, The MIT Press.

DTI (2005a) *Women in the IT Industry: Phase 1, Towards a Business Case for Diversity*, interim report, London: Department for Trade and Industry (DTI).

——(2005b) *Women in the IT Industry: Phase 2, How to Retain Women in the IT Industry*, London: Department for Trade and Industry (DTI).

du Gay, P. and Pryke, M. (eds) (2002) *Cultural Economy*, London: Sage.

Dyson, E., George, G. and Toffler, A. (1994) *Cyberspace and the American Dream: A Magna Carta for the Knowledge Age*, Version 1.2, Progress and Freedom Foundation, www.pff.org/issues-pubs/futureinsights/fil.2magnacarta.html.

Edgerton, D. (2007) *The Shock of the Old: Technology and Global History since 1900*, Oxford: Oxford University Press.

Elefante, P. and Deuze, M. (2012) 'Media Work Career Management, and Professional Identity: Living Labour Precarity', *Northern Lights: Film & Media Studies Yearbook* 10(1): 9–24.

Ellerman, D. (1992) *Property and Contract in Economics: The Case for Economic Democracy*, Cambridge, MA: Blackwell.

Elliott, G. (1993) *Labourism and the English Genius*, London: Verso.

Elmer, G. and Gasher, M. (eds) (2005) *Contracting Out Hollywood: Runaway Productions and Foreign Location Shooting*, Lanham: Rowman & Littlefield.

Entertainment & Leisure Software Publishers Association (2004) *Chicks and Joysticks: An Exploration of Women and Gaming*, London: Entertainment & Leisure Software Publishers Association.

Ewing, D. (1977) *Freedom Inside the Organization: Bringing Civil Liberties to the Workplace*, New York: Dutton.

Feldman, G. (2011) 'If Ethnography is more than Participant-observation, then Relations are more than Connections: The Case for Nonlocal Ethnography in a World of Apparatuses', *Anthropological Theory* 11(4): 375–95.

Ferus-Comelo, A. (2008) 'Mission Impossible? Raising Labor Standards in the ICT Sector', *Labor Studies Journal* 33, No. 2: 141–62.

Fitzgerald, F. Scott (1941) *The Last Tycoon*, London: Penguin.

Fleming, P. and Sturdy, A. (2006) *'Just Be Yourself'* – *Towards Neo-normative Control in Organisations?* Cambridge: University of Cambridge.

Flew, T. (2004) 'Creativity, Cultural Studies, and Service Industries', *Communication and Critical/Cultural Studies* 1(2): 176–93.

Flores, F. and Gray, J. (1999) *Entrepreneurship and the Wired Life: Work in the Wake of Careers*, London: Demos

Florida, R.L. (2002) *The Rise of the Creative Class and How it's Transforming Work, Leisure, Community and Everyday Life*, New York: Basic Books.

Francke, L. (1994) *Script Girls: Women Screenwriters in Hollywood*, London: British Film Institute.

Fröbel, F., Jürgen, H. and Kreye, O. (1980) *The New International Division of Labor: Structural Unemployment in Industrialised Countries and Industrialisation in Developing Countries*, trans. P. Burgess, Cambridge: Cambridge University Press; Paris: Éditions de la Maison des Sciences de l'Homme.

Garnham, N. (1990) *Capitalism and Communication: Global Culture and the Economics of Information*, London: Sage.

——(1990a) 'Public Policy and the Cultural Industries', in *Capitalism and Communication*, London: Sage.

——(2005) 'From Cultural to Creative Industries', *International Journal of Cultural Policy* 11(1): 15–29.

Gereffi, G. and Korzeniewicz, M. (1994) *Commodity Chains and Global Capitalism*, Westport: Greenwood Press.

GeSI and EICC (2008) *Social and Environmental Responsibility in Metals Supply to the Electronic Industry*, Global e-Sustainability Initiative (GeSI) and Electronic Industry Citizenship Coalition (EICC), www.eicc.info/PDF/Report%20on%20Metal%20Extraction.pdf.

Gibson, C. (2003) 'Cultures at Work: Why "Culture" Matters in Research on the "Cultural" Industries', *Social and Cultural Geography* 4(2): 201–15.

Gibson, C. and Klocker, N. (2005) 'The "Cultural Turn" in Australian Regional Economic Development Discourse: Neoliberalising Creativity?' *Geographical Research* 43(1): 93–102.

Gill, R. (2002) 'Cool, Creative and Egalitarian? Exploring Gender in Project-based New Media Work in Europe', *Information, Communication and Society* 5: 70–89.

——(2006) *Technobohemians or the New Cybertariat? New Media Work in Amsterdam a Decade after the Web*, Amsterdam: Institute of Network Cultures, www.network cultures.org/_uploads/17.pdf (accessed 22 February 2012).

——(2009) 'Creative Biographies in New Media: Social Innovation in Web Work', in A.C. Pratt and P. Jeffcut (eds) *Creativity, Innovation and the Cultural Economy*, London: Routledge.

——(2013) 'On Not Saying the "S" Word: Postfeminism, Entrepreneurial Subjectivity and the Repudiation of Sexism Among Cultural Workers', *Social Politics*, in press.

Gill, R. and Pratt, A. (2008) 'In the Social Factory? Immaterial Labour, Precariousness and Cultural Work', *Theory, Culture & Society* 25(7–8): 1–30.

GLA (Greater London Authority) (2012) *World Cities Culture*, www.worldcitiesculture report.com (accessed 6 November 2012).

Global Witness (2009) 'Faced with a Gun, What Can You Do?' *War and the Militarisation of Mining in Eastern Congo*, London: Global Witness.

Goffman, E. (1973) 'Regions and Region Behavior', in *The Presentation of Self in Everyday Life*, New York: The Overlook Press.

Good Electronics, Paula Overeem and CSR Platform (2009) *Reset: Corporate Social Responsibility in the Global Electronics Supply Chain*, Amsterdam: Good Electronics.

Gorz, A. (2004) 'Économie de la connaissance, exploitation des savoirs: Entretien réalizé par Yann Moulier Boutang and Carlo Vercellone', *Multitudes* 15, multitudes. samizdat.net/Economie-de-la-connaissance.

Graham, G. (ed.) (2005) *Journal of Supply Chain Management*, special issue: Exploring Supply Chain Management in the Creative Industries, 10(5).

Graham, M. (2008) 'Warped Geographies of Development: The Internet and Theories of Economic Development', *Geography Compass* 2, No. 3: 771–89.

Greenfield, S., Peters, J., Lane, N., Rees, T. and Samuels, G. (2002) *SET Fair: A Report on Women in Science, Engineering and Technology*, London: The Royal Institute of Great Britain.

Greenspan, A. (2010) 'On the City's Edge', *Transit Labour: Circuits, Borders, Regions*, transitlabour.asia/blogs/citys-edge (accessed 23 January 2012).

Gregg, M. (2007) 'Freedom to Work: The Impact of Wireless on Labour Politics', *Media International Australia*, Special Issue on Wireless Technologies and Cultures, 125 (November): 57–70.

——(2008) 'The Normalisation of Flexible Female Labour in the Information Economy', *Feminist Media Studies* 8(3): 285–99.

——(2010) 'On Friday Night Drinks: Workplace Affect in the Age of the Cubicle', in M. Gregg and G.J. Seigworth (eds) *The Affect Theory Reader*, Durham: Duke University Press.

——(2011) *Work's Intimacy*, Cambridge: Polity Press.

Grindstaff, L. (2002) *The Money Shot: Trash, Class and the Making of TV Talk Shows*, Chicago: University of Chicago Press.

Gross, A. (2012) 'The Economy of Social Data: Exploring Research Ethics as a Device', in L. Adkins and C. Lury (eds) *Measure and Value*, Oxford: Blackwell.

Grossberg, L. (2010) *Cultural Studies in the Future Tense*, Durham: Duke University Press.

Grossman, E. (2006) *High Tech Trash: Digital Devices, Hidden Toxics, and Human Health*, Washington: Island.

Guilford, J.P. (1950) 'Creativity', *The American Psychologist* 5.9: 444–54.

Habermas, J. (1976) *Legitimation Crisis*, London: Heinemann.

——(2001) *The Postnational Constellation*, trans. M. Pensky, Boston: MIT Press.

Haigh, G. (2012) *The Office: A Hardworking History*, Carlton: The Miegunyah Press.

Haines, L. (2004a) *Phase 1, Women and Girls in the Games Industry*, Manchester: Media Training North West (MTNW).

——(2004b) *Phase 2, Why are There So Few Women in Games?* Manchester: Media Training North West.

Hamilton, I. (1990) *Writers in Hollywood 1915–1955*, London: Heinemann.

Hampson, I. and Junor, A. (2010) 'Putting the Process Back in: Rethinking Service Sector Work', *Work, Employment and Society* 24(3): 526–45.

Handy, C. (1995) *The Empty Raincoat: Making Sense of the Future*, London: Random House.

Hardt, M. and Negri, A. (2001) *Empire*, Cambridge, MS: Harvard University Press.

——(2005) *Multitude: War and Democracy in the Age of Empire*, London: Penguin.

Harrod, T. (1999) *The Crafts in Britain in the 20th Century*, New Haven, CT: Yale University Press.

Hartley, J. (ed.) (2005) *Creative Industries*, Oxford: Blackwell.

Harvey, D. (2005) *The New Imperialism*, Oxford: Oxford University Press.

Havens, T., Lotz, A. and Tinic, S. (2009) 'Critical Media Industry Studies: A Research Approach', *Communication, Culture and Critique* 2: 234–53.

Heelas, P. (2002) 'Work Ethics, Soft Capitalism and the "Turn to Life2"', in P. du Gay and M. Pryke (eds) *Cultural Economy*, London: Sage.

Hesmondhalgh, D. (2002) *The Cultural Industries*, London: Sage.

——(2005) 'Media and Public Policy as Cultural Policy: The Case of the British Labour Government', *International Journal of Cultural Policy* 11(1): 95–108.

——(2007) *The Cultural Industries*, 2nd edn, London: Sage.

Hesmondhalgh, D. and Baker, S. (2011) *Creative Labour: Media Work in Three Cultural Industries*, London: Routledge.

Hesmondhalgh, D. and Pratt, A. (2005) 'Cultural Industries and Cultural Policy', *International Journal of Cultural Policy* Vol. 11, No. 1: 1–13.

Hirsch, P. (1972) 'Processing Fads and Fashions: An Organization-set Analysis of Cultural Industry Systems', *American Journal of Sociology* 77/6: 639–59.

Hirst, P. (1989) 'The Politics of Industrial Policy', in P. Hirst and J. Zeitlin (eds) *Reversing Industrial Decline? Industrial Structure and Policy and Britain and her Competitors.* Oxford: Berg.

Hobsbawm, E. (1981) 'The Forward March of Labour Halted?' In M. Jacques, and F. Mulhearn (eds) *The Forward March of Labour Halted*, London: Verso, 279–86.

Hochschild, A.R. (2003 [1983]) *The Managed Heart: Commercialization of Human Feeling*, 20th anniversary edn, Berkley: University of California Press.

Holgate, J. and McKay, S. (2009) 'Equal Opportunities Policies: How Effective are they in Increasing Diversity in the Audio-visual Industries' Freelance Labour Market?' *Media, Culture and Society* 31(1): 151–63.

Holmes, B. (2002) 'The Flexible Personality', eipcp.net/transversal/1106/holmes/en (accessed 2 April 2012).

——(2011) 'Do Containers Dream of Electric People? The Social Form of Just-in-time Production', *Open* 21: 30–44.

Howkins, J. (2001) *The Creative Economy: How People Make Money from Ideas*, London: Penguin.

——(2010) *Creative Ecologies: Where Thinking is a Proper Job*, New Jersey: Transaction Publishers.

Humphry, J. (2009) *Officing: Professionals' Daily ICT Use and the Changing Space and Time of Work*, PhD thesis, University of Western Sydney.

Hutton, W. (2007) *Staying Ahead: The Economic Performance of the UK's Creative Industries*, London: Work Foundation and the Department for Culture, Media and Sport (DCMS).

IFPI (2010) *Investing in Music*, www.ifpi.org/content/library/investing_in_music.pdf (accessed 16 January 2012).

Illouz, E. (2007) *Cold Intimacies: The Making of Emotional Capitalism*, London: Polity Press.

Inglehart, Ronald (2008) 'Changing Values Among Western Publics from 1970 to 2006', *West European Politics* 31(1–2): 130–46.

Institute of Public and Environmental Affairs (2011) *The Other Side of Apple*, Beijing: IPE Reports.

International Federation of Journalists (2006) *The Changing Nature of Work: A Global Study and Case Study of Atypical Work in the Media Industry*, Research Report, www.ifj.org/pdfs/ILOReport070606.pdf.

International Labour Organization (2010) *Sectoral Activities Department* (SECTOR), www.ilo.org/public/english/dialogue/sector/sectors/mining/emp.htm.

Irigaray, L. (1995) 'The Question of the Other', *Yale French Studies* 87: 7–19.

Jackson, K. (2010) *The Worlds of John Ruskin*, London: Pallas Athlene & Ruskin Foundation.

Jarvis, H. and Pratt, A.C. (2006) 'Bringing it All Back Home: The Extensification and "Overflowing" of Work. The Case of San Francisco's New Media Households', *Geoforum* 37: 331–39.

Jaumotte, F. (2003) 'Female Labour Force Participation: Past Trends and Main Determinants in OECD Countries', OECD Economics Department Working Papers, No. 376.

Jenkins, H. (2004) 'The Cultural Logic of Media Convergence', *International Journal of Cultural Studies* 7(1): 33–43.

Jones, O. (2011) *Chavs. The Demonisation of the Working Class*, London: Verso.

Joshi, A. and Roh, H. (2009) 'The Role of Context in Work Team Diversity Research: A Meta-analytic Review', *Academy of Management Journal* 52: 599–627.

Jurik, N.C. (1998) 'Getting Away and Getting By: The Experiences of Self-employed Homeworkers', *Work and Occupations* 25(7): 7–35.

Kalm, Sara. (2001) 'Emancipation or Exploitation? A Study of Women Workers in Mexico's Maquiladora Industry', *Statsveteskaplig Tidskrift* 104, No. 3: 225–58.

Kanngieser, A. (2010a) 'Self-valorisation and Creative Labour', *Transit Labour: Circuits, Borders, Regions*, transitlabour.asia/blogs/self-valorisation-creative-labour (accessed 23 January 2012).

——(2010b) 'Rethinking Regionalism – Some Field Reflections', *Transit Labour: Circuits, Borders, Regions*, transitlabour.asia/blogs/rethinking-regionalism-some-field-reflections (accessed 22 February 2012).

Kanngieser, A., Neilson, B. and Rossiter, N. (2010) 'What is a Research Platform', *Transit Labour: Circuits, Borders, Regions*, transitlabour.asia/blogs/what-research-platform (accessed 22 January 2012).

Kant, I. (1951 [1790]) *Critique of Pure Judgement*, New York: Hafner Press.

Kaufmann, D. (1986) 'Simone de Beauvoir: Questions of Difference and Generation', *Yale French Studies* 72: 121–31.

Keane, M. (2007) *Created in China: The Great New Leap Forward*, London: Routledge.

Keen, A. (2008) *The Cult of the Amateur: How blogs, MySpace, YouTube and the Rest of Today's User-generated Media are Killing our Culture and Economy*, Nicholas Brearley Press.

Kelly, J. (1982) 'Useful Work and Useless Toil', *Marxism Today*, August.

Kennedy, H. (2012) *Net Work: Ethics and Value in Web Design*, Basingstoke: Palgrave.

Kotamraju, N.P. (2002) 'Keeping Up: Web Design Skill and the Reinvented Worker', *Information, Communication and Society* 5(1): 1–26.

Kücklich, J. (2005) 'Precarious Playbour: Modders and the Digital Games Industry', *Fibreculture*, No. 5, five.fibreculturejournal.org/fcj-025-precarious-playbour-modders-and-the-digital-games-industry/ (accessed 19 January 2012).

Landry, C. (2000) The Creative City: A Toolkit for Urban Innovators, London: Earthscan.

Larner, W. and Craig, D. (2005) 'After Neoliberalism? Community Activism and Local Partnerships in Aotearoa New Zealand', in N. Laurie and L. Bondi (eds) *Working the Spaces of Neoliberalism*, Oxford: Blackwell Publishing.

Lash, S. and Lury, C. (2007) *Global Culture Industry: The Mediation of Things*, Cambridge: Polity.

Lash, S. and Urry, J. (1994) *Economies of Signs and Space*, London: Sage.

Latour, B. (2005) *Reassembling the Social: An Introduction to Actor-Network Theory*, Oxford: Oxford University Press.

Lawton, K. and Potter, D. (2010) *Why Interns Need a Fair Wage*, London: IPPR.

Lazzarato, M. (1996) 'Immaterial Labour', in M. Hardt and P. Virno (eds) *Radical Thought in Italy: A Potential Politics*, Minneapolis, MN: University of Minnesota Press.

LDA (2003) *Skills for Creative London*, unpublished notes from seminar, London: LDA.

Leadbeater, C. (1999) *Living on Thin Air: The New Economy with a New Blueprint for the 21st Century*, London: Viking.

Leadbeater, C. and Oakley, K. (1999) *The Independents: Britain's New Cultural Entrepreneurs*, London: Demos.

Leonard, D. and Swap, W. (1999) *When Sparks Fly: Igniting Creativity in Groups*, Boston: Harvard Business School Press.

Leung, I. and Teh, D. (2011) 'Reflections of Transit Labour and Contemporary Chinese Art: A Conversation', Transit, online posting (available email: transit@transitlabour.asia) (31 August 2011).

Levitas, R. (1996) 'The Concept of Social Exclusion and the New Durkheimian Hegemony', *Critical Social Policy* 16(5): 5–20.

Lewis, C.D. (1946) *The Poetic Image*, London: Jonathan Cape.

Liu, A. (2004) *The Laws of Cool: Knowledge Work and the Culture of Information*, Chicago: University of Chicago Press.

Lobato, R. (2008) 'Secret Lives of Asian Australian Cinema: Offshore Labour in Transnational Film Industries', *Studies in Australasian Cinema* 2, No. 3: 213–27.

Losurdo, D. (2011) *Liberalism: A Counter History*, New York: Verso.

Luckman, S. (2012) *Locating Cultural Industries: The Politics and Poetics of Creative Work*, Basingstoke: Palgrave Macmillan.

——(2013) 'The Aura of the Analogue in a Digital Age: Women's Crafts, Creative Markets and Home-Based Labour After Etsy', *Cultural Studies Review*, 19(1): forthcoming.

Lüthje, B. (2006) 'The Changing Map of Global Electronics: Networks of Mass Production in the New Economy', in T. Smith, David A. Sonnenfeld and David Naguib Pellow (eds) *Challenging the Chip: Labor Rights and Environmental Justice in the Global Electronics Industry*, Philadelphia: Temple University Press, 17–30.

Ma, T. (2009) 'China and Congo's Coltan Connection', *Project 2049 Institute Futuregram* 09-003, www.project2049.net/publications.html.

MacCarthy, F. (1994) *William Morris: A Life for our Times*, London: Faber & Faber.

McChesney, R. and Schiller, D. (2003) *The Political Economy of International Communications: Foundations for the Emerging Global Debate about Media Ownership and Regulation*, UNRISD Technology, Business and Society Paper 11, www.unrisd.org.

MacDonald, I. (2007) 'The Struggle for the Silents: The British Screenwriter from 1910 to 1930', *Journal of Media Practice* 8(2): 115–28.

McFall, L. (2004) 'The Culturalization of Work in the New Economy: A Historical View', in T.E. Jenson and A. Westenholz (eds) *Identity in the Age of the New Economy: Life in Temporary and Scattered Work Practices*, Cheltenham: Edward Elgar, 9–33.

MacIntyre, A. (2007) *After Virtue: A Study in Moral Theory*, 3rd edn, London: Bloomsbury.

McKercher, C. and Mosco, V. (eds) (2007) *Knowledge Workers in the Information Society*, Lanham: Lexington.

McKinlay, A. and Smith, C. (2009) *Creative Labour: Working in the Creative Industries*, Basingstoke: Palgrave MacMillan.

McRobbie, A. (1998) *British Fashion Design: Rag Trade or Image Industry?* London: Routledge.

——(2002) 'Clubs to Companies: Notes on the Decline of Political Culture in Speeded Up Creative Worlds', *Cultural Studies* 16(4): 516–31.

——(2011) 'Rethinking Creative Economy as a Radical Social Enterprise', *Variant* 41 (Spring).

Mannix, E. and Neale, M.A. (2005) 'What Differences Make a Difference? The Promise and Reality of Diverse Teams in Organizations', *Psychological Science in the Public Interest* 6: 31–55.

Maras, S. (2009) *Screenwriting: History, Theory and Practice*, London: Wallflower Press.

Marcuse, H. (1941) 'Some Social Implications of Modern Technology', *Studies in Philosophy and Social Sciences* 9, No. 3: 414–39.

Marx, K. (1976) *Capital: A Critique of Political Economy*, Vol. One, Harmondsworth: Penguin.

——(1987) *Capital: Vol. 1: A Critical Analysis of Capitalist Production*, 3rd edn, trans. S. Moore and E. Aveling, and ed. F. Engels, New York: International Publishers.

Maslow, A. (1962) *Toward a Psychology of Being*, Princeton, NJ: D. Van Nostrand.

——(1965) *Eupsychian Management: A Journal*, Homewood, IL: Richard D. Irwin and The Dorsey Press.

——(1971) *The Farther Reaches of Human Nature*, New York: Viking Press.

Mason, P. (2007) *Live Working or Die Fighting: How the Working Class went Global*, London: Harvill Secker.

Mathews, J. (1989) *Age of Democracy. The Politics of Post-Fordism*, Melbourne: Oxford University Press.

Maxwell, R. and Miller, T. (2011) 'Old, New and Middle-aged Media Convergence', *Cultural Studies* 25(4–5): 585–603.

——(2012) *Greening the Media*, New York: Oxford University Press.

Mayer, V. (2011) *Below the Line: Producers and Production Studies in the New Television Economy*, Durham and London: Duke University Press.

Menger, P.M. (2002) *Portrait de l'Artiste en Travailleur: Métamorphoses du Capitalisme*, Paris: Éditions du Seuil et La République des Idées.

Merrill, B. and West, L. (2009) *Using Biographical Methods in Social Research*, London: Sage.

Miege, B. (1989) *The Capitalization of Cultural Production*, New York: International General.

Millar, J. and Jagger, N. (2001) 'Women in ITEC Courses and Careers', Suffolk: Women and Equality Unit (WEU), Department of Trade and Industry (DTI) & Department for Education and Skills (DFES).

Miller, T., Govil, N., McMurria, J., Maxwell, R. and Wang, T. (2005) *Global Hollywood 2*, London: British Film Institute.

Miller, T., Lawrence, G., McKay, J. and Rowe, D. (2001) *Globalization and Sport: Playing the World*, London: Sage Publications.

Miller, T. and Leger, M.C. (2001) 'Runaway Production, Runaway Consumption, Runaway Citizenship', The New International Division of Cultural Labour, *Emergences* 11(1): 89–115.

Milliken, F.J. and Martins, L.L. (1996) 'Searching for Common Threads: Understanding the Multiple Effects of Diversity in Organizational Groups', *Academy of Management Review* 21: 402–33.

Mills, C. Wright (1951) *White Collar: The American Middle Classes*, New York: Oxford University Press.

——(1959) *The Sociological Imagination*, Oxford: Oxford University Press.

Montague, D. (2002) 'Stolen Goods: Coltan and Conflict in the Democratic Republic of Congo', *SAIS Review* 22, No. 1: 103–18.

Morini, C. (2007) 'The Feminization of Labour in Cognitive Capitalism', *Feminist Review* 87(1): 40–59.

Morris, W. (1884) 'A Factory as it Might Be', first published in *Justice* (April–May), www.infed.org/archives/e-texts/william_morris_a_factory_as_it_might_be.htm (accessed 22 September 2011).

——(1885) 'A New Party', *Commonweal*, Vol. I, No. 8 (September): 85, www.marxists. org/archive/morris/works/1885/commonweal/09-new-party.htm (accessed 17 October 2011).

——(1888) 'Signs of Change', *Collected Lectures*, first published Reeves & Turner, www.marxists.org/archive/morris/works/1884/useful.htm (accessed 10 October 2011).

——(1973) *Political Writings of William Morris*, ed. A.L. Morton, London: Lawrence and Wishart.

Mosco, V. (2004) *The Digital Sublime: Myth, Power, and Cyberspace*, Cambridge, Mass.: MIT Press.

Mosco, V. and McKercher, C. (2009) *The Laboring of Communication: Will Knowledge Workers of the World Unite?* Lanham: Lexington.

Mosco, V. McKercher, C. and Huws, U. (eds) (2010) *Getting the Message: Communications Workers and Global Value Chains*, London: Merlin Books.

Mukerji, C. and Schudson, M. (n.d.) *Rethinking Popular Culture: Contemporary Perspectives in Cultural Studies*, 4-7-423, Berkeley: University of California Press.

Munro, R. (2001) 'Calling for Accounts: Numbers, Monsters and Membership', *Sociological Review* 49(4): 473–93.

Murray, R. (1988) 'Life After (Henry) Ford', *Marxism Today* 32(10): 8–13.

Muthyala, J. (2011) 'Call Center Cultures and the Transnationalization of Affective Labor', *Reconstruction* 11(1), reconstruction.eserver.org/111/Muthyala.shtml (accessed 5 March 2012).

Nagy, K.H. and Zhen-Wei Qiang, C. (2010) 'China's Emerging Informatization Strategy', *Journal of the Knowledge Economy* 1, No. 2: 128–64.

Nardono, N., McPherson, A. and Sadique, T. (2009) *Greening Consumer Electronics – Away from Chlorine and Bromine*, Göteborg/Montréal: ChemSec (the International Chemical Secretariat) and Clean Production Action.

Neff, G., Wissinger, E. and Zukin, S. (2005) 'Entrepreneurial Labor Among Cultural Producers: "Cool" Jobs in "Hot" Industries', *Social Semiotics* 15, No. 3: 307–34.

Negri, A. (2006) *Empire and Beyond*, Cambridge: Polity.

——(2007) *Goodbye Mister Socialism*, Paris: Seuil.

Negus, K. (1998) 'Cultural Production and the Corporation: Musical Genres and the Strategic Management of Creativity in the US Recording Industry Media', *Academy of Management Review* 21: 402–33.

Neilson, B. and Rossiter, N. (2005) 'From Precarity to Precariousness and Back Again: Life, Labour and Unstable Networks', *Fibreculture Journal* 5.

——(2010) 'Still Waiting, Still Moving: On Labour, Logistics and Maritime Industries', in D. Bissell and G. Fuller (eds) *Stillness in a Mobile World*, London: Routledge.

Newman, T. (1984) 'Introduction: The Themes of the Exhibition', in *Institute for Contemporary Art, William Morris Today*, London: Institute for Contemporary Art.

Nimpuno, N., McPherson, A. and Sadique, T. (2009) 'Greening Consumer Electronics: Moving Away from Bromine and Chlorine', *Clean Production Action Report*, Springbrook, New York.

Nixon, S. (2006) 'The Pursuit of Newness', *Cultural Studies* 20: 90–106.

Nnorom, I.C. and Osibanjo, O. (2008) 'Overview of Electronic Waste (E-Waste) Management Practices and Legislations, and their Poor Applications in the Developing Countries', *Resources Conservation & Recycling* 52, No. 6: 843–58.

Norman, J. (2008) *Compassionate Economics: The Social Foundations of Economic Prosperity*, Policy Exchange and University of Buckingham Press.

Norman, M. (2007) *What Happens Next: A History of American Screenwriting*, New York: Harmony Books.

Nye, D.E. (1994) *American Technological Sublime*, Cambridge, Mass.: MIT Press.

——(2006) 'Technology and the Production of Difference', *American Quarterly* 58, No. 3: 597–618.

——(2007) *Technology Matters: Questions to Live With*, Cambridge, Mass.: MIT Press.

Oakley, K. (2006) 'Include us out – Economic Development and Social Policy in the Creative Industries', *Cultural Trends* 15: 255–73.

——(2009) *Art Works: A Review of the Literature on Cultural and Creative Labour Markets*, London: Creativity, Culture and Education.

——(2011) 'In its Own Image: New Labour and the Cultural Workforce', *Cultural Trends*, Vol. 20, No. 3–4 (December).

——(2012) 'Rich but Divided … the Politics of Cultural Policy in London', in H. Anheier and Y. Isar (eds) *Cities, Cultural Policy & Governance*, Volume 5, The Cultures and Globalization Series, Sage, 204–12.

Oborne, P. (2011) 'The Moral Decay of our Society is as Bad at the Top as the Bottom', *Daily Telegraph* online, 10 August (accessed 10 October 2011).

O'Connor, J. (1998) 'New Cultural Intermediaries and the Entrepreneurial City', in T. Hall and P. Hubbard (eds) *The Entrepreneurial City: Geographies of Politics, Regime and Representation*, Chichester: John Wiley, 225–40.

O'Connor, J. and Xin, G. (2006) 'A New Modernity: The Arrival of "Creative Industries" in China', *International Journal of Cultural Studies* 9(3): 271–83.

——(2010) 'City of Other People's Dreams', *Transit Labour: Circuits, Borders, Regions*, transitlabour.asia/blogs/city-other-peoples-dreams (accessed 23 January 2012).

Ohmae, K. (1995) *The End of the Nation State: The Rise of Regional Economies*, London: Harper Collins.

Ollilainen, M. and Calasanti, T. (2007) 'Metaphors at Work: Maintaining the Salience of Gender in Self-managing Teams', *Gender and Society* 21: 5–27.

Ong, A. (2006) *Neoliberalism as Exception: Mutations in Citizenship and Sovereignty*, Durham: Duke University Press.

Orage, A.R. (1907) 'Politics for Craftsmen', *Contemporary Review* 91: 787–94.

Pateman, C. (1988) *The Sexual Contract*, Stanford: Stanford University Press.

Peck, J. (2011) 'Creative Moments', in McCann and Ward (eds) *Mobile Urbanism. Cities and Policymaking in the Global Age*, Minneapolis: University of Minnesota Press.

Perren, A. and Holt, J. (eds) (2009) *Media Industries: History: Method, and Theory*, Malden: Blackwell.

Peters, T. (1992) *Liberation Management: Necessary Disorganization for the Nanosecond Nineties*, New York: Knopf.

——(1999a) 'The Work Matters', address delivered in Boston, March 1999, www.providersedge.com/docs/leadership_articles/The_Work_Matters_Movement.pdf (accessed 2 April 2012).

——(1999b) *The Brand You 50, Or Fifty Ways to Transform Yourself from an 'Employee' into a Brand that Shouts Distinction, Commitment, and Passion!*, New York: Knopf.

Phillip, A. and Trinh, T. (2001) 'Image of ICT', London: MORI, commissioned by e-skillsNTO.

Polanyi, K. (1944) *The Great Transformation*, Boston: Beacon Press.

Postone, M. (1993) *Time, Labour and Social Domination: A Reinterpretation of Marx's Critical Theory*, New York: Cambridge University Press.

Powdermaker, H. (1950) *Hollywood: The Dream Factory*, New York: Little Brown and Company.

Powers, W. (2010) *Hamlet's Blackberry: A Practical Philosophy for Building a Good Life in the Digital Age*, New York: Harper.

Pratt, A.C. (2008) 'Cultural Commodity Chains, Cultural Clusters, or Cultural Production Chains?' *Growth and Change* 39(1): 95–103.

Prince, R. (2009) *Assembling the Creative Economy: Epistemic Communities, Policy Transfer and the Geography of Expertise*, unpublished PhD thesis, University of Bristol.

Proctor-Thomson, S.B. (2009) *Creative Differences: The Performativity of Gender in the Digital Media Sector*, unpublished PhD thesis, Lancaster University.

Pun, N. (2008) '"Reorganized Moralism": The Politics of Transnational Labor Codes', in L. Zhang and A. Ong (eds) *Privatizing China: Socialism from Afar*, Ithaca: Cornell University Press.

Purnell, J. (2005) *Making Britain the World's Creative Hub. Creative Britannia: Turning Ideas into Business*, speech to IPPR conference, 16 June, Department for Culture, Media and Sport, www.culture.gov.uk/reference_library/minister_speeches/2050.aspx (accessed 7 February 2006).

Putman, D. (1997) 'The Intellectual Bias of Virtue Ethics', *Philosophy* 72/280: 303–11.

Puwar, N. (2004) *Space Invaders: Race, Gender and Bodies out of Place*, Oxford: Berg.

Pynchon, T. (1984) 'Is it O.K. to be a Luddite?' *New York Times Book Review*, 28 October: 40–41.

Rancière, J. (2002) *Aesthetics and Its Discontents*, Cambridge: Polity.

Randle, K., Kurian, J. and Leung, W.F. (2007) *Creating Difference: Overcoming Barriers to Diversity in UK Film and Television Employment*, Hertfordshire: Creative Industries Research & Consultancy Unit, Business School, University of Hertfordshire.

Ravenscroft, N. and Gilchrist, P. (2009) 'The Emergent Working Society of Leisure', *Journal of Leisure Research* 41(1): 23–39.

Remesh, B.P. (2004) 'Cyber Coolies in BPO: Insecurities and Vulnerabilities of Non-standard Work', *Economic and Political Weekly* 39(5): 492–97.

Renard, S. (2010) 'Unbundling the Supply Chain for the International Music Industry', unpublished thesis, University of Southern New Hampshire, academicarchive.snhu.edu/bitstream/handle/10474/474/int2010renard.pdf?sequence=3 (accessed 23 January 2012).

Reygadas, L. (2002) *Ensamblando culturas: Diversidad y conflicto en la globalización de la industria*, Barcelona: Gedisa.

Rimmer, M. (2009) 'Instrumental Playing? Cultural Policy and Young People's Community Music Participation', *International Journal of Cultural Policy* (15)1: 79–90.

Ritzer, G. and Jurgenson, N. (2010) 'Production, Consumption, Prosumption: The Nature of Capitalism in the Age of the Digital "Prosumer"', *Journal of Consumer Culture* 10, No. 1: 13–36.

Robertson, J.W. (2010) 'The Last Days of Free-market Hegemony? UK TV News Coverage of Economic Issues in Spring 2008', *Media, Culture & Society* 32(3): 517–29.

Robinson, K., DfEE and DCMS (1999) *All Our Futures: Creativity, Culture and Education*, Sudbury: National Advisory Committee on Creative and Cultural Education (NACCCE). Commissioned by the Secretaries of State for Education and Employment (DfEE) and Culture, Media and Sport (DCMS).

Rose, N. and Miller, P. (1988) 'The Tavistock Programme: the Government of Subjectivity and Social Life', *Sociology* 22.2 (May): 171–92.

Ross, A. (2000) 'The Mental Labour Problem', *Social Text* 18: 1–31.

——(2003) *No-collar: The Humane Workplace and its Hidden Costs*, New York: Basic Books.

——(2008) 'The New Geography of Work: Power to the Precarious', *Theory, Culture and Society* 25(7–8): 31–49.

——(2009) *Nice Work if you can get it. Life and Labor in Precarious Times*, New York: New York University Press.

Rossiter, N. (2006) *Organized Networks: Media Theory, Creative Labour*, New Institutions, Rotterdam: Nai Publishers.

——(2009) 'Translating the Indifference of Communication: Electronic Waste, Migrant Labour and the Informational Sovereignty of Logistics in China', *International Review of Information Ethics* 11(10): 36–44, www.i-r-i-e.net/inhalt/011/011-full.pdf (accessed 23 January 2012).

Rossiter, N., de Muynck, B. and Carriço, M. (eds) (2008) *Urban China, Special Issue: Creative China: Counter-Mapping the Creative Industries*, 33.

Rosten, L. (1940) *Hollywood: The Movie Colony, the Movie Makers*, New York: Arno Press.

Ruskin, J. (1903) *The Complete Works of John Ruskin, Vol. III: The Seven Lamps of Architecture*, Cook, E.T. and Wedderburn, A. (eds.), London: George Allen.

Ruskin, J. (1907) *The Stones of Venice, Vol. II: The Sea-Stories*, London: George Routledge and Sons and E.P. Dutton & Co.

——(2010 [1862]) *Unto this Last*, London: Pallas Athene.

Ryan, B. (1991) *Making Capital from Culture: The Corporate Form of Capitalist Cultural Production*, Berlin: Walter de Gruyter.

Ryan, J. (1985) *The Production of Culture in the Music Industry: The ASCAP-BMI Controversy Lanham*, MD: University Press of America.

Sabel, C. (1982) *Work and Politics*, Cambridge: Cambridge University Press.

Samuel, R. (2006) *The Lost World of British Communism*, London: Verso.

Sanyal, K.K. (2007) *Rethinking Capitalist Development: Primitive Accumulation, Governmentality and the Post-Colonial Capitalism*, London: Routledge.

Sarda, S. (2010) '@ Baoshan Electronics Market', *Transit Labour: Circuits, Borders, Regions*, transitlabour.asia/blogs/baoshan-electronics-market (accessed 23 January 2012).

Sassen, S. (2010) 'A Savage Sorting of Winners and Losers: Contemporary Versions of Primitive Accumulation', *Globalizations* 7(1–2): 23–50.

Saundry, R., Stuart, M. and Antcliff, V. (2007) 'Broadcasting Discontent – Freelancers, Trade Unions and the Internet', *New Technology, Work and Employment* 22(2): 178–91.

Sayer, A. (2009) 'Contributive Justice and Meaningful Work', *Res Publica* 15: 1–16.

Sayers, S. (2003) 'Creative Activity and Alienation in Hegel and Marx', *Historical Materialism* 11/1: 107–28.

——(2007) 'The Concept of Labour: Marx and his Critics', *Science and Society* 71/4: 431–54.

Schiller, H.I. (1976) *Communication and Cultural Domination*, New York: International Arts and Sciences Press.

Schultheiss, J. (1971) 'The "Eastern" Writer in Hollywood', *Cinema Journal* 11(1): 13–47.

Sefton-Green, J. (2008) *What Future for the Non-formal Learning Sector?* London Development Agency, www.julianseftongreen.net/wp-content/uploads/2008/07/seftongreen_NFLS_essay.pdf (accessed 8 September 2011).

Seltzer, K. and Bentley, T. (1999) *The Creative Age: Knowledge and Skills of the New Economy*, London: Demos.

Sennett, R. (2002) *The Culture of the New Capitalism*, New Haven, CT: Yale University Press.

——(2006) *The Culture of the New Capitalism*, New Haven, CT and London: Yale University Press.

——(2008) *The Craftsman*, New Haven and London: Yale University Press.

Shank, B. (1994) *Dissonant Identities: The Rock 'n Roll Scene in Austin, Texas*, Hanover, NH: Wesleyan University Press.

Sholette, G. (2010) *Dark Matter: Art and Politics in the Age of Enterprise Culture*, London: Pluto Press.

Singer, J. (1998) 'Online Journalists: Foundation for Research into their Changing Roles', *Journal of Computer-Mediated Communication* 4(1).

Skeggs, B. (2004) *Class, Self, Culture*, London: Routledge.

Skillset (2009) *Employment Census: The Results of the Seventh Census of the Creative Media Industries*, London: Skillset, The Sector Skills Council for Creative Media.

——(2010) *Women in the Creative Media Industries*, London: Skillset, The Sector Skills Council for Creative Media.

——(2011) *Sector Skills Assessment for the Creative Industries of the UK*, London: Skillset, The Sector Skills Council for Creative Media.

Smith, C. and Ngai, P. (2006) 'The Dormitory Labour Regime in China as a Site for Control and Resistance', *The International Journal of Human Resource Management* 17(8): 1456–70.

Snow, C.P. (1987) *The Two Cultures and a Second Look: An Expanded Version of the Two Cultures and the Scientific Revolution*, Cambridge: Cambridge University Press.

Sohn-Rethel, A. (1978) *Intellectual and Manual Labour: A Critique of Epistemology*, London: McMillan Press.

Stahl, M. (2008) 'Sex and Drugs and Bait and Switch: Rockumentary and the New Model Worker', in D. Hesmondhalgh and J. Toynbee (eds) *The Media and Social Theory*, London: Routledge.

——(2010) 'Cultural Labour's "Democratic Deficits": Employment, Autonomy, and Alienation in US Film Animation', *Journal for Cultural Research* 14: 271–93.

——(2013) *Unfree Masters: Recording Artists and the Politics of Work*, Durham, NC: Duke University Press.

Staiger, J. (1982) 'Dividing Labour for Production Control: Thomas Ince and the Rise of the Studio System', in G. Kindem (ed.) *The American Movie Industry: The Business of Motion Pictures*, Carbondale and Edwardsville: Southern Illinois University Press, 94–103.

Standing, G. (1999) *Global Labour Flexibility*, New York: St Martin's Press.

——(2011) *The Precariat: The New Dangerous Class*, London: Bloomsbury Academic.

Stempel, T. (1988) *Framework: A History of Screenwriting in the American Film*, New York: Continuum.

Stevens, A. and Mosco, V. (2010) 'Prospects for Trade Unions and Labour Organizations in India's IT and ITES Industries', *Work Organisation, Labour and Globalization* 4(2): 39–59.

Storey, J., Salaman, G. and Platman, K. (2005) 'Living with Enterprise in an Enterprise Economy: Freelance and Contract Workers in the Media', *Human Relations* 58(8): 1033–54.

Students & Scholars Against Corporate Misbehaviour (2010) *Workers as Machines: Military Management in Foxconn*, Hong Kong: Students & Scholars Against Corporate Misbehaviour.

Sutton Trust (2006) *The Educational Backgrounds of Leading Journalists*, London: Sutton Trust.

Taylor, M. (2008) 'Power, Conflict and the Production of the Global Economy', in M. Taylor (ed.) *Global Economy Contested: Power and Conflict across the International Division of Labour*, London: Routledge.

Taylor, S. and Littleton, K. (2012) *Contemporary Identities of Creativity and Creative Work*, Abingdon: Ashgate.

Terranova, T. (2000) 'Free Labour: Producing Culture for the Digital Economy', *Social Text* 18(2): 33–58.

——(2004) *Network Culture: The Politics of the Information Age*, London: Pluto.

Teubner, G. (2009) 'The Corporate Codes of Multinationals: Company Constitutions Beyond Corporate Governance and Co-determination', in R. Nickel (ed.) *Conflict of Laws and Laws of Conflict in Europe and Beyond: Patterns of Supranational and Transnational Juridification, ARENA Report* No 1/09, Centre for European Studies, University of Oslo.

Thiel, J. (2005) *Creativity and Space: Labour and the Restructuring of the German Advertising Industry*, Aldershot: Ashgate.

Thompson, N. (2002) *Left in the Wilderness: The Political Economy of British Democratic Socialism since 1979*, Chesham: Acumen.

Thrift, N. (2005) *Knowing Capitalism*, London: Sage.

——(2007) *Non-Representational Theory: Space, Politics, Affect*, London: Sage.

Toffler, A. (1983) *Previews and Premises*, New York: William Morrow.

Towse, R. (2006) 'Copyright and Artists: A View from Cultural Economics', *Journal of Economic Surveys* 20/4: 567–85.

Toynbee, J. (2000) *Making Popular Music: Musicians, Creativity and Institutions*, London: Arnold.

——(2010) 'Creativity and Intellectual Property Rights', in H. Anheier and Y. Isar (eds) *Cultural Expression, Creativity and Innovation*, London: Sage.

Trinh, T.M.H. (1987) 'Difference: "A Special Third World Women Issue"', *Feminist Review* 25: 5–22.

Tsing, A. (2009) 'Supply Chains and the Human Condition', *Rethinking Marxism* 2: 148–76.

Tunstall, J. (ed.) (2000) *Media Occupations and Professions: A Reader*, Oxford: Oxford University Press.

Turba, L. (2011) 'A Resource-based Approach to Strategy Analysis in the New Digital Television Arena', *Technology, Analysis and Strategic Management* 23(5): 545–66.

Turkle, S. (2011) *Alone Together: Why We Expect More from Technology and Less from Each Other*, New York: Basic Books.

Tyler, M. (2005) 'Women in Change Management: Simone de Beauvoir and the Co-optation of Women's Otherness', *Journal of Organizational Change Management* 18: 561–77.

Unite (2008) *How Green is My Workplace? A Guide for Unite Members and Representatives in the Electrical Engineering, Electronics and IT Sector*, London: Unite.

United Nations (2002) *Report of the Panel of Experts on the Illegal Exploitation of Natural Resources and Other Forms of Wealth of the Democratic Republic of the Congo*, www.un.org/News/dh/latest/drcongo.htm.

Upadhyay, C. and Vasavi, A.R. (2008) *In an Outpost of the Global Economy: Work and Workers in India's Information Technology Industry*, New Delhi: Routledge.

Ursell, G. (1998) 'Labour Flexibility in the UK Commercial Television Sector', *Media, Culture & Society* 20: 129–53.

——(2000) 'Television Production: Issues of Exploitation, Commodification and Subjectivity in UK Television Labour Markets', *Media, Culture & Society* 22(6): 805–27.

van der Linden, M. (2008) *Workers of the World: Essays toward a Global Labour History*, Leiden: Brill.

van Liemt, G. (2007) *Recent Developments on Corporate Social Responsibility (CSR) in Information and Communications Technology (ICT) Hardware Manufacturing*, Geneva: International Labour Office.

van Zoonen, L. (1998) 'A Professional, Unreliable, Heroic Marionette (M/F): Structure, Agency and Subjectivity in Contemporary Journalisms', *European Journal of Cultural Studies* 1(1): 123–43.

Virno, P. (1996) 'The Ambivalence of Disenchantment', in M. Hardt and P. Virno (eds) *Radical Thought in Italy: A Potential Politics*, Minneapolis: University of Minnesota Press, 1–10.

von Hippel, E. (2005) *Democratizing innovations*, Boston: MIT Press, mitpress.mit.edu/democratizing_innovation_PDF.

Wajcman, J. (2011) 'Gender and Work: A Technofeminist Analysis', in E.L. Jeanes, D. Knights and Martin P. Yancey (eds) *Handbook of Gender, Work and Organization*, Chichester: Wiley.

Wayne, M. (2010) 'The Normative Basis of Creative Labour in Kant and Marx', paper presented to Moral Economies of Creative Labour conference, University of Leeds, 7–8 July.

——(n.d.) *Red Kant: Aesthetics, Marxism and the Third Critique*, London: Continuum Press, forthcoming.

Weber, M. (1949) 'Objectivity in the Social Sciences and Social Policy', in E. Shils and H.A. Fitch (eds) *The Methodology of the Social Sciences*, New York: Free Press.

Weeks, K. (2011) *The Problem with Work: Feminism, Marxism, Antiwork Politics, and Postwork Imaginaries*, Durham: Duke University Press.

West, N. (1939) *The Day of the Locust*, London: Penguin.

Whyte, W.H. (1963) *The Organization Man*, Harmondsworth: Penguin.

Williams, P., Bridge, K., Edwards, J., Vujinovic, N. and Pocock, B. (2009) *Sustainable Lives in Sustainable Communities? Living and Working in Ten Australian Suburbs*, Adelaide: Centre for Work + Life, University of South Australia.

Williams, R. (1980) *Problems in Materialism and Culture*, London: Verso.

——(1981) *Culture*, London: Fontana.

——(1983 [1958]) *Culture and Society 1780–1950*, New York: Columbia University Press.

——(2005) 'Base and Superstructure in Marxist Cultural Theory', in *Culture and Materialism*, London: Verso.

Wills, J. and Simms, M. (2004) 'Building Reciprocal Community Unionism in the UK', *Capital and Class* 82: 59–84.

Winston, B. (2007) 'Let Them Eat Laptops: The Limits of Technicism', *International Journal of Communication* 1: 170–76.

Wittel, A. (2001) 'Towards a Network Sociality', *Theory, Culture and Society* 18(6): 51–76.

Wong, S., Liu, J. and Culpan, T. (2010) 'Life and Death at the iPad Factory', *Bloomberg Business Week*, 7–13 June: 35–36.

Wood, E.M. (1986) *The Retreat from Class. A new 'True' Socialism*, London: Verso.

Wood, H. and Skeggs, B. (2008) 'Spectacular Morality: Reality Television, and the Re-making of the Working Class', in D. Hesmondhalgh and J. Toynbee (eds) *Media and Social Theory*, London: Taylor and Francis, 177–94.

Woodmansee, M. (1996) *The Author, Art and the Market: Rereading the History of Aesthetics*, New York: Columbia University Press.

Wordsworth, W. (1979 [1805]) 'The Prelude', in J. Wordworth, M. Abrams and S. Gill (eds) *The Prelude 1799, 1805, 1850: Authoritative Texts, Context and Reception, Recent Critical Essays*, New York: Norton and Co.

Work Foundation (2007) *Staying Ahead: The Economic Performance of the UK's Creative Industries*, London: Department for Culture, Media and Sport.

Yoon, H. and Malecki, E.J. (2010) 'Cartoon Planet: Worlds of Production and Global Production Networks in the Animation Industry', *Industrial and Corporate Change* 19(1): 239–71.

Zechner, M. and Kanngieser, A. (2010) 'Future Functions: Aspirations, Desire and Futures', *Transit Labour: Circuits, Borders, Regions*, transitlabour.asia/blogs/future-functions-aspiration-desire-and-futures (accessed 23 January 2012).

Zeitlin, J. (1989) 'Local Industrial Strategies', *Economy and Society* 18(4): 367–73.

Zhiguo, F. and Xiaoliang, Z. (2010) 'Cluster-based Supply Chain Study of Cultural Creative Industry', *Proceedings of 2nd International Conference on e-Business and Information Security*, Wuhan, May: 1–4.

Films

Adaptation (2002) written by Charlie Kaufman and Donald Kaufman, directed by Spike Jonze. USA: Columbia Pictures.

Barton Fink (1991) written by Joel Coen and Ethan Coen, directed by Joel Coen. USA: Circle Films and Working Title Films.

Episodes (2011–present) created by David Crane and Jeffrey Klarik, directed by James Griffiths and Jim Field Smith, UK and USA: Hat Trick Productions.

Sunset Boulevard (1950) written by Charles Brackett, Billy Wilder and D.M. Marshman Jnr, directed by Billy Wilder. USA: Paramount Pictures.

Index